Renku Reckoner

Also available by this author from Darlington Richards Press:

the Little Book of Yotsumonos by John Carley with Hortensia Anderson, Lorin Ford, Carole MacRury, Sandra Simpson, William Sorlien and Sheila Windsor

RENKU RECKONER

John Carley

Darlington Richards Press
South Africa and Ireland

Copyright © 2013 John Carley

All rights reserved. No part of this book may be used or reproduced in any manner whatsoever without written permission except in the case of brief quotations embodied in critical articles and reviews.

First printing: 2015
Edited by Norman Darlington and Moira Richards
Design by Darlington Richards Press
Front cover and illustrations by John Carley

ISBN 978-09869763-3-9

Published by Darlington Richards Press
South Africa & Ireland
www.darlingtonrichards.com

This book is dedicated to all the sincere people that it gratuitously mocks. Myself included. Above all it is dedicated to my wife, my son, and my daughter for keeping that sense of mockery alive.

cob-web fingers fitting the 11,001st angel on a pinhead
Johannes S. H. Bjerg

CONTENTS

Foreword	4
Renku Just Being Renku: John Carley's *Renku Reckoner* Introduction by Chris Drake	8
Preface	13

The Forms of Renku
descriptions, schemas, appraisals, examples

How to Read the Schemas	16
Kasen the thirty-six splendid immortals	19
Rokku renku rocks on	27
Tankako an excursion in verse	34
Triparshva past, present and future	40
Nijuin twenty times around	46
Imachi waiting for the moon	51
Hankasen and Demikasen halfway to hell	57
Shisan a significant occasion	62
New Shisan with an eye on tradition	66
Junicho a twelve-tone scale	68
New Junicho turning the tables	72
Yotsumono four things	76

Renku Theory and Practice

Link & Shift: An Overview — nothing more fundamental ... 82

Beginnings and Endings — more than a few ku ... 85

A Dynamic Pattern — pacing with jo–ha–kyu ... 89

Link: Making the Connection — manners and methods of linkage ... 92

More About Shift — some practicalities ... 97

Thematic Renku — reasons to join the circus ... 103

The Mechanics of the White Space — in the void between verses ... 106

Occurrence and Recurrence — variety and change in a renku sequence ... 109

The Three Rs — how to avoid going backwards ... 120

On Backlink — no better way to waste your time ... 124

Cut or Uncut? — haiku, hokku, and hopping mad ... 127

Know Your Enemy — haikai stanzas in Japanese ... 131

Know Yourself — haikai stanzas in English ... 138

The Seasons of Renku — what, where, when and why ... 146

What Price Kigo? — the function of seasonal reference in renku ... 151

Explaining it all Away — strictly need to know ... 155

Exercises — snatching the pebble ... 159

The Minimum Conditions — what does it take to be Shofu renku? ... 168

Conducting a Sequence — how to make enemies of your friends ... 170

Publication Credits ... 178

Foreword

John Edmund Carley, virtuoso haikai poet and theorist, died on the last day of 2013, following a long battle with mesothelioma. He was 58. During his last 15 years he led hundreds of linked-verse sequences and translated a significant number of Edo-period kasen, breathing a new life into traditional collaborative verse forms in English. His central contention was that renku is not a Japanese art form, but an art form that has arisen in Japan.

Carley was a multi-faceted man who was easily approachable and never stood on his learning. He will be greatly missed by the many people who had the good fortune to cross his path, from the Bengali and Pashtun poets of Lancashire in the 1990s to writers of renku on every inhabited continent since the turn of the century. I count myself lucky to have been able to number him among my friends.

Raised in the north of England, he lived for a time in France and Italy, and spoke French, Italian and Piedmontese fluently. As a percussionist and sound engineer, he was a key figure in the Bristol music scene during the late 1970s and early 1980s, performing and recording in such bands as the Spics, the Radicals and Scream and Dance. He would later muse that his experience as a musician, together with the fact that his dyslexia forced his aural experience to centre stage, played a major role in his focus on phonics and rhythm in poetry, an area receiving scant attention in English-language haikai, especially haiku.

In his 20s, Carley's interest in haikai was awakened when he first opened Nobuyuki Yuasa's translation of Matsuo Basho's *Oku no hosomichi* (*Narrow Road to the Deep North*). Remembering the occasion later, he said,

> I recall as if it were yesterday my shock at hearing Basho speak. The sensation is there still: how could this long dead bloke from an alien culture communicate so directly when most poetry in my own language left me cold?

In the field of haikai aesthetics Carley acknowledged Professor Yuasa as Master, and the latter's influence remained a constant in his work.

In the 1990s Carley began editing the poetry magazine *Pennine Ink*, and during this period he developed an interest in work in minority languages, promoting poetry readings in languages such as Farsi and Urdu. This culminated in the publication of his translation from Bengali of Ala Miah's *Light of Keshob Pur* (Big Lamp) in 2000.

In 1999, in response to the fierce but inconclusive debate around English-language haiku prosody, he proposed the zip, a short, flexible fixed-form stanza designed to show the natural cadences of English to best advantage. As an analogue to Japanese *teikei* haiku, it encompasses 15 syllables in two lines, each of which is split by a mid-line caesura. The zip approach would later be adapted to renku with some considerable success. An example from the inventor's pen:

> had I the strength   I'd blow away
>   the last   of the willow-herb

At the same time, his interest in collaborative poetry was growing, and in 1999 he published *What a Performance* (Big Lamp), a book of performance poems for more than one voice, with two other poets. In 2002 he launched the Young Renga Project, whereby he visited schools throughout Lancashire and

Manchester, teaching the principles of linked verse to students and collecting a body of work which he published on his Villa Rana website. In the same year, he established the first listserv forum dedicated to linked verse, The Renkujin Palace, where he hosted numerous collaborative compositions.

This interest brought him into contact with Japan's Association for International Renku (AIR) and resulted in a long and fruitful collaboration with Eiko Yachimoto. Her influence in the area of current Japanese practice is evident in Carley's work from this period onwards, and the two would collaborate on numerous translations of Basho-school kasen.

With the launch of the online journal *Simply Haiku* in 2003, Carley joined the editorial board as renku editor. In this capacity he was successful in promoting new thinking and breathing new life into an art form which had been to some degree misapprehended in the west. In addition to publishing collaborative work by new poets, he was the first to publish and promote new western renku formats such as the triparshva. Leaving *Simply Haiku* in 2006, he took up the position of renku coordinator at *Moonset* where he continued his pioneering work.

As well as those poets well known in the world of English-language haikai, such as William J. Higginson and Susumu Takiguchi, Carley went on to engage in collaborations with leading academics in the field of Japanese literature such as Herbert Jonsson, Chris Drake and Cheryl Crowley. When in 2005 he was invited by Nobuyuki Yuasa to participate in a landmark kasen to commemorate the 300th anniversary of the death of Basho's disciple Takarai Kikaku, he felt he had in some way come full circle. Little had he imagined when his eyes were first opened to the magic of haikai some 30 years earlier by Yuasa's *Narrow Road*, that he would one day participate in a linked verse session led by this Master. The resulting kasen was published in the booklet *Springtime in Edo* in 2006 (Keisuisha).

> A name engraved on a beach
> One summer day long ago.   Sosui (Nobuyuki Yuasa)

> The heather-lined road
> To Scarborough fair,
> The purple of her lips.   John

In searching ever more deeply for the essence of Shofu, or Basho-school renku, Carley eventually reached back to the Chinese Tang-dynasty four-line form of *jueju* or 'puzzle poem' (known as *zekku* in Japanese), concluding that the aesthetic values and techniques advanced by Basho could be successfully encompassed in a poem of just four stanzas. This ultimate distillation of renku he called *yotsumono*, or 'four things.' In 2012 he published *the Little Book of Yotsumonos* (Darlington Richards Press), which contained, in addition to an introduction to the principles of renku and to his new form in particular, 60 examples of the yotsumono, ten each penned by Carley with six different poets including the late Hortensia Anderson. Said Sonja Arntzen upon reading the book: "This form of four short verses can compass an astonishing amount of ground, time and emotion, while the resonating space between the verses and between the voices reaches to infinity."

Lingering Heat

> lingering heat —
> chrysanthemums drop
> from her kimono   Hortensia Anderson

    some men say the scarab

    worships moonlight   John

    once again

    the exterminator

    comes to pay a call   Hortensia

    who will weep

    upon this pauper's grave?   John

On Christmas 2011, Carley's son gifted him a copy of the famed *Fifty-Three Stations of the Tōkaidō* by Utagawa Hiroshige, a series of *ukiyo-e* woodcut prints inspired by the artist's travels along the coast road between Edo and Kyoto, published in 1833-34. The gift so inspired Carley that he immediately began composing a hokku to accompany each image, and the resulting combination of image and poetry was published as the delightful *nothing but the wind* in 2013 (Gean Tree Press). To accompany Hiroshige's snowy depiction of Kanbara, Carley wrote:

    a winter's night

    held fast beneath the snow

    a deeper silence

Carley was tireless in his efforts to promulgate the writing of renku in English. Subsequent to his early activities at The Renkujin Palace, he engaged ceaselessly in collaborations with poets the world over, by email as well as in specialised forums such as The Renku Group and Issa's Snail. Rather than a Japanese art form, he regarded renku as an art form that happened to have originated in Japan. He did not see renku as an esoteric practice tangled in a myriad rules and prohibitions, but as readily comprehensible and governed by a small number of key principles. His position was that all aspects of Shofu renku aesthetics and technique may be understood in any cultural context and emulated in any human language.

Carley published essays on renku theory in periodicals such as *Journal of Renga & Renku*, as well as on his own Renku Reckoner website, which was regarded as a resource of exceptional value by renku poets, both beginner and advanced. During his last year, he revised and expanded his body of theoretical essays, and assembled what he referred to as his "haikai manifesto;" it is this work which we are honoured to present here. *Renku Reckoner* comprises 19 chapters on renku theory and practice, including a series of carefully planned exercises, as well as descriptions, seasonal schemas, appraisals and full example poems of 12 traditional and modern renku forms, including his new adaptation of the hankasen, to which he gave the name *demikasen*. It is hoped and envisaged that this authoritative work will stand as a lasting witness to the author's genius.

Those many fortunates who worked with Carley will remember him as endlessly patient, always ready to take the time to explain the finer points of any argument. His deep knowledge was always tempered with a self-deprecating humour and an endearing sense of the absurd. Nor was his gift with words confined to poetry. Here is how he signed off an email to me in late 2013:

The sun is well nigh over the horizon, let alone the yard arm, and the insidious muezzin of beeriness calls from the minaret of The Griffin Inn.

Let's all raise a pint of Sunshine (his favourite tipple) to the memory of a great man!

Norman Darlington, Bunclody, Ireland

Renku Just Being Renku: John Carley's *Renku Reckoner*
Introduction by Chris Drake

At last we have a book about renku in English that is also at the creative cutting edge of renku worldwide, one so full of new ideas and compelling images that it deserves to be widely read even in Japan, where renku made its first appearance. *Renku Reckoner* is based on a solid understanding of how renku, originally called haikai no renga, or, simply and more commonly, haikai, emerged both as an art and as an extremely popular social phenomenon in late medieval and early modern Japan before being largely replaced during the rush to modernize by haiku and other poetic forms influenced by western poetry. Luckily this down period was followed by a small but significant renku renaissance in the second half of the twentieth century, and John Carley's book is not only a brief but reliable guide to renku forms and history but is itself one of the high points of the recent renku renaissance. At the same time, Carley stresses from the outset that he is writing a manifesto about what renku must become if it is to establish itself as a form of poetry in English as well as a global art form. In this sense, *Renku Reckoner* is ultimately a book about the future and about the past as future. It's a kind of poetic survival kit for life in the twenty-first century, since Carley is confident that renku will put down roots in English and become more conscious of itself in English and other languages as a form with major artistic achievements and possibilities.

Carley likes to think big, though most of his sentences, are small, pithy, and to the point, and he makes his points clearly and humorously, always providing a guiding thread of logic for the reader to follow. He writes as a renku poet, as a sabaki who has guided numerous outstanding sequences, and as a theorist with as many ideas as verses up his sleeves. His basic stance shows in the style of the book, which is often humorous, ironic, or even verse-like, and in the structure of the book, which has two linked halves that resemble a great hokku and wakiku. The book is intended for readers of all types and levels, and they can pick and choose which sections to read first, although a systematic reading is also highly recommended. So is a zigzag reading that moves back and forth between the halves, since the actual practice of renku, outlined in the first half, and matters of structure and theory, discussed in the second half, are intimately related. Then again, a crazy-quilt reading itinerary will no doubt seem most natural to many readers. *Renku Reckoner* is so packed with interesting links and ideas coming at the reader from so many directions that only multiple readings are likely to satisfy true lovers of renku.

The book's first half, The Forms of Renku, introduces and discusses what Carley judges to be the twelve most important renku formats now being used by renku poets around the world. It is not, however, simply a dry list of rules and abstract characteristics. It is rich in esthetic judgments as well as in details and practical hints for renku writers and is clearly designed for a wide range of readers, from students of comparative literature to the most experienced renku poets. Not content with the standard schemas of the most typical distribution of various verse types in each form, Carley also gives an overview for each as well as remarks on the strengths and limitations of the form from the point of view of a renku poet and sabaki. He also points out how the schemas can be used creatively and templatitis avoided. Finally, and best of all, Carley also includes an example renku for each form. All the examples are of outstanding quality and need to be read and interpreted many times before they can be fully appreciated. The mere fact of gathering all these fine renku sequences into one place should have a bracing effect on the future development of renku in English.

In Japan, where thousand-verse and ten thousand-verse renga and renku sequences were once fairly common, the hundred-verse *hyakuin* form is still considered a relatively normal format, though the thirty-six-verse kasen form has been the most popular format for more than three centuries. Carley's lineup of major renku forms, which reflects contemporary trends and tastes in the English-speaking world, also tends toward the shorter end of the historical renku format spectrum, beginning with the medium-length kasen (though the experimental and flexible rokku form can theoretically extend itself indefinitely), continuing through shorter forms, and ending with the fetching four-verse yotsumono form. Contrary to common belief, Basho did not establish the kasen form, though he and his followers did some jaw-dropping things with it. There was a general move in the middle and late seventeenth century toward the kasen led by all sorts of commoner haikai poets, most of whom, like Basho, had not been trained as traditional renga masters. Linking mainly with groups of busy urban commoners, these haikai masters were attracted to the kasen form above all because it was short enough to complete in a single sitting—a very important consideration before the rise of the Internet—yet capacious enough to give each poet several verses on various topics and to allow the development of clearly contrasting base-rhythms and tonalities, leaving poets with a feeling of having gone on a substantial renku journey. To exemplify the kasen form, Carley has chosen his resourceful and very lively translation of a famous kasen done by Basho and Kikaku, the founder of the Edo-za school of urban haikai. This dynamic translation is in my opinion one of the core parts of *Renku Reckoner* and shouldn't be missed. A rapid reading is also not advised.

The example renku sequences given for the other eleven renku forms, both traditional and nontraditional, are also truly outstanding, and none of them should be missed by serious lovers of renku. Because of its futuristic outlook, I'd especially like to mention the example renku given for the twenty-two-verse triparshva, which Carley considers one of the most successful modern renku formats. The example triparshva appears to be a ryōgin sequence done by two poets but is actually a dokugin solo sequence done by Carley with another version of himself. He is, however, following Japanese precedent. Dokugin single-poet sequences were fairly common in both medieval renga and Edo-period haikai, especially in the hundred-verse format, and in renga it was customary for a poet who wrote a solo sequence to consciously try to imagine he was seven or eight different people and to write from all seven or eight points of view simultaneously. In Japanese culture the self has generally been considered to be an intensely social and contextually rooted identity-cluster capable of taking many points of view in daily life without seriously contradicting itself, and a renga or renku sequence—except for the hokku—was conceived of as a series of fictional verses written from different points of view, so the writer of a solo renku simply utilized the many voices and perspectives that competed for space within his own mind. Carley, however, obviously felt the need to develop his triparshva in the form of a poetic dialog between explicitly different sub-selves. The sequence is a brilliant virtuoso performance by Carley (one aided by the length and structure of the triparshva form), and one can only hope its success will inspire similar two- or even multi-self single-poet renku in English, since in English the development of explicitly and strongly different points of view may be more difficult for single renku poets to achieve without the use of explicit personas attached to different names.

In the last part of the book, Renku Theory and Practice, Carley deals with aspects of composing and interpreting renku using his unique style that is humorous yet eminently serious and logical. His easy-going yet rigorous style allows him to smuggle in almost unnoticed a series of crucial theoretical and esthetic questions about, ultimately, What is renku? Carley's lively and constantly morphing narrator's voices are able to blend practical and theoretical concerns rather smoothly, so the chapters in this passionately argued section are definitely not the type of theoretical reading you'd want to do in order to cure insomnia, for instance. All the basic information about renku rules and composition protocol are covered in this last section, and the discussion of each topic is direct and clear. It is also deliberately tendentious, since Carley is arguing the case for Shofu *(shōfū)* or Basho-style renku, which Carley regards as the only renku tradition in Japan to have reached the very highest levels of linking and artistic self-consciousness. In this Carley follows the dominant view in contemporary Japan, though other views exist. Shofu is also important for Carley, however, because its adherence to a high level of artistry and non-representational linking based ultimately on scent linking made possible achievements of contemporary experimental renku, which he considers to be the modern form of Shofu.

The explanation of the mechanics of renga and renku forward motion, often referred to as "link and shift," is the clearest I've seen, partly because of a helpful series of diagrams[1], and there are things of interest here for both beginner and veteran. The discussion of the three-movement jo-ha-kyu structure is also lucid, and Carley's use of musical metaphors is very effective, although Carley recognizes that other methods of pacing and overall rhythmic patterning are also possible. Also outstanding are his discussions of how to achieve change and variety, of using rules flexibly and artistically, and his criticisms of simplistic prohibitions against "back-linking." Carley also has some trenchant things to say about the importance of euphony, assonance, alliteration, onomatopoeia, and many kinds of tropes and sound patterns in renku verse, and he skillfully shows why syllable-counting in Japanese is a very different process than it is in English: 5-7-5 mora-based syllables in Japanese simply do not equate with the same number of syllables in English, leaving the question of English renku meter noticeably open—and allowing Carley to present his own solutions to the English renku metrical conundrum here. He also gives extensive treatment to *hiraku* or renku inner verses (those that follow the hokku) in the process deconstructing myths such as the common belief that inner verses shouldn't contain dashes or cutting words. As Carley points out, pauses and syntactic breaks aren't that uncommon in inner verses. What distinguishes inner verses from the hokku is that when inner verses have two parts, the parts are not strongly contrastive or superimposed but instead work together as part of a single image, often functioning to strengthen emphasis or clarify meaning or act as ellipses. Their breaks and pauses are therefore not the internal gaps of the hokku. For doubters, in a document that can be found on the Internet the renku poet and teacher Higashi Meiga made a list (in Japanese) of inner verses by Basho and his followers that contain kireji.

Carley's semiotically-based analysis of the four "loci" of change in renku in Occurrence and Recurrence will change your perception forever about the way various rules regarding seriation, distribution, and the avoidance zones for various topics and subtopics affect the artistic aspects of renku, and this chapter is recommended for readers who enjoy the esthetics of structural features. Likewise, on a more practical level, two gems of chapters that definitely should not be skipped are placed at the very end of the book. I hope readers have the passion and stamina to get as far as Exercises, which describes and explains several traditional exercises, along with three exercises devised by Carley himself, that will almost surely raise your sensitivity to many details of linking and stimulate you to try to raise your linking ability. These exercises have to be practiced, so simply reading this chapter is not enough. The same can be said for the final chapter, Conducting a Sequence, which is based on Carley's many years of experience as a member of renku-writing *za* or groups and as a sabaki. The wide-ranging tips he offers are based on conclusions he's reached during a long process of trial and error, and they cover the most important aspects of composing in a group.

Running through all the chapters in the second half of *Renku Reckoner* are the names Basho and Basho-style. Carley, in my opinion, sometimes exaggerates slightly the importance of Basho in renku history, but this is understandable given the hagiographic tone perceptible in the writings of the majority of contemporary Japanese writers who deal with renku history. Only in recent decades have haikai poets in other schools, such as the Danrin and Edo-za schools, come to be read and discussed in Japanese universities, and although commentaries on non-Basho-style renku are increasing, they are still few and far between. In English, few literary translations are available of renku outside of those written by Basho and by those, like Buson, who led the Back-to-Basho movement in the eighteenth century. In this situation detailed, substantial debate about various historical renku schools and styles in English is very difficult, so using Basho as the heroic "great man" who elevated renku to an artistic level equal to that of waka and renga is a valid and productive approach that can point out, as Carley has done so well, the many ways Basho and later poets who followed the Basho style played a crucial role in the revival of renku that took place in the twentieth century inside and outside Japan. By invoking Basho, Carley is able to show very clearly that artistic renku has the potential to surpass renku written mainly as performances or as forms of social communication or works written to achieve practical goals.

Carley summarizes his conception of Shofu or Basho-style renku in The Minimum Conditions, a chapter near the end of the book that in some ways deserves to be placed at the beginning of the second half as a methodological preamble. In this summary Basho is presented as a universal artist whose renku demonstrate the same respect for the transcendental power of the imagination and intuition that was later demonstrated by the Romantics and some modernists and postmodernists in English poetry. Basho thus raised renku to a level which allowed it to transcend the boundaries of Japan and the Japanese language and develop into newer forms of artistic renku expression in contemporary Japan, the west, and elsewhere—forms that Basho himself never imagined.

Perhaps Basho's greatest discovery, according to Carley, was the *nioi-zuke* or scent link. Basho reportedly said the name is somewhat similar to what medieval waka poets called *yosei*, floating traces of delicate feeling that can be perceived if one pays close attention but that are beyond verbal description or definition. According to Basho's followers, Basho said he used this word to mean a link that operates without reference to verbal or logical similarities, links that are impossible to predict and rely primarily on mood, intuition, and instinctive feeling. He also used it more generally to mean the importance, in all kinds of renku links, of thinking beyond standard semantic links and familiar images and thus linking in ways that cannot be fully explained or analyzed. To do this, Basho prized non-rational, artistic connections between verses even when that meant loosening traditional rules a bit and ignoring standard traditional associations between words and situations. Scent links ultimately allowed Basho to link in ways that assume that renku can attain a condition close to that of music. As Carley explains in the chapter The Mechanics of the White Space, scent linking allows sensitive readers to discern almost inaudible tonalities, rhythms, movements, and textures, and he feels that focused and attuned readers of Basho-style renku—including, presumably, the original poets—are able to obliquely perceive what he calls the "white space" that pervades and surrounds a well-done renku. By this Carley seems to mean an overall ambiance that transcends the borders between the individual verses and transforms the renku from a linear series of verses into "sinuous unity" in which every verse can reverberate and share energy with every other verse in a dimension that lies beyond all the traditional rules prohibiting near and far semantic and phonic repetition as well as other non-linear behavior.

Carley believes Basho was influenced by the mandalas of the Shingon school of Tantric Buddhism in Japan and considered kasen to be verbal mandalas in which every verse is linked to every other in the transcendental unity of the mandala. This view is speculative, and only further research will tell whether Basho had mandalas in mind or not. The concept of barely perceptible transcendental unity was not exactly a major topic in Basho's day, however, and it surely owes much to Schelling and Coleridge, who are now as popular in Japan as they are elsewhere. Ultimately it doesn't matter whether Basho thought in terms of mandalas or not, since Basho clearly did expand waka *yosei* and discovered non-rational and non-referential scent links, which are themselves the crucial link for Carley between historical Japanese renku and global, universal renku. It is from this point of view that Carley criticizes thematic renku. For Carley, renku is not mainly about external reference or prosaic themes at all. Above all renku is about simply being itself. Freed from prosaic references, scent-linking can initiate a process of collective intuition of rhythms, tenors, shapes, and movements impossible to otherwise perceive yet powerful enough to bring people together on a transcendental, global level of energy sharing. Other views of thematic renku and renku reference to its historical context are of course possible, but I feel thankful Carley didn't take that route and end up leaving us with a bland, boring synthesis. He passionately believed in scent links and white space and intuition of unspecifiable renku unities. They resonated with his artistic and philosophical sensibilities, and he pushed this way of thinking further than it had ever been articulated before him.

Instead of coming to a conclusion I would like to wipe the dust off one more way of writing and reading renku that is buried away in *Renku Reckoner* so deeply as to be almost invisible: *renku wave*—"a long passage of verse that builds and breaks thanks to an extended chain of non-cognitive association" (p. 30). The concept of renku wave is an innovation of contemporary renku poets in Japan, and it, too, raises questions of large-scale interaction between verses. Carley regards a wave as a single group or chain of verses linked by scent and tonality rather than by semantics or rationality, while in Japan it is also conceived of as non-contiguous verses that flash or vibrate here and there in a renku in a strong way that links the verses despite their formal distance from each other. Both conceptions of renku wave are about intuiting and articulating oblique relationships that are not immediately perceptible yet are emotionally, esthetically, and spiritually significant. Renku waves can be interpreted as signs of a non-definable renku unity, or they can be enjoyed empirically as long rhythms that have somehow appeared in the perceptible world. After the publication of *Renku Reckoner*, however, neither of these alternatives can simply be taken for granted. Reading and writing renku is no longer an innocent activity, and those who take renku seriously will surely be followed around by sudden waves and basic questions from here on in.

---

[1]Carley's diagrams use icons of scissors to represent shifting—what Carley aptly refers to as the "disassociation" or semantic severing of the newest linked verse from the uchikoshi or penultimate verse. His scissors icons suggest to me that it's time to recognize that it is more accurate to speak of cutting here than of shifting, which can imply small-scale changes. Each new verse must turn away from and leave behind each penultimate verse, an act of moving on and relinquishing that was often compared by Japanese renga and renku poets to releasing or giving up one's attachment to the penultimate verse, so the phrase "cut and link" would be more precise than shift and link and also suggest cutting verbal attachments. Moreover, the term "shift" is needed to describe something else equally essential: what happens to each renku verse after a newer verse follows it and causes it to shift in meaning and/or tone in relation to the latest verse. Some renku sequences written in English seem closer to a series of single verses rather than a series of constantly shifting, dialogical verse pairs, so if renku motion were described as a triple movement, "cut, link, and shift," with shift referring to the transformation of the verse linked to, this might aid understanding of the actual triple-movement process. I use "cut" first in the three-term series because cutting must take place before appropriate linking or shifting can be completed.

Preface

The book

The book is a haikai manifesto. It is not an academic treatise. There are no citations. And no footnotes.

The book advances a series of arguments—purely by assertion—on the basis that if you don't like the assertions you will make some of your own.

The book contains schematic layouts, narrative descriptions, and personal appraisals of some of the renku patterns current in English. Or else plucked out of the air.

The book uses the word English to describe a language, not a nationality.

The types of renku

- Renku is different to the high style of medieval Japanese linked verse called *ushin renga*.
- Renku is different to the comedic style of medieval Japanese linked verse called *mushin renga*.
- Renku is unrelated to the experimental English forms which incorporate *ren* or *enga* in their names.
- Renku is sometimes misapplied to trivial forms of Edo period *haikai no renga*.

This book deals solely with haikai no renga as written by the *Shomon*—the immediate Basho school—later close disciples, and those of the renku revival who further that approach. It is therefore limited to *Shofu* renku—linked verse written in the Basho style.

The author

The author is a wholly decrepit individual who will shortly be composting back into the more anonymous parts of Lancashire.

A former musician and professional liar, the latter part of his life has been spent crouched over the paraffin stove in his garden shed, plotting revenge.

During this time he claims to have led hundreds of linked verse sequences. Translated or co-translated a significant number of Edo period kasen. Swapped secrets on prosody with enemy agents via short wave radio. And scoured the pages of Health and Efficiency Magazine for the key terms *renga* and *renku*. Until they hurt.

The hidden agenda

- Renku is not a Japanese art form. It is an art form that has arisen in Japan.
- Art transcends time and space.
- There is no absolute distinction to be drawn between Japanese and non-Japanese renku.
- There is no absolute distinction to be drawn between Edo period and modern renku.
- All aspects of Shofu renku aesthetics may be understood in any cultural context.
- All aspects of Shofu renku technique may be emulated in any human language.

John Carley, August 2013

The Forms of Renku

descriptions, schemas, appraisals, examples

THE FORMS OF RENKU

How to Read the Schemas
sticking to the plan

Caveat lector

The use of schematic guides has been a feature of the spread of renku worldwide. They are not a new phenomenon, and are still used in Japan. However, though they are often called *circles*, Japanese renku groups tend to be run along traditional lines. Authority is organised vertically and composition is likely to be directed by a person of acknowledged seniority who will vary the outline at will.

There are few such specialists elsewhere. And there is perhaps less appetite for what is perceived as hierarchy. Who needs to be told what to do, when a glance at a crib sheet will suffice?

Schematic guides are a boon. They give rapid access to an unfamiliar format, and they empower all present in the decision making process. But they are limited. And therefore, ultimately, they are limiting.

By their very nature the schematic guides presented here are as flawed as any others. They are optimised. They are idealised. Though hopefully not entirely neutered. The reader is respectfully reminded that these layouts are illustrative only and represent a fraction of those possible. Anyone with the patience to read the rest of this book will be able to modify them at will. At a minimum it is advisable to skim the description and appraisal that accompany each guide.

Renku Reckoner is dedicated to the contemporary exercise of Shofu renku in English. *Shofu* means *in the manner or style of Basho*. This is not a question of layouts or schematics but of aesthetics and techniques. There is absolutely no reason why poets with a little experience should not go beyond the present guides and come up with fresh ideas.

Header, description and appraisal

For each type of sequence, the first line of the page header is the name of the format. The second carries a strap line. Where the name is a romaji rendering of the Japanese, the strap line is generally a free translation. The third line details the originator or populariser of the format plus an approximate date for its emergence.

There follows an overall verse count and a description of the principal structural features. In the main this section is limited to form and function. However, where the originator considered particular aspects of the architecture to have a bearing on technique, related injunctions, and their consequences, are outlined.

An appraisal appears below every chart and its respective key. This is more subjective. It discusses the aesthetic choices implicit in a format and may compare one type of sequence with another. It also ascribes a stylistic tendency, varying from the classical to the avant garde. These latter are offered as a rule of thumb. The reader may choose to ignore them.

More certain are the references to later chapters that appear in both the description and appraisal. They point to further reading that will illuminate specific points of contention, particularly those which are most frequently misunderstood.

It is not recommended to attempt composition of any sort in the absence of a working knowledge of the basic generative mechanism of renku described in the chapter *Link & Shift: An Overview*.

The chart

Where the sequence divides formally into parts, movements or sides, the chart is likewise divided into sections. These are either named for the traditional folio divisions (see *Kasen: Description*) or numbered. If applicable, each section also carries an indication of its dynamic phase drawn from the jo–ha–kyu pacing paradigm (see *A Dynamic Pattern*). The chart is otherwise arranged vertically.

The first column at left gives the name or number of each verse position followed by its status as a long or short verse. The named verses have special compositional characteristics (see *Beginnings and Endings*). In so far as *long* and *short* are fluid concepts in much English haikai, the reader might wish to refer to the chapter *Know Yourself*.

In some sources generic verse positions are numbered according to their place on the side of a writing sheet—be it real or notional. This is particularly the case for the kasen and those sequences such as the tankako and nijuin which are thought to resemble it. However, given that not all renku sequences divide in this way, and those that do vary from authority to authority, for the sake of consistency the present diagrams number them sequentially from start to finish.

All but the most experimental work starts from the season in which composition is begun. Accordingly the remainder of the columns are headed autumn, spring, summer or winter. Sequences follow down. In order to give some indication of the flexibility available, autumn and spring have two layouts each.

Some sources, particularly those dealing with historic or Japanese practice only, will give distributions for a fifth season—new year. As an entity in its own right new year has become increasingly marginal. For our present purposes it is discarded (see *The Seasons of Renku*).

The symbols

All verse positions carry a season/non-season designation. The seasons are coded **sp**—spring, **su**—summer, **au**—autumn, and **wi**—winter. Non-season verses, otherwise known as *miscellaneous* verses, are coded **ns**. In rare cases the reader will encounter an *all-season* position—**sn**. This permits any of the four seasons to appear, but does not allow a treatment as non-season.

Almost invariably season verses appear in groups of two or more. Should a season be brought forward or delayed, the verses move as a group.

Some verse positions may also feature traditional fixed topics. These are coded **bl**—blossom, **mn**—moon, and **lv**—love. A modern alternative to blossom, the more generic flower, is coded **fl** whilst the rokku adds the quirk of asserting a rock position—**rk**. The positions shown for the love verses are indicative only. If brought forward or delayed, they also move as a group.

The forward slash / indicates a choice of designation for that particular verse position—the most commonly chosen option being listed first. Therefore **fl/bl** is a choice between flower or blossom figuring in that verse—flower being the more likely. Likewise **sp/au** is a choice between spring or autumn, with spring being the default.

Particular attention should be paid to season options of this sort. Where the identical order and choice appears in successive verses, the verses will change together. There may also be implications for subsequent choices. A pair of verses coded **wi/su**, **wi/su** early in a poem will typically find their counterpart **su/wi**, **su/wi** further on. In this instance, if the most common option of winter is chosen for the first pair, the reciprocal summer must be chosen for the latter, and vice versa.

Single verses may behave in the same way, though the counterpart will just as frequently appear in the verse immediately following as at a distance. Therefore **su/ns** may follow hard on **ns/su**. Here, if non-season is chosen first, summer appears second. And so on.

THE FORMS OF RENKU

If in doubt, the key at the foot of the chart sets out the relevant conditions.

Square brackets **[...]** indicate a single option between one or more verse positions. The choice is either/or. For examle, where **[mn]** appears in both the hokku and at verse #5, moon will appear as the fixed topic in one only of these verses.

Parentheses **(...)** indicate that a topic may appear at that verse position or be ignored. For example, where **(bl)** appears in the hokku an additional blossom verse is possible there, but not obliged.

Caveat scriptor

The schematic guides are designed to help writers avoid some of the more obvious pitfalls of a particular type of sequence. Persons new to the genre are advised to adhere to the limited options indicated, at least in the first instance. But the ability to faithfully follow a diagram has little to do with poetry. Simply meeting the criteria for a verse is not the same as writing the verse, any more than expressive singing involves simply hitting the right notes.

Kasen
the thirty-six splendid immortals
per Matsuo Basho 1680s

Kasen—36 verses: Description

The kasen—meaning *splendid immortals*—takes its name from the practice of creating ideal groups of thirty-six artistic forbears. In outline the kasen predates Basho but his subsequent refinements earned it such popularity that the format has been identified with him ever since. Before the 1650s most sequences were one hundred verse *hyakuin*, or fifty verse *gojuin*. By the time of Basho's death the kasen predominated.

The macro structure of the kasen reflects the number of standard writing sheets—*kaishi*—needed to record it. If the scribe's brushwork is suitably neat, a kasen requires two sheets. Both sides are written on.

The front of the first sheet—*sho-ori no omote*—records any title or foreword plus the six verses of the preface—*jo*. The back of the first sheet—*sho-ori no ura*—carries the first twelve verses of the development movement—*ha*. The front of the second sheet—*nagori no omote*—holds the further twelve verses of ha, whilst the finale—*kyu*—is carried on the reverse—*nagori no ura*—along with a record of the who, where and when of composition.

Historically, the division of the central section into two movements of twelve verses is a function of their physical separation. However in the writing of the immediate Basho school, and subsequent generations of Shofu poets, it is often possible to discern a difference. The second twelve may be more swift moving and challenging, exhibiting deliberately disruptive dynamic and phonic properties. Some renku theorists, writing in English, therefore distinguish between the two halves of ha, referring to the first as the *development* and the second as the *intensification*.

Given that it was Basho's format of choice, the general parameters of the kasen are to be found in many contemporary sources aimed at persons new to renku. In order to be both brief and intelligible, such descriptions are necessarily simplified. Unfortunately, the consequent standardisation can give the impression of an unrelenting orthodoxy. This in turn places an apparent premium on conformity—the implication being that the genre is both formulaic and dull.

The reader should be aware that the précis given here, and illustrated by the schematics, is an indication only of how the kasen may be written. Moreover it describes the contemporary approach which, influenced by the cautious conservatism of recent years, is less flexible than in times past. Words such as *must*, *will*, *never* and *only* are frequently encountered in respect of the kasen but, in the corpus of Basho's own work, there are many exceptions that would doubtless cause the modern editor to quail and perplex the more didactic of our worthy authorities.

Assuming there are any trees left to pulp, elsewhere in this screed of cant the chapter *The Seasons of Renku* discusses the forces that govern the order and duration of seasonal passages in all forms of renku. It is the basis for the layouts charted below. Familiarity with it will allow writers to exercise an appropriate degree of flexibility.

Though Basho's own work shows a preponderance of the former, in theory a kasen divides more or less equally between season and non-season (miscellaneous) verses. Of the season verses, spring and autumn are more prominent than summer and winter by a ratio of approximately 5:3. Spring and autumn verses typically appear in threes—a number that may extend to four or five, as was common in the Edo period. Summer and winter likewise appear in pairs or singly, with the possibility that the run will extend to three. A feature of the earlier literature is that a series of season verses will often be found to cross the boundary between one side of a writing sheet and the next, or to transition between sheets. By contrast, in contemporary practice there is a tendency to regard the folio and seasonal boundaries as co-terminous, with a consequent emphasis on the breaks between movements.

Over the course of a poem, and other than for poems begun in spring, the major seasons—spring and autumn—feature twice, whilst summer and/or winter may be represented by a single group of verses. For poems begun in spring, the season makes three separate appearances. In all cases, the fixed topic of spring blossom appears twice: as the penultimate verse on the back of the first sheet—at #17—and as the penultimate verse of the sequence as a whole—verse position #35. These positions are referred to as the place or throne of blossom—*hana no za*—and are very rarely brought forward or delayed.

In the kasen a blossom verse is never treated as the more generic topic of *flower*—it remains the preserve of cherry or plum—though far more irreverent tones are possible than would have been thinkable in medieval renga. Some of Basho's sequences contain puns that disguise the topic altogether.

In total the moon makes three appearances: as the penultimate verse of the preface—position #5, at or around the seventh position on the back of the first sheet—verse #13, and as the penultimate verse on the front of the second sheet—position #29. These are *tsuki no za*—the place of the moon. Two of the moons are almost invariably set against autumn, that of jo—unless the season itself is displaced—and that towards the close of the second part of ha. The third moon takes a different season—generally summer or winter, rarely spring—and may be relatively underplayed. Unlike blossom verses, the moon positions more readily shift—#13 being most likely to be brought forward or delayed.

The other fixed topic to have survived the radical downsizing from renga—love—typically appears as a pair or trio of verses somewhere in the middle of both of the longer passages of verse. Basho tended to treat love rather freely whereas others of his school, and later writers, often choose to mirror the train of emotions inherited from the classics. We can therefore expect to see a naive attraction become physical consummation, only for the whole farrago to end in disillusion—circumstances in which it can take skill to avoid straightforward narrative progression. A love run may also be preceded by a verse which indirectly sets up the general subject. This is *koi no yobidashi*—the usher of love. Less common is *koi banare*—the end of love—a tag verse whose figurative reading implies some form of suitably sententious moralisation.

In the work of the immediate Basho school the special compositional characteristics of hokku, wakiku, daisan and ageku (see *Beginnings and Endings*) are rarely modified and never ignored. Likewise only the most intimate sequences fail to honour the duty to code for the appropriate greetings, leave-taking or augury.

Modern kasen are little different, especially where—as is common in Japan—composition marks a ceremonial occasion such as an anniversary. Though many new types of sequence have been proposed in the last fifty years, a wholesale revision of the kasen has not. The only appreciable difference is that—as indicated by the following diagram—contemporary poems tend not to employ a very long run of verses set in single season.

Kasen: Schemas

first sheet, front—preface—jo

	autumn	autumn	spring	spring	summer	winter
hokku	au	au [mn]	sp	sp	su	wi
wakiku	au	au [mn]	sp	sp	su	wi
daisan	au	au	sp	sp	su/ns	wi/ns
4 short	ns	ns	ns	ns	ns	ns
5 long	su mn	ns/wi	ns	wi mn	au mn	au mn
6 short	su	wi	au mn	wi	au	au

first sheet, back—development—ha part 1

	autumn	autumn	spring	spring	summer	winter
7 long	su	ns	au	ns	au	au
8 short	ns lv	ns	au	ns	ns	ns lv
9 long	ns lv	ns lv	ns lv	ns	ns	ns lv
10 short	ns (lv)	ns lv	ns lv	ns	ns (lv)	ns (lv)
11 long	ns	ns (lv)	ns (lv)	au	ns lv	ns
12 short	wi	su [mn]	ns	au [mn]	wi	ns
13 long	wi mn	su [mn]	su mn	au [mn]	wi mn	su mn
14 short	ns	ns	su	ns	ns	su
15 long	ns	ns	ns	ns	ns	ns
16 short	ns	sp [bl]	ns	sp	sp	ns
17 long	sp bl	sp [bl]	sp bl	sp bl	sp bl	sp bl
18 short	sp	sp	sp	sp	sp	sp

THE FORMS OF RENKU

second sheet, front—development/intensification—ha part 2

19 long	sp	ns	sp	ns	sp	sp
20 short	ns	ns	ns	ns (lv)	ns	ns
21 long	ns	ns	ns	ns lv	ns (lv)	ns
22 short	ns	ns lv	ns	ns lv	su (lv)	ns
23 long	su	ns lv	wi	su (lv)	su lv	wi
24 short	su (lv)	su (lv)	wi	su	ns/wi lv	wi
25 long	ns lv	su	ns/su	ns	ns	ns (lv)
26 short	ns lv	ns	ns lv	ns	ns	ns lv
27 long	ns	ns	ns lv	ns	ns	ns lv
28 short	au	au [mn]	au	au	au	ns
29 long	au mn	au [mn]	au mn	au [mn]	au mn	au mn
30 short	au	au	au	au [mn]	au	au

second sheet, back—finale—kyu

31 long	au	ns	au	ns	au	au
32 short	ns	ns	ns	ns	ns	ns
33 long	ns	ns	ns	ns	ns	ns
34 short	sp/ns	sp	sp/ns	sp	sp/ns	sp/ns
35 long	sp bl	sp bl	sp bl	sp bl	sp bl	sp bl
ageku	sp	sp	sp	sp	sp	sp

Notes

sp/ns – spring is the more likely option
ns/wi – likewise non-season
ns/su – likewise non-season
su/ns – likewise summer
wi/ns – likewise winter
ns – non-season (miscellaneous) position
bl – blossom position
[bl] – alternate blossom position—for each adjacent pair the choice is either/or
mn (moon position)
[mn] – alternate moon position—for each adjacent pair the choice is either/or
lv – love position, indicative—love verses move as group
(lv) – additional love position, optional, indicative—love verses move as group

Kasen: Appraisal

Writing a kasen is like playing the banjo. It is easy to do badly.

Renku is poetry, not a credit check. The idea that we may succeed purely by dint of meeting some criterion or other is anathema. Shofu sequences are neither a game, nor an entertainment. If you have bought this book on a different understanding, please burn it immediately. Should you be reading a virtual copy, please smash your hard-drive, or other digital storage medium, with a hammer. A large one.

Given its antecedents it is hardly surprising that the kasen is wonderful. But it is also unforgiving. In order to prosper one must understand, and be able to exploit, the techniques brought to bear by the Basho school. Minimum requirements are a fine control of relative pacing (see *A Dynamic Pattern*) and the ability to generate powerful linear movement involving non-thematic forms of cohesion (see *The Mechanics of the White Space*). It also helps to have a conscious control of form and phonics (see *Know Your Enemy* and *Know Yourself*), plus a distaste for flummery. In their absence it is unlikely that a poem will gain sufficient shape to reward the readers' willingness to engage.

Similarly, unless the participants are few in number, highly talented, and have a good grounding in the genre, a poem needs to be directed by an experienced leader—a *sabaki*. The length of the movements is such that a purely picaresque approach will fail. The six verses of the preface or finale are enough to require an overview. Devoid of guidance, the twenty-four verses of the development and intensification can be a very long haul indeed.

For all but a genius, or a fool, thirty-six verses can also take some time to complete. Particularly in the case of remote composition—by correspondence, email or social media—the sheer number of exchanges needed to achieve a full text can cause the poem, or enthusiasm for it, to founder. A less ambitious project may be wise. At first.

But a facility with the kasen remains essential to the development of excellence in Shofu renku. People who limit themselves to the shorter modern forms are unlikely to develop the highest artistry the genre permits. It is not that the kasen is best avoided. Only that it can be daunting for the novice.

Perhaps the best counsel is to read some of the classics first in translation—always avoiding Mr Miner and Ms Odagiri. As the moons, blossoms, loves, and familiar seasons recur, but do so without repeating, we are reminded that the best renku do not strive after absolute novelty. In the hands of a Master, both the structure and execution of the kasen demonstrate that fine writing has more to do with periodicity and interlocking cycles, with tonal control, evolution and recontextualisation.

All of us can aspire to this. It simply takes time to learn.

THE FORMS OF RENKU

Kasen: Example

Drinking debts get run up here and there
For a man to live past 70—well, that's rare   Tu Fu

Purveyors of Verse

purveyors of verse
gorging year on year
these sake debts —   Kikaku   詩あきんど年を貪る酒債かな

a winter lake at dusk,
horses hauling carp   Basho   冬湖日暮て駕馬に鯉

billhooks blunt
some brutes are yet
let past the barrier-gate   Basho   干鈍き夷に関をゆるすらん

shamisen—our demons
brought to tears   Kikaku   三線人の鬼を泣しむ

moonlight on my sleeve
a cricket
drowsy on my lap   Kikaku   月は袖 蟋蟀眠る 膝の上に

binding the wings of a snipe
how dark the night   Basho   鴫の羽しばる夜深き也

    * * * *

that shameless monk
do they sneer at him?
swathes of silver-grass   Basho   恥知らぬ僧を笑ふか草薄

Yamazaki drizzle,
the paper-brolly dance   Kikaku   しぐれ山崎からかさを舞う

a bamboo patterned
quilted kimono
deep-dyed indigo   Basho   笹竹のどてらを藍に染めなして

the hunting ground in cloud,
longing for his prince   Kikaku   狩場の雲に若殿を恋

a noble girl-child
sent to be fostered
by the village boss   Basho   一の姫里の庄家に養はれ

that famous snorer, I'd say
has been an awful topic   Kikaku   鼾名に立つと云題を責めけり

mountain cuckoo, its echoing call the ghost of remorse	Basho	ほとゝきす怨の霊と啼かへり
clinging to this life, scrawny from cold scraps	Kikaku	うき世に泥む寒食の痩
petals for my shoes so poor, my hat a rice-straw lid	Basho	沓は花貧重し笠はさん俵
thus Basho our host smites a butterfly	Kikaku	芭蕉あるじの蝶たたく身よ
all gone to rot, the pye-dogs too will likely eat haikai!	Basho	腐れたる俳諧犬も食はずや
itching and scratching restless night, restless moon	Kikaku	ほちほちとして寐ぬ夜ねぬ月

* * * *

the groom will join her shortly as the fulling beat begins	Kikaku	聟入の近づくままに初砧
battle being spent kudzu holds no grudge	Basho	戦ひ止んで葛うらみなし
cast in gold just to jeer at little Madame Violet	Kikaku	嘲りに黄金は鋳る小紫を
Otoku's nipples black as any bream	Basho	黒鯛黒しおとく女が乳
her hair a wrack to coil and crack the horns from a turban shell	Kikaku	枯藻髪さざえの角を巻折らん
this storm-tossed cape the demon's acolyte	Basho	魔神を使とす荒海の崎
take up your bow of iron, go forth to face the warring world	Kikaku	鉄の弓取猛き世に出よ
a tiger at her breast, with child by break of day	Basho	虎懐に姙るあかつき

THE FORMS OF RENKU

the mountain cold,
four sleepers lie abed
blown by a gale   Kikaku   山寒く四睡の床を吹く嵐

banked embers spent
I see by finger tip   Basho   うづみ火消て指の灯

mistress slattern
grown jealous of morning
closes out the moon   Kikaku   下司后朝をねたみ月を閉

a watermelon
wrapped in silk, no less!   Kikaku   西瓜を綾に包むあやにく

       * * * *

such sorrow,
the bush-clover of Miyagi Moor
withered by the wind   Basho   哀いかに宮城野のぼた吹凋るらん

Michinoku's wild-men
couldn't spot a quern   Kikaku   みちのくの夷 しらぬ石臼

the warrior slumbers
in full armour
borrowing his pillow   Basho   武士の鎧の丸寝枕貸す

eight calls from the colt
to warn of snow to come   Kikaku   八声の駒の雪を告げつつ

purveyors of verse
gorging blossoms fair
oh sake debts!   Kikaku   詩あきんど花を貪る酒債哉

a vernal lake at dusk,
palanquins piled with song   Basho   春湖日暮て駕輿に吟

Winter 1682

Matsuo Basho
Takarai Kikaku

Rokku
renku rocks on
Haku Asanuma (2000)

Rokku—x6 verses: Description

The rokku is a variable length sequence that can be tailored to fit the circumstances of composition. It comprises a flexible number of six verse movements, typically in the range of three to six. The shortest variant is eighteen verses, a longer variant—thirty or thirty-six. Three movements are a minimum. There is no stated maximum.

The name combines the Japanese words for *six* and *verse*, but also echoes the transliteration of the English word *rock*—as in *rock and roll*—a wry reminder that poets are expected to rebel.

In practice the rokku mixes traditional and modern characteristics in equal proportion. It is paced strictly according to jo–ha–kyu. The first six verses are therefore jo. They observe the constraints associated with more formal sequences and will typically include a moon verse at position #5. The closing movement is kyu. It closes with spring blossom and ageku in the regulation manner, though the latter may sometimes be non-season. The special characteristics of hokku, wakiku, daisan, and ageku are retained, honorific functions included—so willing.

All other sections of the rokku are ha. It is a stipulation that the penultimate six verses of a poem should adopt some form of experimental prosody. In Japanese, where haikai of all sorts normally employs strict-form (see *Know Your Enemy*), this movement is comprehensively freed up. Conversely in English, when the overall approach is effectively free verse, it may be that at this point there is a switch to something more regular. Writers employing the supple stanzas advocated in a later chapter (see *Know Yourself*) are faced with a dilemma—to loosen further, or to become more obviously strict-form. In any event Asanuma-san's intention is clear—for the last movement of ha, experimentation is the order of the day.

As noted, the moon verse of the first movement, and the blossom verse of the close, reflect the values implied by their familiar positions. In all but the shortest variants, further moon and blossom verses appear in one or more movements of ha. These are less conventional. Blossom can become the more generic flower, while moon embraces an assortment of seasons and may sustain the occasional indignity. Autumn moon, with its claim to better treatment, features only once in a poem.

A pair, or pairs, of love verses also appear in one or more movements of ha alongside a new fixed topic, the eponymous *rock*. This is a mini category containing *rock* (stone), *ice cube*, and *rock music*. The default is *rock* (stone). Sequences with more than one rock position use a different reference for each. The frequency and ratio of blossom, moon and love verses reflect those of the wider literature—rock being analogous to blossom. We may therefore expect to see moon every nine to twelve verses whilst blossom, rock, and a pair of love verses will appear somewhere in the order of once every fifteen to eighteen verses.

In the desire to avoid any conceivable instance of reversion, the rokku lays great emphasis on the importance of shift (see *More About Shift*). Therefore, despite the anomalous nature of some of the earliest pieces published in Japanese, there is an absolute injunction against a tone or topic persisting for more than two verses. This includes the seasonal context. The sole exception is the ageku, which is afforded the compositional latitude typical of an Edo period kasen. Therefore, in sequences where the antepenultimate and penultimate verses take spring, ageku may also do the same. But even here non-season is preferred.

A poem still begins with the season in which it is composed and draws to a close on spring. Beyond this, and the newly introduced ban on more than two like verses appearing together, all other aspects of seasonal distribution are left open. Individual season verses, or pairs of verses, may change without an intervening non-season verse. Seasons may simply alternate, minor seasons outnumber major, etc. Which being the case, the layouts below err on the side of caution.

THE FORMS OF RENKU

Rokku: Schemas

	jo	jo	jo	jo	jo	jo
	autumn	autumn	spring	spring	summer	winter
hokku	au	au mn	sp	sp	su	wi
wakiku	au	au	sp bl	sp	su rk	wi
daisan	ns	ns	ns	ns	ns	ns
4 short	ns	ns	ns	ns	ns	ns
5 long	su mn	ns	wi mn	au mn	au mn	su mn
6 short	ns	su rk	wi	au	au	ns
	ha part 1	*ha*	ha part 1	ha part 1	ha part 1	ha part 1
7 long	ns rk	*ns*	ns	ns	ns	ns lv
8 short	sp	*ns lv*	ns lv	su	ns lv	ns lv
9 long	sp bl/fl	*ns lv*	au lv	ns rk	wi lv	au
10 short	ns	*wi*	au	ns lv	wi	au
11 long	ns lv	*wi*	ns rk	wi lv	ns	ns rk
12 short	wi lv	*ns*	ns	ns	ns	ns
	ha part 2	kyu	ha part 2	*ha part. 2*	*ha part 2*	ha part 2
13 long	ns	ns	ns	*ns*	*ns*	wi mn
14 short	ns	su	ns	*ns*	*sp mn*	ns
15 long	au mn	ns	su mn	*sp*	*ns*	ns
16 short	au	ns	su	*su*	*ns*	ns
17 long	ns	sp bl	ns	*su mn*	*au rk*	sp bl/fl
18 short	ns rk	sp	ns	*ns*	*ns*	sp

ROKKU

	ha part 3	ha part 3	kyu	kyu	ha part 3
19 long	*su*	*wi rk*	ns	su	*ns rk*
20 short	*ns*	*ns lv*	wi	ns	*su*
21 long	*ns lv*	*ns lv*	ns	ns	*ns lv*
22 short	*ns lv*	*au*	ns	sp	*ns lv*
23 long	*wi mn*	*au mn*	sp bl	sp bl	*au mn*
24 short	*wi*	*ns*	sp	ns/sp	*au*
	kyu	kyu			kyu
25 long	ns	ns			ns
26 short	ns	su			wi rk
27 long	ns	ns			ns
28 short	sp	sp			ns
29 long	sp bl	sp bl			sp bl
30 short	ns/sp	ns/sp			sp

Notes

ns/sp – non-season or spring—the default is non-season
ns – non-season (miscellaneous) position
bl – blossom position
bl/fl – blossom position, a treatment as flower is possible
mn – moon position
lv – love position, indicative—love verses move as group
rk – rock position—an element from the rokku category: rock (stone), ice cube, rock music
italic – verses in italics form part of the experimental (penultimate) movement of ha
verse number - designations that do not apply in all cases are greyed out

Rokku: Appraisal

Though at first sight startlingly radical, the rokku is in fact an intriguing blend of old and new.

Until the advent of the rokku a consistent theme of the renku revival had been the search for ever shorter sequences. Asanuma-san's proposal runs counter to this, or rather, offers a more nuanced solution. With a minimum length of eighteen verses, and no upper limit, he offers us a sequence for all occasions. At least in theory.

As with the kasen and triparshva, six verses apiece for the preface and finale are sufficient to explore their dynamic potential. Whether the same can be said for a single movement of ha is less certain. If, as indicated, jo and kyu are approached in classic mode, it will take some ingenuity to avoid the sensation that such a short central section is anything other than harsh and abrupt. The more so since, as the penultimate movement of the poem, it is also expected to use experimental prosody. In sum—an eighteen verse sequence looks tricky.

Two or more sections of development are a different proposition. It is possible to argue that the individual movements are still too short to facilitate the *renku wave*—a long passage of verse that builds and breaks thanks to an extended chain of non-cognitive association (see *The Mechanics of the White Space*). But Haku Asanuma takes ha in a different direction. His mercurial disregard for the seasons and fixed topics is intended to complement the modern, highly juxtapositional, approach that has evolved from the vogue for compact forms. Writing in this style continuously challenges, changes, and searches out new ground so that, in a well executed rokku, the experimental prosody of the penultimate movement is no more than a furtherance of what has gone before.

It seems likely therefore that the majority of rokku will be written as four, five or six movements in total—twenty-four, thirty or thirty-six verses—which devote two, three or four movements respectively to ha. Handled well these should yield balanced sequences. The same may be true of forty-two and forty-eight verse variants, but there is little obvious appetite for renku sessions this long.

The introduction of *rock* as a new fixed topic is little more than a pleasant whimsy, but the decision to limit all love or same-season verses to two in a row is highly significant. Hitherto this arrangement has occurred only by happenstance—as a result of lack of space, such as we see in the junicho and shisan. Many less practiced writers consider this a happy outcome as it limits the scope to unwittingly loop back. Asanuma-san takes the argument further. With the rokku he contends that any element of consonance between an added verse and the verse before last is always de facto reversion (see *The Three Rs*). When it comes to link and shift, shift must be absolute. Even if the space available is infinite, nothing may extend beyond the adjacent pair.

The assertion may seem unexceptional. Even self evident. But it does run counter to the theory and practice of the Basho school as it has stood for the past 300 years whereby relative degrees of shift may occur which are nonetheless sufficient to guarantee a non-thematic strand (see *Thematic Renku*). This is not to suggest that Asanuma-san's approach is unreasonable, or indefensible, but it is rather maximal. It would be unfortunate if it encouraged a simplistic understanding of the forces which govern variety and change in Shofu renku.

Should this be enough to have you counting sheep, or dancing with the angels and pin-heads? No. Anyone in search of serious insomnia is advised to attempt three or four simultaneous rokku with people from assorted time zones. Each variant of a different length. In a different language. As poem leader.

Rokku: Example

A Cup of Snow

laughing with delight
a cup of snow
a moon-eyed girl   jc

half gone, the last jar
of ginger jam   cm

roadside shop,
the chain-saw artist
asks me my sign   mdw

a faint glow in the sky
before sunset   as

first chill night
the smell of cedar
in the quilts   ha

tic by toc
the leaves begin to fall   jc

　　* * * *

dab, dab, dabbing
at her cards the old lady
yells 'bingo!'   cm

a mosquito bite
on the toddler's cheek   mdw

their second date
she drinks him
under the table   as

we roll with the waves
of the water bed   ha

and bathe eche veyne
in swich licour
of which engenderéd...   jc

the scent of wild rose
in the birthing suite   cm

* * * *

    deepening depression
    the telephone
    stops ringing   mdw

    a late-night diner
    the hum of the fridge   as

    constant as the
    poverty of poets
    autumn moon   jc

    three generations
    peddling fallen walnuts   cm

    left-over candy
    the pumpkin's toothy grin
    starts to sag   mdw

    candle wax obscuring
    the way of light   ha

* * * *

    tamarisk honey
    the el-tarfah of dry tears   as

    with each breath
    the desert's fire and dust   cm

    searching for an airplane
    without wings   jc

                              affair the after
    way wrong the home coming   mdw

    each snowflake different
    his wife's kiss   ha

    the lack of a sharp knife
    and a whetstone   as

* * * *

abattoir...
the apathetic gaze
of man and beast   cm

from rock to rock
the grizzly's nose   mdw

the sniper scope
adjusted
on the Canon Sure Shot   as

fighting through the shed
to reach the mower   jc

we fill our pails
with plum blossoms
and then?   ha

the spring dawn
spills down the mountain   cm

January to May 2008

Hortensia Anderson
John Carley (sabaki)
Carole MacRury
Alan Summers
Michael Dylan Welch

Tankako
an excursion in verse
Kagami Shiko (1700s)

Tankako—24 verses: Description

As the 4/8/8/4 verse structure suggests the tankako is a 2/3 scale kasen—a comparison which holds true for all the principal features. Hokku, wakiku, daisan, and ageku are generally treated in a conservative manner although the slight air of innovation which attaches itself to the tankako means that the kasen remains the format of choice for the most formal compositions.

Though they are shortened, the jo–ha–kyu dynamic pattern remains tied to the nominal four sides of a pair of writing sheets. The initial four verses therefore make up the preface—jo. The next eight constitute the first part of the development movement—ha. The second part, the erstwhile intensification, takes a further eight, whilst the poem concludes with four verses dedicated to the finale or rapid close—kyu.

The sequence allows for two moon verses, one of which is always set against autumn. Moon normally appears at verse positions #5 and #19. However, for sequences begun in autumn, the first is brought forward to figure in either the hokku or daisan. In these circumstances both moon verses will take autumn.

As with the kasen, each writing sheet has blossom as the penultimate verse—positions #11 and #23—though, for sequences begun in spring, the first may be brought forward to the hokku. Blossom is always treated as the classic cherry or plum, never as the more generic *flower*. In common with other types of Shofu sequence, where it is not nominated as a fixed topic, a reference to the latter may appear at any point in the poem as long as it does not diminish the prominence of the blossom verse proper.

Love normally appears twice, as a pair of verses somewhere towards the middle of each part of the development. A more extended treatment is possible at either of these locations while those of the second sheet may be held back to appear in the finale.

A run of spring verses generally appears twice, those of other seasons once only. Exceptions apply to sequences begun in spring which may have as many as three groups of spring verses, and those begun in autumn that may see a second group of autumn verses appear later in the poem—in which case one of the minor seasons may be omitted altogether.

Overall there is a slight preponderance of season verses, though a run of non-season verses may extend to four in a row. In almost all cases the central run of spring verses crosses from one sheet to the next whereas the border between jo and ha, and ha and kyu, is bounded on one or both sides by a miscellaneous verse.

Tankako: Schemas

first sheet, front—preface—jo

	autumn	autumn	spring	spring	summer	winter
hokku	au [mn]	au [mn]	sp	sp [bl]	su	wi
wakiku	au	au	sp	sp	su	wi
daisan	au [mn]	au [mn]	sp	sp	ns	ns
4 short	ns	ns	ns	ns	ns	ns

first sheet, back—development—ha part 1

	autumn	autumn	spring	spring	summer	winter
5 long	ns	ns	au mn	ns	au mn	su mn
6 short	wi/su	su/wi	au	wi/su	au	su
7 long	wi/su lv	su/wi lv	au lv	wi/su mn	au lv	ns
8 short	ns lv	ns lv	ns lv	ns lv	ns lv	ns lv
9 long	ns	ns lv	ns	ns lv	ns	ns lv
10 short	ns	ns	ns	ns	ns	ns
11 long	sp bl	sp bl	sp bl	su/wi [bl]	sp bl	sp bl
12 short	sp	sp	sp	su/wi	sp	sp

second sheet, front—development/intensification—ha part 2

	autumn	autumn	spring	spring	summer	winter
13 long	sp	sp	sp	ns	sp	sp
14 short	ns lv	ns	ns	ns	ns	ns
15 long	ns lv	ns	ns/[su/wi]	ns lv	ns	ns lv
16 short	ns	ns	[su/wi]/ns	ns lv	ns lv	ns lv
17 long	ns	ns	ns lv	au mn	ns lv	ns

18 short	au	wi/su	ns lv	au	wi	au
19 long	au mn	wi/su mn	wi/su mn	au	wi mn	au mn
20 short	au	ns	wi/su	ns	ns	au

second sheet, back—finale—kyu

21 long	ns	ns lv	ns	ns	ns	ns
22 short	ns	ns lv	ns	ns	ns	ns
23 long	sp bl	sp bl	sp bl	sp bl	sp bl	sp bl
ageku	sp	sp	sp	sp	sp	sp

Notes
wi/su – adjacent pairs take the same season—whichever pair is selected first the alternate pair is selected second (where available)
su/wi – ditto
[su/wi] – summer or winter in one only of the adjacent verses—a pair taking the alternate season will appear after
ns – non-season (miscellaneous) position
bl – blossom position
[bl] – alternate blossom position—the choice is either/or
mn (moon position)
[mn] – alternate moon position—the choice is either/or
lv – love position, indicative—love verses move as group

Tankako: Appraisal

As a student Shiko was a member of Shomon—Basho's inner circle. He learnt his lessons well.

If the scope of the tankako is to appreciably shorten the Basho-school kasen whilst retaining as many of the original features as possible it must be counted a success. It looks and feels familiar. The seasons and their related fixed topics turn up with a frequency, and in places, that ease the writer towards the continuance of Shofu—the Basho style.

Inevitably there are compromises. With only four verses available the preface can be a little tight. As the first three verses have special compositional requirements, it is none too easy to establish a lasting sense of decorum with only verse #4 available to calm any turbulence. The temptation is to always settle on a hokku that will set an agreeable tone, and then opt for the least disruption.

The decision to retain position #5 as the default for the first moon verse also generates conflict. Not only are we no longer in the preface, this position is now the first of the development movement and is expected to lend the poem a distinct forward momentum. The more reflective palette typical of a classic autumn moon holds few of the correct colours.

It is also questionable whether four verses will suffice to fully satisfy the demands of the finale – at least not as specified by Master Zeami (see *Beginnings and Endings*). There is a tendency to reinforce the popular misconception that kyu is either uniformly brash, or a staid mirror of the poem's opening.

The complaint therefore is that the tankako makes demands to which its structure is not best adapted. But such a criticism is excessive. An awareness of the potential difficulties with the preface and finale should be enough to see them overcome. Certainly the eight verse passages of the development movement permit all but the most remarkable feats of concatenation. And anyone capable of that level of skill has the kasen readily available.

The tankako has much to recommend it for poets who are familiar with the Shomon approach to the kasen and do not wish to stray too far, or for those who have hitherto only written compact sequences and would like to experience a fresh set of challenges without running the risk, inherent to the longest forms, that the project might become unwieldy.

Somewhere under this desk is a rubber stamp that says *passed*. Now, where did I put that ink?

THE FORMS OF RENKU

Tankako: Example

The Kite Contest

frogs, toads —
the unsuspected beauty
of their voices   bd

a lotus-stem lengthens
in the mirror lake   vm

between the rows
a flash of knives and hoes,
women weeding   jc

the kite contest begins
to shouts of glee   kr

* * * *

crunching, crunching
we share pieces
of peanut toffee   ac

her hair all in a flutter
on a cobble bench   sy

snowbound silence,
just the warmth of
breathing from their bed   jc

bereft of stars
the winter moon, alone   kr

not a hope
but the fight with cancer
goes on anyway   vm

tea spurts from the child's mouth
down his shirt   sy

with the squash blossoms
art students
drift into the Rialto   bd

hovering over the menu
a late sun   ac

* * * *

TANKAKO

digging for diamonds,
is the mud colour
this deep from blood?   kr

by tooth and talon
they harrow all hell   jc

a stubborn battle,
both cocks end up
diced in the blanquette   vm

fumbling at the keys
my piano frowns back   ac

the stave
betrayed by moonlight and smoke
his life as a fox   bd

hairs rise on young necks
the touch of frail grass   sy

a burnt clearing,
hunters and beaters
ready for the shoot   vm

caught in the long jump
athletes pedal air   kr

* * * *

tracing down
the faded spines of books
a narrowed eye   bd

the Master checks the metre
of my verse   jc

our dusty street
filled with plum blossoms
and swallows   ac

a cool touch upon the pond,
a rippled breeze   sy

April to May 2013

Ashley Capes   Vasile Moldovan
John Carley (sabaki)   Kala Ramesh
Bill Dennis   Steven Yaschuk

Triparshva
past, present and future
Norman Darlington (2005)

Triparshva—22 verses: Description

The name triparshva is derived from the Sanskrit meaning *trilateral* or *facing three ways*. It has three movements or sides, each dedicated to a component of jo–ha–kyu—the performance paradigm elaborated by the Noh master Zeami and subsequently applied to other Japanese art forms, notably, in the case of haikai no renga, by Basho in his refinement of the kasen.

The first side is jo. Its six verses echo the opening of the kasen. Hokku, wakiku and daisan have full scope to unfold and may deal in honorifics if desired. Verse #4 takes the preface quietly forwards. Moon—albeit not autumn—is at the familiar position #5. Verse #6 rounds off the movement at leisure.

The second side is ha. Concluding with a run of autumn verses, and typically featuring autumn moon at the penultimate position, it recalls the second development movement of the kasen. At ten verses it has sufficient space to cope with forceful writing.

Kyu is also familiar. Uncluttered with extraneous obligations, it is long enough to permit a suitable flourish before closing with the ever amenable blossom and the lingering resonance of a classic ageku.

Each movement of the triparshva contains two distinct seasons. Autumn and spring verses appear in groups of two or three. Winter and summer appear singly or in pairs. Seasons do not straddle the boundaries between sides. The distinction between movements is clear cut.

Of the two moon verses, one is always autumn—normally that of #15—whilst the other takes a different season. However, for sequences begun in autumn, the moon at #5 may be brought forward to the hokku, in which case—if the other is not also brought forward from #15—both may be set in autumn.

Sequences begun in spring may have blossom in the hokku as well as at the close. In all cases, though blossom is generally treated as cherry or plum, other flowering and fruiting deciduous trees may feature—including those that are used for hedging. In so far as some flower relatively late, care must be taken to avoid anachronism in the overall run of verses (see *The Seasons of Renku*).

Love takes two or three verses towards the middle of the development movement. Treated freely or formally, this number may extend to four if *koi no yobidashi* and/or *koi banare* are involved (see *Kasen: Description*).

Triparshva: Schemas

side 1, preface—jo

	autumn	autumn	spring	spring	summer	winter
hokku	au	au mn	sp	sp bl	su	wi
wakiku	au	au	sp	sp	su	wi
daisan	ns	au	ns	sp	ns	ns
4 short	ns	ns	ns	ns	ns	ns
5 long	su/wi mn	wi/su	su/wi mn	wi/su mn	sp/wi mn	sp/su mn
6 short	ns	ns	ns	ns	sp/ns	sp/ns

side 2, development—ha

7 long	ns	ns	ns	ns	ns	ns
8 short	ns	ns	ns	ns	ns	ns
9 long	wi/su (lv)	ns	ns	su/wi lv	ns/sp (lv)	ns/sp
10 short	wi/su lv	su/wi	wi/su (lv)	su/wi lv	wi/sp lv	su/sp (lv)
11 long	ns lv	su/wi [mn]	wi/su lv	ns lv	ns lv	ns lv
12 short	ns (lv)	ns lv	ns lv	ns	ns (lv)	ns lv
13 long	ns	ns lv	ns (lv)	au [mn]	ns	ns (lv)
14 short	au	au	au	au	au	au
15 long	au mn	au [mn]	au mn	au [mn]	au mn	au mn
16 short	au	ns	au	ns	au	au

side 3, finale—kyu

17 long	ns	ns	ns	ns	ns	ns
18 short	su/wi	wi/su	su/wi	wi/su	wi	su
19 long	ns	ns	ns	ns	ns	ns
20 short	sp	sp	sp	ns	sp	sp
21 long	sp bl	sp bl	sp bl	sp bl	sp bl	sp bl
ageku	sp	sp	sp	sp	sp	sp

Notes

su/wi – whichever season appears first an alternate pair appears second, reverting to a single verse of the original thereafter—same season pairs change together
wi/su – ditto
sp/wi + sp/ns – for a sequence begun in summer—jo will contain a pair of spring verses or a single winter verse, the opposite occurring in ha—same season pairs change together
sp/su + sp/ns – for a sequence begun in winter—jo will contain a pair of spring verses or a single summer verse, the opposite occurring in ha—same season pairs change together
ns – non-season (miscellaneous) position
bl – blossom position.
mn – moon position.
[mn] – alternative moon position—the choice is either/or
lv – love position, indicative—love verses move as group
(lv) – additional love position, optional, indicative—love verses move as group

Triparshva: Appraisal

It is difficult to offer a critical appraisal of something which is to all intents and purposes flawless. But the triparshva is the result of human ingenuity, so defects there must be. Perhaps if I were to split my personality...

It looks strange... Having abandoned the polite fiction that it is recorded on conventional writing sheets, the poem does divide into three not four. But of course this number makes complete sense in respect of jo–ha–kyu.

Its proportions are lopsided. Whoever heard of 6/10/6?... Except that the doubling of size between preface and development is no magic bullet in itself. Consider the 4:8 ratio of the tankako. Eight verses are ok for a development movement, especially where there is a second one to follow. But four is tight for the preface or finale (see *Tankako: Appraisal*). And that 6:12 ratio, made so famous by the kasen, is itself a lopsided adjustment from the mediaeval hyakuin's 8:14. The strength of the triparshva is that the movements are optimised. The shape is a function of that.

Well the seasons follow the calendar then... No they don't. In some parts of some distributions, if you choose certain options, you *may* end up with calendar order. But there are always sufficient miscellaneous verses to make this a tractable problem at worst, and, if you want to avoid the whole issue in the first place, just choose other options.

It's a funny name. Foreign. It's enough to put me off... Yes. That would appear to true for some people.

Perhaps if it was called the *sanmen*—three facets—it would achieve an even greater diffusion. The triparshva is a relatively recent proposal. It has met with almost universal acclaim. At the time of writing, good quality examples have been published in something like a dozen languages. Japanese is not amongst them.

There is no absolute reason why the wish to spread knowledge of renku should imply a commensurate willingness to receive it. But this is a shame as the triparshva has achieved the holy grail. It permits the full exercise of the Basho style in only twenty-two verses. Funny name or not.

THE FORMS OF RENKU

Triparshva: Example

A Long Way Home

who knows where
this icy moon will lead —
a long way home   rj

my flower bed
could use a quilt of snow   jc

fizzing gently
in the bathroom—
gin and Alka-Seltzer   rj

the rumours spread
that such and such is...   jc

little lambs cavort
as well they ought
on picture postcards   rj

a dew drop lensing
rhapsodies of green   jc

   * * * *

light your chillum,
rock your splay toed feet
you mad mad monk   jc

dzap dzabba zooom
the ghost of New Orleans   rj

viscous in the heat
a ceiling fan
to stir the hours   jc

what God has joined
let no man put asunder   rj

imagining
the muzzle flash
his catamitic smile   jc

nothing but disgust
at Wilde's retraction   rj

oriental epigrams
these trifles
that are called 'haiku'   jc

falling leaves
a childless couple scamper   rj

arpeggio—
above the serried rooftops
autumn moon   jc

a carbonised potato
in the ash   rj

     * * * *

our alchemist insists
he always has been
fond of lead   rj

Bay Watch beauties
glimmer in the sun   jc

how wonderful,
here's half a dozen poets
that agree!   rj

nuthatches and creepers
track the sap   jc

cherry blossom
clinging
to the undertaker's hat   rj

so that's the promise:
death and resurrection   jc

November to December 2005

John Carley
Rachel Joyne

Nijuin
twenty times around
Meiga Higashi (1980s)

Nijuin—20 verses: Description

Despite its compact size, the folio structure of the nijuin is considered analogous to that of the kasen. The movements take their names from the same theoretical pair of writing sheets and correspond to the traditional dynamic pattern. The first four verses are the preface—jo. The following six comprise the first part of the development movement—ha. The nominal front of the second sheet carries the six verses that complete the development, and the four verses of the reverse are the finale—kyu.

Poems start with the season in which composition is begun and finish with a traditional run of spring verses including blossom and a seasonal ageku. Verse distributions for sequences begun in spring are therefore adjusted so that it features both at the opening and the close. Otherwise each season appears once only—spring and autumn as a group of three verses, summer and winter as a pair or, on occasion, as a single verse. Seasons do not cross over between sides or writing sheets. The individual movements are clear-cut.

There are two moon verses, one of which is set in autumn. For sequences begun in autumn, the first will therefore pull up from its default position at #5 in order to figure in either the hokku or daisan. Other constraints of verse distribution oblige the later moon position to roam the front of the second sheet.

With the exception of sequences begun in spring, blossom appears once only—in the conventional penultimate position. Those begun in spring may feature blossom both in the hokku and at the close, but the majority do not. In all cases the expectation is that the topic is treated in a conventional manner. Classical references are applauded.

Love generally appears as a pair of verses somewhere in each half of the development movement. A more extended treatment will typically involve either a set-up verse—koi no yobidashi—or a commentary verse—koi banare (see *Kasen: Description*). In these circumstances the total run would not exceed three verses, and the topic itself be limited to a single appearance.

Nijuin: Schemas

first sheet, front—preface—jo

	autumn	autumn	spring	spring	summer	winter
hokku	au [mn]	au [mn]	sp [mn]	sp (bl)	su	wi
wakiku	au	au	sp	sp	su	wi
daisan	au [mn]	au [mn]	ns	sp	ns	ns
4 short	ns	ns	ns	ns	ns	ns

first sheet, back—development—ha part 1

5 long	ns	ns	su [mn]	wi mn	au mn	au mn
6 short	ns lv	ns	su lv	wi	au	au
7 long	ns lv	ns lv	ns lv	ns	au lv	au lv
8 short	su/wi	ns lv	ns	ns lv	ns lv	ns lv
9 long	su/wi	wi/su lv	ns/wi	ns lv	ns	ns
10 short	ns	wi/su	wi/ns	su/ns lv	ns	ns

second sheet, front—development/intensification—ha part 2

11 long	ns	ns	ns	ns/su	ns	su [mn]
12 short	ns	ns	ns	ns	wi [mn]	su [mn]
13 long	ns lv	ns	au lv	ns	wi [mn]	ns
14 short	wi/su lv	su/wi	au lv	au	ns	ns lv
15 long	wi/su mn	su/wi mn	au mn	au mn	ns lv	ns lv
16 short	ns	ns	ns	au	ns lv	ns

second sheet, back—finale—kyu

17 long	ns	ns	ns	ns	ns	ns
18 short	sp	sp	sp	ns	sp	sp
19 long	sp bl	sp bl	sp bl	sp bl	sp bl	sp bl
ageku	sp	sp	sp	sp	sp	sp

	su/wi – whichever is selected first its counterpart is selected after—both verses change together
	wi/su – likewise
	ns/wi – whichever is selected first its counterpart is selected after
	su/ns – likewise
Notes	**ns** – non-season (miscellaneous) position
	bl – blossom position.
	(bl) – additional blossom position, optional
	mn – moon position
	[mn] – alternate moon position—the choice is either/or
	lv – love position, indicative—love verses move as group

Nijuin: Appraisal

The originator of the nijuin, Meiga Higashi, was a central figure in the renaissance of renku during the latter part of the last century. Always widely respected in Japan, and popular elsewhere as interest in the genre began to spread, Higashi-sensei demonstrated the ability to think freely and act judiciously. The nijuin is proof of both.

Abandoning Shiko's earlier caution (see *Tankako: Appraisal*) the format takes the axe to the kasen—slashing it almost in half. Excepting those sequences begun in spring, it does away with the central tenets of circularity and recurrence. Only the moon necessarily appears twice, and then always in a different season. With no element allowed to cross the divide, the folio divisions and the dynamic phases are treated as one and the same. The blade-work is nothing if not neat.

At the same time there is much that is familiar. Moon, blossom, and love are saved from any scandal. The distribution of the seasons, their relative proportions, and those of the intervening miscellaneous verses—all establish benchmarks for how the kasen might contract. Most obvious of all is the folio structure with its bow in the direction of writing sheets and scribes.

Yet it is here that the train hits the buffers. Neither the four verses of the preface nor the six verses of a development movement are enough to give the Basho style free rein. There is too little elbow room—too many constraints. There is not quite enough rope for us to hang ourselves. The four part division looks comforting enough, but it is not truly fit for purpose.

That, at least, is the accusation. But it may be as misdirected as it is churlish. Was it Higashi's aim to create the perfect mini-kasen, or to encourage and facilitate the writing of renku? We can judge from the thousands of subsequent poems that he certainly succeeded in the latter.

The nijuin broke the mould. It is clear and straightforward—easily assimilated—and has a certain style of its own. Though it may be that the triparshva more closely approaches the kasen, the nijuin is always good to write.

Nijuin: Example

Early Morning Heat

a line of ants
in the courgette flower —
early morning heat   ss

perhaps you'd care
to share my parasol?   jc

country-western
and native songs,
a circle round the drum   ws

she pastes her happy snaps
to a favourite page   cr

   * * * *

seeking, hiding
way beyond the curfew
shadows and moon   lf

in the blackberry basket
a taste of river fog   ss

the chameleon's tail
curls between
red, orange, yellow   cr

with a shiver of silk
her stocking hits the floor   jc

everyone answers
to the name of Smith
at Honeycomb Hotel   lf

the street sweeper
returns a gallic shrug   ss

   * * * *

misunderstood
a frog jumps into ~ whoops
the bouillabaisse   lf

a smear of something
stains my new saijiki   jc

THE FORMS OF RENKU

    snowbound highways
    lined with deer,
    the moon in every eye   ws

    lemmings stream across
    a frozen lake   cr

    over and over and over
    on hold
    the first four bars of Bach   ws

    all that Dresden china
    turned to dust   jc

        * * * *

    granddad hides his stash
    of sticky toffee
    in the glove box   cr

    a blackbird tugs a worm
    out of a hole   lf

    rising above
    the dry-stone wall
    waves of white blossom   ws

    between our dreams of spring
    a bridge of sand   ss

January to February 2013

John Carley (sabaki)
Lorin Ford
Cynthia Rowe
Sandra Simpson
William Sorlien

Imachi
waiting for the moon
Shunjin Okamoto (1984)

Imachi—18 verses: Description

The imachi is an undivided format offering a continuous run of eighteen verses. The absence of separate sides or movements—originally a function of the way longer work was recorded—earns it the epithet a *single sheet* poem (see *Kasen: Description*). The dynamic phases of jo–ha–kyu, normally associated with the folio divisions, are still present, but more fluid.

Each season appears once only. The ratios between season and non-season verses, and amongst the seasons themselves, are conventional. Spring and autumn take three verses apiece. Summer and winter, a pair. The overall proportion between season and non-season verses is therefore 10:8. At first sight this looks slightly unbalanced. But given that sequences begin with a run of season verses and end on another, or with a sole non-season verse, there are sufficient non-season positions to comfortably allow well spaced distributions. In time honoured fashion, the starting season is that of composition. Thereafter only the more generic constraints apply to the order in which they appear (see *The Seasons of Renku*).

Imachi means *to sit and wait*. In this case we are waiting for moonrise on the evening of the 18th day of the lunar cycle. This occurs noticeably later than at other times and was traditionally the occasion for either extended contemplation or extended revelry on the part of part of poets, thinkers and assorted drinkers. The name is therefore a wry suggestion that, as far as the arrival of the moon is concerned, events may unfold in a haphazard manner.

An alternative name for the imachi is *debana* which can be loosely given as *blossom takes its turn*. Both these titles indicate that the sequencing of the fixed topics may be irregular, but they are still treated according to precedent. Therefore, whilst some variants exist which allow for one only, the imachi typically has two moon verses, one of which is always autumn. The single blossom verse will be cherry or plum, and love is unlikely to step too far from its conventional terms of reference.

It must be said that those terms are often misunderstood by occidental poets whose interpretation of love may be at once too loose and too narrow. Whilst very explicit content is avoided, and any thematic development a sign of bad writing, in Shofu renku a run of love verses deals only with those attractions which might ultimately find sexual expression. In such circumstances, verses predicated on affection for animals, or aged relatives, would be inconceivable. Or rather—they would appear elsewhere in the poem.

Conversely, as the sexual mores of the Edo period were in some ways similar to those of present-day liberal democracies, it is very common for the liaisons in question to be homosexual—most frequently male/male. As Japanese grammar allows gender to be more motile this point has tended to be obscured. Or, given the violent prejudices of the past, even where a translator has understood a verse correctly, a less challenging interpretation has often won out.

There is no obligation to include or exclude a particular facet of adult sexuality in a poem, but it is well for writers to be aware of their choices. The same is true for the approach to hokku, wakiku, daisan and ageku.

Given that the imachi looks rather novel it is unlikely to be written in the most exalted company, so it will rarely be the case that the opening verses are expected to code for formal greeting. But whilst certain facets of the format are indeed radical, the treatment of the fixed topics is traditional, and, even for sequences begun in summer and winter, the wakiku shares its season with the hokku. Taken together, these factors suggest that the hokku and wakiku will be tightly paired, leaving daisan to function as a conventional break-away verse (see *Beginnings and Endings*).

THE FORMS OF RENKU

The free approach to season verse distribution means that, at the close, a blossom verse is rarely in attendance to guide us to the exit. Extra emphasis is therefore placed on the ageku to round off the poem. It does however gain extra flexibility as the happy glow that accompanies spring may be replaced by something else entirely.

Imachi: Schemas

there are no divisions in the imachi

	autumn	autumn	spring	spring	summer	winter
hokku	au [mn]	au [mn]	sp [bl]	sp [bl]	su [mn]	wi
wakiku	au	au	sp	sp [bl]	su [mn]	wi
daisan	au [mn]	au [mn]	sp [bl]	sp	ns	ns
4 short	ns	ns	ns	ns	ns	ns
5 long	ns	ns	ns	ns	ns	au [mn]
6 short	ns (lv)	su/wi	ns	wi	sp	au
7 long	su (lv)	su/wi lv	wi/su [mn]	ns	sp bl	au [mn]
8 short	su lv	ns lv	wi/su [mn]	ns	sp	ns
9 long	ns lv	ns lv	ns	ns	ns	ns lv
10 short	ns	ns (lv)	ns lv	au	ns lv	ns lv
11 long	sp [bl]	wi/su	ns lv	au mn	ns lv	ns lv
12 short	sp [bl]	wi/su mn	su/wi lv	au	wi (lv)	su
13 long	sp	ns	su/wi	ns	wi (lv)	su mn
14 short	ns	ns	ns	ns	ns	ns
15 long	ns	ns	ns	ns lv	ns	ns
16 short	wi/ns	sp	au	su lv	au	sp
17 long	wi mn	sp bl	au mn	su lv	au mn	sp bl
ageku	ns/wi	sp	au	ns	au	sp

Notes
- **wi/ns** – whichever is selected first its counterpart is selected after
- **su/wi** – likewise—both verses change together
- **wi/su** – likewise
- **ns** – non-season (miscellaneous) position
- **bl** – blossom position
- **[bl]** – alternate blossom position—the choice is either/or
- **mn** – moon position
- **[mn]** – alternate moon position—the choice is either/or
- **lv** – love position, indicative—love verses move as group
- **(lv)** – additional love position, optional, indicative—love verses move as group

Imachi: Appraisal

Imachi or nijuin—which best facilitates Shofu renku? Simplistic questions beget simplistic answers. But a comparison between the two is informative nonetheless.

Master Okamoto and Master Higashi make many of the same core choices. The ratio of season to non-season verses is nearly identical, as are the proportions of the seasons themselves. There are the same number of moon verses, one of which is always set in autumn with its attendant demand to be respected. Blossom likewise dominates spring and must be feted in time honoured fashion. Even the recommended treatment of love is to all intents and purposes indistinguishable.

This common understanding between two such pivotal figures of the renku renaissance is reassuring. We have a baseline against which later experimentation can be judged. It is surely no coincidence that the triparshva, for instance, builds on the same criteria.

But the differences are crucial.

Most obviously the imachi abandons the pretence that we are still grinding our ink stones as we jealously guard a dwindling supply of writing sheets. There are no folio divisions, and therefore no clear-cut breaks to help orchestrate the poem. Jo–ha–kyu may still be applied, but the transition from one dynamic movement to the next relies purely on the power of the text.

Appearances to the contrary, the inherent fluidity of a single bloc of verses, whilst not easy to handle, more closely reflects the Edo period approach to side and sheet boundaries than does most contemporary practice. Modern writing tends to treat the boundaries between the sides of the writing sheets and the dynamic phases of jo–ha–kyu as co-terminous. As they are now one and the same, they may be subsumed into the idea of conveniently distinct *movements*.

In the immediate Basho school, by contrast, we frequently see a given run of season verses breach the divide between sides or leap from one sheet to another. At the same time, the more circumspect tenor of jo might persist into what is theoretically ha, whilst kyu is frequently identified as starting somewhere around verse #28. Passages of ha can be relatively quiet and, just occasionally, the close of a poem turns out to be so heavily freighted it is difficult to reconcile it with kyu at all. When Basho and Etsujin are the guilty parties, we can be sure the effect is deliberate.

The search for greater fluidity drives Okamoto-sensei's other, highly significant, decision—more freedom for the season distribution. Though a poem still starts with the time of year that obtains, it no longer necessarily ends with spring.

The effect goes well beyond basic structural variation. After centuries of precedent—not all of it formal, but simply as the accumulation of artistic practice—the seasons carry with them an associated palette of topics and tones. These colours are neither obligatory, nor always evident—haikai is after all reliant on adding the proletarian and tweaking the privileged—but they are present nonetheless. How many spring verses have you read that involve a great deal of bloodshed?

The joys of the imachi go beyond the uncertainty to do with moonrise. As the seasons may occur in almost any order, the poem can take on a completely different psychological shape to that of more conventional formats.

Here we return to the absence of folio divisions and the consequent lack of visual differentiation in a single bloc of verses. The lesson of Basho's successful implementation of jo–ha–kyu in the kasen is not that there is a sole dynamic pattern suitable for renku. It demonstrates only that the treatment of passages of verse as emotive phases is essential if a poem is to feel rewardingly coherent. There is absolutely no reason why a poem should not start loud, go quiet, drift, and then suddenly burst into flame at the ending. So willing, the eighteen verses of the imachi allow us to do just that.

A glance at the list of Italian terms used in musical notation is a reminder of what can be achieved. But let us finish on two distinct similarities between the nijuin and the imachi which can otherwise slip under the radar.

How short can a poem go, and still be said to contain all of creation? The idea of renku as a mandala, of containing the ten thousand things, is an historical constant (see *Thematic Renku*). One of the reasons the kasen can be daunting for the novice is that its thirty-six verses draw in an astounding number of subjects. The poem proves to have an appetite that it is very hard to feed. But at twenty verses? Eighteen? Are we still in the same territory? If the answer is *no* the poem may well be more tractable, but what does that do for the aesthetics? Are these shorter sequences necessarily impoverished?

Short though it may be, the imachi shares another characteristic with the nijuin—both allow more than two verses in a row of the same denomination. We may see three spring verses, three autumn verses, and just possibly a run of four dedicated to love. The significance of this must be judged against the background of how shift has come to be viewed in much modern practice—not least as a consequence of the search for ever more compact sequences (see *More About Shift*). These issues may be framed rationally (see *Rokku: Description*) or so erratically as to be worthless (see *On Backlink*), but an understanding of the pros and cons of the argument is essential. Not just so that we can cope with sequences longer than the nijuin or imachi. But in order to engage creatively with those that are even shorter.

Imachi: Example

Between the Jagged Rocks

the sainted pond,
a tao of tadpoles
flexes once again   jc

young grasses bow
between the jagged rocks   nd

hawthorn blossom
red, as if the Saxons
shed your blood   jc

a rope tied here and there
with holy knots   nd

every seven years
the book says
all the slaves go free   nd

snow so high we
couldn't get to school   jc

a moonlit dram
my only fuel
this freezing night   nd

sweet poetry
the mistress of excess   jc

sheathed in silk
and pheromones and fags
those rugged pecs   jc

my lover's lover's face
a distant land   nd

the carbon tax
does little to offset
our sense of guilt   jc

disagreeing to agree
the G8 summit   nd

a heat wave forecast
in the near abroad
let's go serfing!   nd

THE FORMS OF RENKU

    f*** the blarney stone
    just kiss my ass   jc

    Fibonacci's fingers
    fiddle with his
    worry beads   nd

    numbering the faithful
    crescent moon   jc

    a cool wind blows
    the memories of ash
    across Manhattan   jc

    the falling leaf
    knows only now, and now   nd

May to June 2007

John Carley
Norman Darlington

Hankasen and Demikasen
halfway to hell
Unknown (17th century), John Carley (2013)

Hankasen—18 verses: Description

Hankasen means *half kasen*. The poem is the initial folio of a kasen considered as a piece in its own right.

Other than for the occasional adjustment to ensure that both summer and winter appear, season verse and fixed topic distributions mirror those of the first two sides of a full sequence. Particularly in the case of Edo period poems, or those written in close imitation, an extended run of spring or autumn verses may cause the number of non-season verses to be reduced.

The treatment of hokku, wakiku, daisan and ageku is unchanged. Attitudes tend to the formal.

Despite the downsizing, the first six verses remain the preface and are subject to the attendant restraints of topic and tone. The poem then moves into the development phase. Skilled writers might attempt to draw the dynamic feel of kyu—the finale—into the close of the poem. The upper portion of the schematic diagram of the full kasen therefore applies (see *Kasen: Description*).

Demikasen—18 verses: Description

The demikasen dispenses with the remnants of the kasen's folio divisions to present as a single bloc of eighteen verses. It fully implements jo–ha–kyu.

The number, relative proportions and ordering of the season verses are typical of the first sheet of a contemporary kasen, with the exception that summer and winter always take at least one verse.

There are two moon verses, one of which is set in autumn. Spring blossom appears as the penultimate verse. Exceptionally, sequences begun in spring may also feature blossom in the hokku.

Love will either figure briefly and freely or receive a longer conventional treatment. The hokku and wakiku can likewise signal a formal greeting, or simply be written as a closely linked pair (see *Beginnings and Endings*).

Note: the layouts below are those of the demikasen, not the hankasen proper.

THE FORMS OF RENKU

Demikasen: Schemas

the demikasen is a single sheet poem

	autumn	autumn	spring	spring	summer	winter
hokku	au [mn]	au [mn]	sp	sp (bl)	su	wi
wakiku	au	au	sp	sp	su	wi
daisan	au [mn]	au [mn]	sp	sp	ns	ns
4 short	ns	ns	ns	ns	ns	ns
5 long	ns	ns	ns	wi mn	au mn	au mn
6 short	wi	ns	au [mn]	wi (lv)	au	au
7 long	su (lv)	wi	au [mn]	ns lv	au	au
8 short	su lv	wi	au	ns lv	ns	ns lv
9 long	ns lv	ns lv	ns lv	ns (lv)	ns (lv)	ns lv
10 short	ns (lv)	ns lv	ns lv	ns	ns lv	ns (lv)
11 long	ns	ns (lv)	ns (lv)	au	ns lv	ns
12 short	wi	su	ns	au [mn]	wi (lv)	su
13 long	wi mn	su mn	su mn	au [mn]	wi mn	su mn
14 short	ns	ns	su	ns	ns	ns
15 long	ns	ns	ns	ns	ns	ns
16 short	sp	sp	ns	sp	sp	sp
17 long	sp bl	sp bl	sp bl	sp bl	sp bl	sp bl
ageku	sp	sp	sp	sp	sp	sp

Notes

- **su/ns** – summer is the more likely option
- **wi/ns** – likewise winter
- **ns** – non-season (miscellaneous) position
- **bl** – blossom position
- **(bl)** – additional blossom position, optional
- **mn** – moon position
- **[mn]** – alternate moon position—the choice is either/or
- **lv** – love position, indicative—love verses move as group
- **(lv)** – additional love position, optional, indicative—love verses move as group

Hankasen: Appraisal

Part man, part fish, dragging its entrails through the mires of hell—the hankasen might have issued from the disturbed mind of Pieter Bruegel.

Why would anybody want to listen to half a symphony? Or view half a sculpture? Whilst it may be completed relatively rapidly, the hankasen is so ugly and unbalanced that it barely serves as a practice piece. The emollient Mr Higginson (see *New Shisan*) once opined that many early hankasen were the result of a haikai session being cut short. But humans had discovered fire at least 200,000 years earlier. Why were the incomplete manuscripts not simply burnt?

The persistence of the form into the 18th and 19th centuries is a worrying indication of quite how superficial and degenerate much linked verse had become. Shiki, it would seem, had a point.

On the plus side—the manifest deficiency of the hankasen as a short stand-alone sequence has been a principal factor in the search for more satisfactory solutions over the course of the last several decades. The renku revival, and the spread of the genre beyond the shores of Japan, has seen the emergence of any number of more effective alternatives.

As we know, a really good poet can perform miracles. There are, in the historical record, many examples of hankasen that showcase writing of the highest quality. But this is achieved despite the form. Not because of it. Modern writers with an interest in the evolution of the literature might find themselves compelled to attempt a traditional hankasen.

One will be enough.

Demikasen: Appraisal

Can a pig really be made to fly?

The demikasen is the result of the present author reverse-engineering the nijuin and imachi. The general proportion of season and non-season verses is therefore common to all three, as are the totals and associations of the fixed topics. Given that the demikasen shares with the nijuin the obligation to end on spring, distributions for sequences begun in spring are likewise a little skewed.

The demands of a traditional rotation of the seasons (see *The Seasons of Renku*), and familiar locations for moon and blossom, mean that the demikasen shares the nijuin's relative lack of structural flexibility. However the abandonment of any reference to folio divisions gives considerably more scope for dynamic control.

Unlike the imachi, the overall shape of the demikasen strongly suggests that the poem will respond best to jo–ha–kyu in conventional order (see *A Dynamic Pattern*). But it shares with the imachi the possibility to choose the precise point at which a poem changes gear. Although this effect is more difficult to achieve without visual cues (see *Imachi: Appraisal*) the elbow room gained allows for a more fluent treatment of extended passages of verse.

More conservative than the imachi. More liberal than the nijuin. With the demikasen, having dipped our fingers in the trough, it is just possible that we have chanced upon the proverbial silk purse.

Demikasen: Example

Knee-deep in Daisies

bluebirds merge
into a cloudless sky,
knee-deep in daisies   pc

my bare toes cool
between the little stems   mw

another glass?
our words glide easily
across the water   pn

melodies
climb upward on the stave   jc

on nights like these
the roots of rhumba
conjure with the moon   jc

snared in her web
two red leaves, dangling   pn

he kisses
the scuppernong juice
from his lover's lips   pc

topsy turvy moments,
catching their breath   mw

00.00 am
time to ponder
being alone—again   mw

velvet elvis waits
by the recycle bin   pc

no backup plan
just fuzzy dice, and a
dashboard jesus   pn

lighting candles,
the sleet gives way to snow   jc

as though tethered
to that old pine,
a crisp white moon   pn

grandpa paints rainbows
over a faded bench   pc

with the grind
of ink on stone
my head begins to clear   mw

beneath the bark
a surge of rising sap   jc

at the poet's house
a blossoming plum tree
by an open gate   pn

a butterfly
unfolds its golden wings

August to September 2013

Pris Campbell
John Carley (sabaki)
Pat Nelson
Mary White

Shisan
a significant occasion
Kaoru Kubota (1970s)

Shisan—12 verses: Description

The shisan is a twelve verse sequence consisting of four movements of three verses each. The movements are treated as preface, development part one, development part two, and rapid close. To the extent that the four part division is taken to reflect that of the kasen, the shisan also lays claim to the topical and tonal characteristics of the jo–ha–kyu pacing paradigm.

As with all formal renku the shisan starts with the season in which composition takes place. Unusually the seasons then appear in calendar order with one season featuring per movement. Typically spring and autumn will take a grouped pair of verses, whereas summer and winter are represented by a single verse apiece. However, for sequences begun in summer or winter, the wakiku would also be expected to take that season as the shisan invites a relatively conventional treatment.

The majority of moon and blossom verses will be set against autumn and spring respectively—the order in which they appear, and the characteristics of the relevant movement, being dependent on the demands of the calendar. In more experimental sequences the blossom position may be treated as the more generic *flower*. In all cases, a pair of love verses will appear in one of the central movements, normally the one that does not feature moon or blossom.

The word *shisan* may be read in several ways. Primarily *shi* means *four*, and *san* means *three*. When written in kanji *shi* may read as *tamawari*—something bestowed—and *san* as *bansankai*—a formal meal. The suggestion is that participants are invited to a significant occasion—reflecting the expectation that all will respect the finer points of style.

Shisan: Schemas

side 1

	autumn	autumn	spring	spring	summer	winter
hokku	au mn	au	sp bl	sp [mn]	su	wi
wakiku	au	au	sp	sp [mn]	su/ns	wi/ns
daisan	ns	ns	ns	ns	ns	ns

side 2

	autumn	autumn	spring	spring	summer	winter
4 short	ns/wi	wi/ns [mn]	ns/su lv	ns/su	ns	ns
5 long	wi/ns	ns/wi [mn]	su/ns lv	su/ns	au mn	sp bl
6 short	ns	ns	ns	ns	au	sp

side 3

	autumn	autumn	spring	spring	summer	winter
7 long	ns/sp [bl]	ns/sp lv	ns/au [mn]	ns/au	ns	ns lv
8 short	sp	sp lv	au	au lv	wi/ns lv	su/ns lv
9 long	sp/ns [bl]	sp/ns	au/ns [mn]	au/ns lv	ns/wi lv	ns/su

side 4

	autumn	autumn	spring	spring	summer	winter
10 short	ns lv	ns	ns	ns	ns	ns
11 long	su/ns lv	su/ns [fl]	wi/ns	wi/ns [fl]	sp bl	au mn
ageku	ns/su	ns/su [fl]	ns/wi	ns/wi [fl]	sp	au

Notes

su/ns – (wakiku only)—where the hokku is summer, wakiku may be non-season
wi/ns – (wakiku only)—winter likewise
sn/ns or **ns/sn** – (elsewhere)—whichever is selected first its counterpart is selected after
ns – non-season (miscellaneous) position
bl – blossom position
[bl] – alternate blossom position (when season selected)—the choice is either/or
[fl] – alternate flower position (when season selected)—the choice is either/or
mn – moon position
[mn] – alternate moon position (when season selected)—the choice is either/or
lv – love position, indicative—love verses move as group

Shisan: Appraisal

What is the difference between an appraisal and an opinion? Perhaps *appraisal* sounds more judicious. In which case what follows is an opinion.

Published in 2010, *Wind Arrow 2* is a bi-lingual anthology by the Association for International Renku (AIR)—a forward looking literary organisation based in Tokyo. *Wind Arrow 2* is dedicated entirely to the shisan. In part, explains Tateshi Tsukamoto—a leading light—this is because the shisan is an ideal introduction to renku. It is simple. And easy to learn.

In terms of raw form—how many bits of what, where—Tsukamoto-san and his colleagues have a point. The shisan is compact, the seasons are logical, and the fixed topic associations will be familiar to anyone who has read a few haiku. But in practice the shisan is far from easy.

jo–ha–kyu – while the generality of its application may be honoured in such things as avoiding awkward topics for the first few verses, and finishing with a flourish, there are problems. Jo is very crowded. Given that the shisan relies on tradition, each constituent verse has special compositional requirements. Daisan is particularly conflicted, being at once a conventional break-away verse but also, as the last verse of the first movement, being expected to generate a degree of pause.

Ha is also compromised. The short movements make it hard to introduce challenging topics in either of the development sections as there is not enough room to modulate their effect by contextualisation and transformation. Either they become isolated and overly prominent, or they are avoided altogether and we end up with something rather more anodyne.

Kyu may finish boldly, as is the popular perception, or create the lingering resonance of the deep and silent pool, as Master Zeami decreed the true purpose of the elegant ending to be. But, with only three verses to play with, it is difficult to achieve both.

cadences – always assuming that our verses have any cadences in the first place (see *Know Yourself*), approximately 1000 years of linked verse tradition condition the eye and ear to expect long verse followed by short verse, two by two, until the ark is full. The schematic above confirms that no movement in a shisan retains the traditional pattern. Each movement contains three verses. All are therefore obliged to end with a long verse, or start with a short verse.

seasons – at first sight the logical succession of the seasons is a welcome simplification of the more arcane formulae that reign elsewhere. But the compaction of the shisan means that there is often only one clear verse between designated season positions. Occasional distributions such as **au, ns, wi** are inevitable, the virtual synchrony being more likely to generate reversion.

Even where there is a two verse separation the strongly associative pull of natural logic can make it hard to establish sufficient distance to avoid a general feeling of regression. There is also a tendency for the mind to impute chronological or seasonal references to the interstitial miscellaneous verses so that what appear to be thematic chains emerge.

passages – it is one of the defining characteristics of Shofu renku that it moves beyond the rolling recombination of cameo pairs to permit powerful non-thematic linear cohesion over extended passages of verse (see *The Mechanics of the White Space*). For all that it may be handled lightly, the shisan pauses and relaunches every three verses. It cannot sustain long riffs.

To be clear: these observations are not made in order to illustrate that the shisan is in some way worthless or defective. Rather that, though the activists of AIR clearly hold the contrary opinion, it pushes the boundaries of Shofu renku and can be very hard to handle.

But the intricacies, the differences, and the challenges peculiar to the shisan are also its attraction. It is nothing if not unusual. Done well it is both striking and beguiling. The only caveat is that, for purposes other than the exchange of pleasantries, it is not best suited to the beginner.

Of course the way to find out is to try writing one yourself. Now would be a good time!

Shisan: Example

The Scent of Lemons

across the empty beach
a butterfly —
the dawning moon						fw

the rust reds of his beard
shot with silver						jc

something special
for sale in a bag
in a back street bar						dp

   * * * *

fourteen years hard labour
in Van Diemen's Land						jc

now they sleep
safe from the tyrant's rage
and winter's storm						dp

my sheepskin coat returns
to Oxfam's window						fw

   * * * *

like candy floss
like powder-puffs, like clouds,
like... cherry blossom						dp

polishing his bells for
the well-dressing dance						jc

train approaching...
through the narrow gorge
white rapids roar						fw

   * * * *

a round of applause
as they renew their vows					fw

our second scoop of sorbet
growing sticky
in the heat						jc

along a dusty road
the scent of lemons						dp

John Carley (sabaki)						October to November 2003
Dick Pettit
Frank Williams

New Shisan
with an eye on tradition
William J. Higginson, after Kaoru Kubota (2004)

New Shisan—12 verses: Description

The new shisan is a variant on the pattern proposed by Kubota-san. The core characteristics of the original are retained bar one—the order of the seasons.

Whereas some elements of the shisan permit a degree of leeway, the new shisan elicits a more conservative response. Moon and blossom appear in association with their primary seasons—autumn and spring respectively. Love is treated in a traditional manner, and the special compositional characteristics of the hokku, wakiku, daisan and ageku are scrupulously adhered to. While the full application of jo–ha–kyu (see *A Dynamic Pattern*) remains problematic in such a short sequence the topical exclusions of jo are most certainly honoured.

The number and proportion of season verses is unaltered but they are redistributed so that calendar-order is avoided. Typically we might expect to see something like:

- spring, winter, autumn, summer
- summer, spring, winter, autumn
- autumn, summer, winter, spring
- winter, autumn, summer, spring

Other permutations are possible. For poems begun in summer or winter, the wakiku will always take the same season. It is never a miscellaneous verse.

Additional information on season verse distribution is contained in the chapter *The Seasons of Renku*. Readers are encouraged to explore their own variations for this and other types of sequence.

New Shisan: Appraisal

Ever generous and considered in his opinions, William J. Higginson (WJH) believed in renku as art. His published views on seasonal reference in general, and season words in particular, are the polar opposite of the polemical rants found between these covers. His work is therefore recommended reading, not least because it will provide balance.

In his views on haikai WJH was something of a conservative, but it was no simple attachment to orthodoxy that prompted him to question the calendar-order succession of the verses in Kubota-san's shisan. The appraisal of the original, overleaf, discusses the potential conflicts that arise from such linear structures in a very compact poem. It is possible to work round them. And arguably, in so doing, one refines one's skills as a writer. But conflicts they remain.

WJH side-steps the problem—if the shisan is attractive, apart from the seasonal distribution, we simply re-order the seasons by drawing on more classical norms. Sheer consistency then suggests that the various stylistic options are also treated with caution and, presto, we have the new shisan—a pattern which retains the majority of the original's intriguing features whilst lending itself to a more traditional treatment.

New Shisan: Example

Summer Rain

all those insects
washed out of the sky —
summer rain

looking for a virgin
in a haystack

gather round then
man or monkey
here your tale begins

    * * * *

kukazu? che cazzo!
pass the sake Jack

blossom viewing
somewhere up the nick
of Shiki's arse

a mad march hare
is sent for counselling

    * * * *

good intentions
make the rich man proud
to starve the poor

this whipping winter wind
the scourge of God

blood and incense,
cheap amalgam
fills my crown of teeth

    * * * *

if that's a skull then
this must be a Harley

whistling softly
corner boys sneak off
to count their conkers

wisps of moon
to warm the sudden night

June 2007

John Carley, solo

- kukazu: the rule governing topic duration in longer renga
- che cazzo: a very coarse Italian exclamation

THE FORMS OF RENKU

Junicho
a twelve-tone scale
Shunjin and Seijo Okamoto (1989)

Junicho—12 verses: Description

The junicho or twelve-tone is a *single sheet* poem; it does not separate into sides or movements.

The convention that the major seasons predominate is retained (see *The Seasons of Renku*). Spring and autumn are therefore each represented by a grouped pair of verses, whereas summer and winter take a single verse each. For sequences begun in winter or summer, the wakiku—verse two—has the option of taking the same season as the hokku in accordance with general practice or moving immediately to a miscellaneous verse (non-season).

A single bloom verse appears in association with any chosen season. The topic is generally treated as *flower*, i.e. a bloom of any description, but conventional blossom verses are possible when circumstances combine to yield a familiar position. Likewise the single moon verse—though the occasional classic autumn moon will be found—is very often set against a different season and handled experimentally. Love is also approached more liberally than the norm. A grouped pair of verses may appear in any position other than the very beginning or end of the poem. Though still retaining its adult association, love is freed from the last of the lingering renga conventions that governed its passage from joy to despair.

Barring ceremonial conventions, the particular compositional characteristics of hokku and ageku are always respected, but those of wakiku and daisan may well be discarded. The topical and tonal exclusions common to the opening passages of most types of sequence are also lifted, as is the suggestion that the poem should be formally paced according to jo–ha–kyu. Instead participants are enjoined to prioritise variety.

Junicho: Schemas

there are no divisions in the junicho

	autumn	autumn	spring	spring	summer	winter
hokku	au	au mn	sp	sp fl/bl	su	wi mn
wakiku	au	au	sp	sp	ns/su	ns/wi
daisan	ns	ns	ns lv	ns	ns	ns
4 short	ns	ns lv	ns lv	wi/su	ns	ns lv
5 long	su/wi mn	ns lv	wi/su	ns lv	sp/au mn	ns lv
6 short	ns	su/wi	ns	ns lv	sp/au	au/sp
7 long	ns lv	ns	ns	ns	ns lv	au/sp
8 short	sp lv	ns	au	au [mn]	wi lv	ns
9 long	sp	wi/su	au fl	au [mn]	ns	su fl
10 short	ns	ns	ns	ns	ns	ns
11 long	ns	sp fl/bl	ns	su/wi	au/sp fl/bl	sp/au
ageku	wi/su fl	sp	su/wi mn	ns	au/sp	sp/au

Notes

su/wi – whichever is selected first its counterpart is selected after
wi/su – likewise
sp/au – likewise—both verses change together
au/sp – likewise—both verses change together
ns/su – (wakiku only)—where the hokku is summer authors may use summer for the wakiku
ns/wi – (wakiku only)—winter likewise
ns – non-season (miscellaneous) position
fl – flower position
fl/bl – flower position, a treatment as blossom is possible
mn – moon position
[mn] – alternate moon position—the choice is either/or
lv – love position, indicative—love verses move as a group

Junicho: Appraisal

The junicho is optimised for experimentation and flexibility. Shunjin and Seijo Okamoto were acknowledged renku masters and one suspects that they sought to push the boundaries as far as they dared whilst retaining sufficient connection to their source tradition not to be declared apostate. They succeeded.

As an indicator of their innovative and internationalist outlook, the name twelve-tone recalls the musical systems of Hauer and Schönberg. Given the formal injunction to seek out variety, it is sometimes taken as an invitation to consider each verse as a distinct pitch or colour.

But it would be unfortunate if the inference were drawn that the junicho is composed of twelve separate stages, each of which seeks to be as distinct as possible. The musical analogy reminds us that in high quality renku there are always elements of coherence to balance those of divergence. Whilst a well written junicho will be swift moving, the pursuit of diversity at all costs is unlikely to yield anything other than a strident cacophony.

The junicho loosens very many fixed topic conventions, increases the options surrounding the opening of a poem and offers more scope to decide on the pattern of pacing. But, whilst not exactly peripheral, none of these properties define the Basho style. The core techniques remain the same. As does the aesthetic impetus. It may look very modern. But the junicho remains Shofu.

The sheer mutability of the structural parameters raises an interesting question though—does this radically enhanced flexibility make the junicho easier or more difficult to work with for writers new to renku?

Naturally the default response of all freethinkers is to heartily proclaim *Easier!* But those of us who still salivate when a certain bell rings know that people sometimes feel more safe with boundaries.

Junicho: Example

November Sky

the leaves no longer
part of the tree —
dark November sky

searching for redemption
in a bottle

well then darling,
shall we risk the
Shiraz or Grenache?

mummy says we
just turn left at Poland

honeysuckle
reaching out to grasp
a twist of air

haiku heaven
turns out to be concrete

snow, they say,
is falling thickly—
moxa on my skin

quarks and leptons
streaming from his pen

ask the grandkids
sugar sprinkles
add that touch of class

early plum—
a petal bathed in moonlight

on the screen
a bloom of entrails
as the belt explodes

this game of solitaire
too quickly won

November 2006

John Carley, solo

New Junicho
turning the tables
Ashley Capes (2011)

New Junicho—12 verses: Description

The new junicho is a single sheet poem without breaks or divisions. It rejects the *adagio–mosso–crescendo* dynamics associated with jo–ha–kyu, requiring authors to create an individual pattern of intensity for each piece.

In contrast to most other forms of renku, the order and duration of the seasons is not the mainstay of structure. A poem may begin in any season or none. The conventional functions of hokku, wakiku, daisan and ageku are otherwise retained, though the topical restrictions common to the start of more conventional sequences are lifted (see *Beginnings and Endings*).

As long as loops, repetitions and gross incongruity are avoided, a strong sense of the natural world may be evoked by any verse referencing any season at any time—up to and including the use of conventional kigo (season words). The erstwhile fixed topics of moon and blossom may still occur, but are no longer mandatory features nor the principal focus of a verse. Where present, moon and blossom may appear in any order and in association with any season or none. Love, likewise, becomes an entirely optional sub-topic.

A new junicho is composed of three categories of verse—*cultural*, *gendai* and *shasei*—whose distribution, though not number, is decided by the authors. This act of ordering loosely fixes the parameters of a poem. It therefore takes care to minimise the risk of reversion (see *The Three Rs*).

The cultural category comprises half the poem. It contains six topics: art, film, literature, music, politics, and religion. Each appears once, in any order.

Gendai and shasei are descriptions of style, not content. The terms reflect their usage amongst contemporary writers rather than a strictly academic interpretation.

There are two gendai verses. These are intentionally modernist, atypical or otherwise challenging in terms of structure, style and/or content. They tend to be prominent.

The four shasei verses are more flexible. They draw directly on lived experience, are observational, uncontrived, and devoid of compositional artifice—qualities generally associated with the maxim *to sketch from life*.

New Junicho: Schemas

There are no divisions in the new junicho

	cultural	shasei	gendai	cultural	gendai	cultural
hokku	cultural	shasei	gendai	cultural	gendai	cultural
wakiku	cultural	cultural	cultural	cultural	gendai	shasei
daisan	shasei	cultural	cultural	gendai	cultural	shasei
4 short	shasei	shasei	gendai	gendai	cultural	cultural
5 long	cultural	shasei	shasei	cultural	cultural	cultural
6 short	cultural	cultural	shasei	shasei	shasei	shasei
7 long	gendai	cultural	cultural	shasei	shasei	gendai
8 short	gendai	gendai	cultural	cultural	cultural	cultural
9 long	cultural	gendai	shasei	cultural	shasei	gendai
10 short	shasei	cultural	shasei	shasei	shasei	cultural
11 long	shasei	cultural	cultural	shasei	cultural	shasei
ageku	cultural	shasei	cultural	cultural	cultural	cultural

Notes

cultural – 6 verses—one per topic: art, film, literature, music, politics, religion
gendai – 2 verses—modernist—atypical structure, tone, content
shasei – 4 verses—sketched from life—lived experience, observational, uncontrived

Caution: the two rightmost columns above involve a de facto risk of reversion

New Junicho: Appraisal

The new junicho represents a radical departure from the general thrust of modernisation in contemporary mainstream Shofu renku which has concentrated on loosening the strictures inherited from the Edo period whilst retaining a recognisable attachment to seasonal distributions and the fixed topics of moon, blossom and love. With a bow in the direction of ushin renga, the new junicho stands all this on its head.

In the absence of so many conventional comforts, participants must address what it is to write renku. We are reminded that moons, blossoms, and summer loves are nothing more than designated topics. They may very well be the starting point for an excellent verse, but they do not confer worth of themselves. The same goes for a tick-box approach to the seasons—poetry-by-numbers is best left to machines.

With the old topics gone there is room for the new. Art, film, literature, music, politics, and religion—the cultural category is nothing if not modern. Yet the paradox is that, were we to read *film* as *drama*, this selection might just as easily have been drawn from medieval renga. Of the list of fixed topics that dropped out of the kasen, all that are missing are travel and ill health. Interestingly they also tend to be universal in a way that some seasonal references are not. When was the last time you listened to a piece of music? Or plastered the ridges between your rice paddies?

The style categories are welcome as a concept. A verse, after all, is made of more than just content. Most English writers come to renku via haiku and so will be familiar with the idea of *shasei*—a term drawn from Masaoka Shiki's championing of unaffected realism as a foil to artifice. The *gendai* category reminds us that, despite the shortcomings of free verse discussed elsewhere in this book (see *Know Yourself*), talented poets from Takarai Kikaku to Haku Asanuma have identified the dangers that arise from an over reliance on strict form. With his gendai verses, Mr Capes obliges us to experiment.

There are, however, dangers. By designating half of them as *cultural*, the new junicho can readily generate a surfeit of verses that deal with human activity. This forces the shasei verses, and indeed the gendai, in the direction of *anything but* if we wish to see a balance between person and place (see *More About Shift*). Though it is debatable how closely any short poem can come to the ideal of being all embracing (see *Thematic Renku*), by formally including the four seasons, the conventional junicho does at least guarantee a certain sense of fullness or completion.

But too much can be made of this. A new junicho may very readily include the annual cycle. There is no more reason for a *literature* verse to preclude a reference to *winter moon* than there is for a *winter moon* verse to avoid all hint of *literature*. Likewise there is no reason why a *cultural* verse must necessarily feature directly drawn protagonists. Everything rests on the skill of the poets. On their attentiveness and imagination.

It may be that, without the way-markers provided by classical fixed topics, the folio divisions, the familiar dynamics, and the roughly cyclical reappearance of the seasons, this radical approach pioneered by Mr Capes will not prove so effective for longer sequences.

But the new junicho is not a longer sequence. It is a challenge. And an education.

New Junicho: Example

Earthquake Season

earthquake season —
the avocado
rolls this way & that   ss   shasei

wave upon wave
a rainbow in curved air   jc   cultural—music

so beautiful
this time of year
the moon over Hiroshima   ws   cultural—politics

the bitter aftertaste
of my twig tea   as   shasei

dead roach
buried in the flower pot
hastily snuffed out   bd   shasei

the doors of perception
rapidly closing   lf   cultural—literature

100 billion neurons
tapped deep
to granite secrets   lf   gendai

they swap their faces
back again they swap   jc   gendai

amid the smell of paint
he coaxes
a small smile from her   ss   cultural—art

blind in the fragrance garden
witch-hazel   bd   shasei

flies all swatted,
the lightest touch
on the divining rod   ws   cultural—religion

we gasp at the delights
of Tokusatsu   as   cultural—film

February to March 2011

John Carley (sabaki)	Sandra Simpson	• Tokusatsu—a genre of sci-fi fantasy
Bill Dennis	William Sorlien	action movie heavily reliant on special
Lorin Ford	Alan Summers	effects and implausibility

Yotsumono
four things
John Carley (2010)

Yotsumono—4 verses: Description

First proposed by the present author in 2010, the yotsumono—*four things*—is a four verse sequence comprising hokku, wakiku, daisan and ageku. The name recalls mitsumono—*three things*—the medieval practice of attaching particular importance to the first three verses of a writing sheet. The yotsumono, by contrast, is complete in its own right.

The structure of the yotsumono mirrors that of the Tang dynasty *discontinuous poem*—the jueju. Known in Japanese as the zekku, its four part progression is thought to have influenced both popular song and the emergence of linked verse. Each stanza of the zekku is named according to its function—*kiku, shoku, tenku* and *kekku*, combining the suffix ku—*verse*—with the elements ki—*description*, sho—*furtherance*, ten—*break*, and ketsu—*determination* or *outcome*.

The yotsumono equates these functions to those of the hokku, wakiku, daisan and ageku—shorn of erstwhile greetings or felicitous parting sentiments. Whereas the zekku is written by a single author, and its degree of turn may be no more than a pleasant digression, the yotsumono is dialogic, being intended for an alternating pair of voices. It also breaks and shifts decisively. Most importantly of all, as with all Shofu renku, it is avowedly anti-thematic.

There are no topical or tonal exclusions in the yotsumono. In terms of jo–ha–kyu, the tenor is that of ha rather than jo or kyu. The poem is swift moving, never uniform. Though the seasons are no longer essential to structure, a strong sense of the natural world may be present at any point in the poem. Formal and informal kigo—season words—and classical fixed topics may either be prominent, or notable for their absence.

Excepting those cases where the ageku incorporates deliberate echoes of the hokku or wakiku for specific expressive purposes, great emphasis is placed on the avoidance of any hint of reversion or regression (see *The Three Rs*). This extends to register, grammar and syntax. Poets are encouraged to pay particular attention to the phonic properties of their work, not least in achieving balanced and proportional cadences between verses.

In order to prevent the unwitting development of thematic subtexts, encourage instinctual responses, and ensure that writers have no greater access to additional information than their readers, participants are enjoined to set aside all discussion of their intentions until composition is complete.

Yotsumono: Schemas

more conventional

	autumn	autumn	spring	spring	summer	winter
hokku	au [mn]	ns (lv)	sp [bl/fl]	ns	su fl	wi (fl)
wakiku	au [mn]	ns (lv)	sp [bl/fl]	ns	ns	ns (lv)
daisan	ns	au [mn]	ns (lv)	sp [fl/bl]	sn (mn)	sn lv
ageku	ns	au [mn]	ns (lv)	sp [fl/bl]	sn/ns	sn mn

less conventional

	open	open	open	open	open	open
hokku	sn lv	sp mn+bl	ns	sn	ns	wi/su (mn)
wakiku	ns lv	sp	ns	ns lv	sn lv	ns
daisan	ns	ns	sn fl	ns lv	sp bl	ns lv
ageku	au bl+mn	wi/au	au mn	sn	ns	su/wi lv

Notes

- **sn** – all-season position—or *any other* season (where a named season is also present)
- **sn/ns** – all-season or non-season
- **wi/au** – winter or autumn
- **wi/su** – whichever is chosen first its counterpart is chosen after
- **ns** – non-season (miscellaneous) position
- **bl** – blossom position
- **[bl/fl]** – alternate blossom or flower position—either/or at one location only
- **bl+mn** – blossom and moon both appear
- **fl** – flower position
- **[fl/bl]** – alternate flower or blossom position—either/or at one location only
- **(fl)** – optional flower position
- **mn** – moon position
- **[mn]** – alternate moon position—the choice is either/or
- **mn+bl** – moon and blossom both appear
- **(mn)** – optional moon position
- **lv** – love position, indicative—love verses move together
- **(lv)** – optional love position, indicative—love verses move together

Yotsumono: Appraisal

Shofu renku? As the courtesan once remarked to the abbot—it looks rather small. So the obvious question, when faced with a yotsumono, is to wonder if it is renku at all.

It depends on what you were expecting. As the abbot doubtless retorted.

Perhaps the oldest form of linked verse, and still the shortest, is the tanrenga—a single exchange of long and short verse between two poets. The yotsumono comes in at twice the size. It opens, broadens, develops and resolves. So, given that the distinction between renga and haikai is one of tone not form, and despite the courtesan's obvious disappointment, there is no reason why a yotsumono, written in the correct spirit, cannot be haikai no renga—aka renku.

But Shofu?

Certainly. If the term *haikai* is something of a catch-all—embracing everything from Basho's most refined work to the drasty margins of zappai—*Shofu* is more easily defined. Above all it is a question of aesthetic values. Fueki ryuko, kogo kizoku, fuga no makoto (see *Minimum Conditions*), none of these rely on length of sequence. The same is true for karumi—the principal driver of his mature style. And short as it may be, there are some aspects of the yotsumono that make it more mainstream than not.

The emphasis on balanced and proportional cadences between verses, and on the poetics of utterance in general, highlights a vital aspect of renku that has received scant attention as the genre has spread into English. The importance of phonology to individual verse structure, linkage, and the wider sense of cohesion cannot be overstated (see *Know Your Enemy*).

The yotsumono also obliges a thorough facility with the particular characteristics of each constituent verse. Description, furtherance, turn, and outcome. Head verse, support verse, breakaway, and close. These functions are vital to the success of any renku sequence but the yotsumono certainly concentrates the mind. The ageku in particular is placed under the spotlight and can no longer escape by mouthing lukewarm platitudes. Though its task remains that of finding a symbolic and emotional fit rather than providing some form of logical conclusion, it is obliged to be much more focused. We are directed away from a generic sense of closure towards *ketsu*—an overarching outcome.

More problematic is the question of variety and change. Clearly, at only four verses, the yotsumono cannot contain the *ten thousand things* of Buddhist metaphysics. Yet this objection may be leveled just as readily at a junicho, or at all poems shorter than the kasen itself. In any event, the suggestion that omni-valence is the product of a surfeit of materials is contentious at best (see *Thematic Renku*). The anti-thematic, all embracing, nature of Shofu renku lies in its aesthetics, not the quantity of scrawl on the page—or else we mistake effect for cause.

The yotsumono side-steps the issue. Participants are directed to avoid all discussion of their intentions, the meaning of any given stanza, or of the linkage between stanzas, either before or during composition. Ergo—the poem cannot be thematic.

Where it is adhered to, this injunction has the welcome effect of boosting the importance of empathy in linkage and heightening the general awareness of phonics. It also gives rise to an intriguing paradox. A skillfully written ageku generates such a strong sense of coherence across the span of the poem that it feels as if it must have been agreed from the outset. It is a further paradox that any attempt to contrive such an outcome by working to a prearranged plan tends to yield a weaker poem.

Renku is a dialogic form of writing, but it is not just an excuse for some genial chat (see *Explaining It All Away*). It takes courage to compose a yotsumono on the fly. But the end result may very well surprise.

Yotsumono: Example

Vivaldi

in raindrops
with no colour of their own
the garden—myself   sw

a lean-to shed,
the seasons come and go   jc

Vivaldi
from the cutting room,
these days always spring   sw

as ever in between
the scent of orange   jc

November 2012

John Carley
Sheila Windsor

Renku Theory and Practice

Link & Shift: An Overview
nothing more fundamental

Early days

The earliest evidence that interest in renku had spread beyond the shores of Japan is believed to be a five day writing session sponsored by the publisher Gallimard in the basement of a Parisian hotel. This was the early spring of 1969. Key persons present were the Mexican, Octavio Paz, the Frenchman, Jacques Roubaud, the Italian, Edoardo Sanguineti, and the Englishman, Charles Tomlinson.

The largely free-form collaborative inter-lingual work the writers produced is perhaps more properly viewed as a precursor to what would later become known as *renshi*. Be that as it may, this was a seminal moment. The genie had escaped the bottle.

In her address to the Global Renku Symposium in Tokyo, October 2000, the poet and literary commentator Ai Yazaki, advanced an argument first made by Meiga Higashi in his paper *Renku no Fukkatsu to Sono Shorai* published in the founding issue of the influential magazine, *Kikan Renku*. Master Higashi wrote:

> *The linking verse is deduced from the preceding verse but it has no other logical connection with the leap-over verse. A work is composed by repeatedly linking a succession of such a verse ad libitum. This ingenious process of poetry composition was developed indigenously by our ancestors and has been found in no culture other than Japanese. In the final analysis, any verse that embodies this characteristic dynamic should be recognised as renku regardless of its mode and other principles of composition.* Translation: Fusako Matano.

Master Higashi was a commanding figure in the development of modern renku during the latter part of the 20th century. By the early 80s he had identified the pressing need to go beyond a narrative description of the genre and identify principles. His purpose, like that of the later Symposium, was to accommodate change whilst preserving integrity. The misunderstanding and rancour that had accompanied the spread of haiku into the western world was a salutary lesson to all.

The argument is made elsewhere in these pages that the stipulation of a sole defining parameter by Higashi and his supporters may in fact be too liberal—that other considerations must come into play. But one thing is certain: it is *impossible* to write renku without an instinctive feel for the paradox that is *link & shift*.

What and where?

Link & shift is the motor of renku. It draws its energy from the forces of connection and disassociation that develop across the arc of a trio of verses. Any trio. And every trio. Technical wonks therefore give these three parts a name, reckoning back each time a new verse is proposed.

Take a look. Below are four verses **A, B, C, D**. For the moment our trio is **A, B, C**.

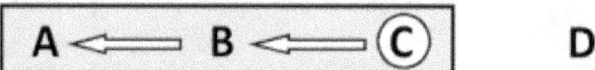

We have already completed verses **A** and **B**. Now we are working on **C**. And the convention is that we name our trio from this point back. So **C**, the verse under consideration, is the *added verse*. The Japanese name is *tsukeku*. **B**, the verse to which we are linking, is the *preceding verse*. The Japanese is *maeku*. And **A**, the last but one, to which **B** was linked, is called the *leap-over verse* or the *verse before last*. In Japanese: *uchikoshi*.

There is no mystery here. Once all are happy with the text of verse **C** our poem moves on and we now have a new verse, **D**, to consider.

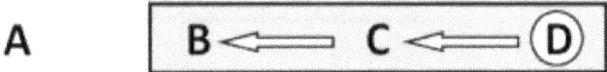

Given that the same dynamic forces govern any three verses in a row, our part names now apply to the new trio. Our added verse is now **D**. Our preceding verse is now **C**. And the verse before last is **B**. Ad libitum, as our elegant translation would have it!

Link—tsukeai

What we have described so far is *link*. In Japanese *tsukeai*. It is unexceptional. Each added verse brings something new to the poem but retains a connection to the preceding verse. Even if it is the product of lateral thinking, the new verse springs forth naturally at some level. It does not arrive unannounced.

The history of world literature is crammed with different takes on linked verse. Likewise contemporary work across the globe. The vast majority of experimental English forms that lay claim to Japanese influence do so on the basis that they are collaborative and reflect some aspect of Japanese styles of linkage.

But, in Shofu renku, link is only half the picture. And it is the obvious half at that. To grasp what is going on below the surface we need to understand the function of the last but one verse in our generative trio. And for that we must understand *shift*.

Shift—tenji

Each time a verse is added to a renku sequence it must link to the preceding verse whilst showing sufficient difference to be interesting. It should also bring something new to the poem as a whole. But, neither the specific differences to the preceding verse, nor the general quality of newness to the poem, are what is meant by the technical usage of *shift*.

In the quotation above Master Higashi is unequivocal. Shift, in contemporary renku theory, requires that each added verse—*has no logical connection with its leap-over verse.*

So, returning to our original trio of **A**, **B**, **C**—as we work on the linkage between **C** and **B**, we must also ensure that no aspect of **A** carries forward to exercise a lingering influence on **C**. Or, to state it the other way round, **C** must link to **B** whilst moving comprehensively from **A**.

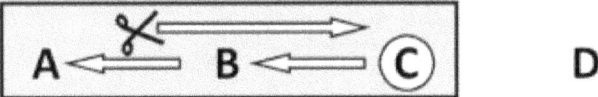

For all that it is easily represented in a diagram, shift, at first sight, is counterintuitive. The reader is cordially invited to pause and consider its implications for a moment.

Were our poem to employ a single, or occasional, instance of shift, all would be well. But the generative forces of link & shift are at play within any trio of verses. Every trio of verses. So, moving on to the composition of verse **D,** we begin to see the dynamic paradoxes of connection and disassociation develop.

Now it is **B** which must not be allowed to colour the tone or content of **D**. Otherwise put: **D** must link to **C** whilst moving comprehensively away from **B**.

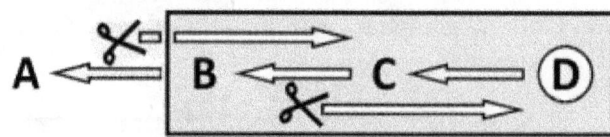

It is the rolling superposition of this set of relations, for the duration of the poem, that makes the more refined forms of renga and renku unique to world literature.

Elsewhere in these pages both link and shift are examined in detail. Clearly it is the case that there might be *degrees* of shift. But, for the avoidance of doubt, it is well to state here that, in Shofu renku, the application of shift is such that any narrative, logical or thematic development is impossible.

This does not mean that shift reduces a renku sequence to nonsense. But it does mean that poets are obliged to find different ways in which to make sense. Therein lies the artistry.

Beginnings and Endings
more than a few ku

The long and the short

The word *ku* means *verse* or *phrase*. In all but the most experimental or dysfunctional renku sequences long verse follows short verse, follows long verse, follows short. Which is straightforward enough, until the cynic asks what precisely is meant by *long*. Winded, perhaps? And for short—how about *tempered*? Sadly the cynic is right.

A mere lick of thumb and forefinger away the chapter *Know Yourself* looks in detail at how English renku stanzas might be constructed. For the moment let us agree that in Japanese at least the notion of long and short has meaning. Therefore the first ku to come before us are generic terms for any long verse or any short verse. A long verse is *chouku*. A short verse is a *tanku*.

Three stooges

The basic generative mechanism of renku exists within each and any trio of verses. The constituent parts of such a trio take their names from the moment we add a new verse. This added verse (the one we are working on) is *tsukeku*. The preceding verse (to which we are linking) is *maeku*. And the verse before that, often called *the leap over*, is none other than *uchikoshi no ku*. Known to its friends as *uchikoshi*—the one from which we must shift.

Stick around renku circles long enough and you'll be tossing these names around like an old pro. But mostly the Japanese terms you'll encounter refer to the first few verses of a sequence, or else the last—the closing verse. The reason these verses have special names is that they have special functions. And these in turn impose particular compositional characteristics.

Hokku—verse one

Hokku means *head verse*. It is the first verse of a renku sequence, the font from which all else springs. On the strength of this some theorists get misty eyed about it, and will not allow the repeat of a single syllable elsewhere in the poem (even though Japanese doesn't use syllables).

The hokku normally references the season in which composition takes place, though not necessarily in a precise way. Longer renku sequences start with a run of several same-season verses, and the order of the run is chronological. Consequently there can be pressure on the hokku to represent the early stages of whichever time of year the participants take as their base. Though the verse will seem true to life in the manner of Shiki's *shasei*, it may in fact be a skillful construct that communicates naturalness.

In the historic literature the hokku frequently codes a greeting to an individual present, salutes the assembled company, comments on the particular circumstances of composition, or augurs well for the renku session to come. Matsuo Basho could do all of these things. With a word. In the blink of an eye. And in Japan at least the practice is still common, specially in formal composition when the poem marks an occasion. Modern English writers, by contrast, often treat the hokku as indistinguishable from a haiku. A figurative reading is absent.

The chance to write the hokku is considered an honour. Traditionally this was the preserve of the most senior poet present or offered as a mark of respect to a noted guest. Alternatively, specially when the writing team comprised Master and students, all present would be invited to compete—each student offering as many candidates as possible before the balloon went up. The pressure to perform under such circumstances led to the convention that hokku candidates could sometimes be composed in advance.

Occasionally a hokku would be lifted from the work of an acknowledged great, those present tagging on a complete or partial sequence. This was a practice called *wakiokori*. It persists as an exercise. Long before any notion of copyright, the greater part of the borrowed hokku were drawn from the dim and distant past, not to avoid the lawyers, but in the hope that something worthwhile might rub off.

The hokku is generally written as a bipartite cut verse, employing the techniques of juxtaposition and combination typical of a modern haiku. The two parts pivot on, and their relationship is inflected by, a cutting word—a *kireji*. Even where the hokku is written as a single-object *verse*, up to and including the use of unitary syntax, it is expected to be able to bear consideration as an independent poem.

In many types of sequence, notably the kasen and those drawn on it, the opening movement is subject to restrictions of tone and topic. However the hokku is exempt from all prohibition and may address any subject it likes, in any manner. It is rare though for the verse to be unrelievedly bleak or brutal. As it turns out the misty eyed theorists had a point. A very harsh treatment at the head of the poem casts such a long shadow that it takes a lot of effort to throw off.

Wakiku—verse two

The second verse of a renku sequence is called the wakiku, a name which means *flanking* or *supporting* verse. Its primary function is to complement the hokku.

In all but the shortest and most recent types of sequence, the wakiku automatically takes the same season as the hokku. The linkage between the two will tend to be tight, the new verse pulling back to show the backdrop against which the action takes place, or else focusing in on some detail to enhance the depth and detail. Other than in the most radical of modern styles, in no case is the relationship between the wakiku and the hokku antagonistic. Hokku and wakiku work together, not against each other.

Some sources compare the relationship between hokku and wakiku to that of the upper and lower sections of a traditionally constructed tanka. Others find a similarity to tan renga. It is true that any such tightly linked pair will generate a sense of sufficiency and closure. But there is a crucial difference. Whilst it is the avowed purpose of a tanka or a tan-renga to resolve and close out, the wakiku does not aim for such finality. There are other verses to come. To some degree at least the wakiku must remain open.

In much of the historic literature, and in modern formal settings, whilst the hokku is the preserve of the honoured guest, the wakiku is written by the person hosting the composition. In the case of those with more wealth than talent, this can lead to a bumpy start. The coded greeting of the hokku attracts more ebullience than grace.

Crucial to an understanding of wakiku is the appreciation that its principal power springs from its place in sequence. The wakiku is not some form of crypto-haiku which might be lifted out of context and still perform adequately as an independent verse. The same holds true for all subsequent verses. Though they may feature a pause in syntax, or a degree of disjuncture between images, they will not demonstrate the strong cut and turn typical of a stand-alone verse.

Daisan—verse three

Daisan is the third verse. The word itself means *third topic*. Theorists like to point out that daisan is the first *true* verse of a renku series in that it is the first which has both a preceding verse to which it must link (the wakiku) and a verse before that from which it must shift (the hokku).

Whereas hokku and wakiku present something of a single unit, the function of daisan is to break away, to open fresh ground. It is here that the sequence begins to unfold.

Linkage between daisan and wakiku is more open than that between wakiku and hokku. In the more traditionally styled longer sequences, despite the constraints placed on the opening movement, daisan will differ markedly from the initial pair even though it may share the same season. In the shorter modern sequences the verse is most likely to be a miscellaneous or non-season verse and may also mark a comprehensive change of tone. In both cases the task facing the poet is to achieve a suitably tangential impetus without completely fracturing the reading experience.

In Japanese, daisan is expected to end with a verb taking the *te* conjugation. This indicates an action or state in continuance. There is a degree of similarity to the present progressive in English or, in some constructions, the present perfect. Whilst there is no consensus on how the *te* ending might be emulated in modern English, it is certainly true that—whereas the wakiku offers a degree of closure—both sense and syntax of daisan are expected to open outwards. It is both germinal and unfinished, suggestive of multiple possibilities.

Like the hokku and the wakiku, daisan is considered a prestigious verse position—one which might be awarded to the most senior person present who has yet to feature.

The poet who thinks they are better than they are tends to get given daisan.

At last—ageku

The closing verse of a renku sequence is the ageku, a name which implies not just an ending but also the fulfillment of anticipation. The sense is not so much of *final* as of *finally*.

In conservative forms of renku, ageku almost always follows spring blossom and takes the same season. However, in recent variants, spring blossom may be located elsewhere in a sequence, or be entirely absent, and ageku may take any season, or none.

Whatever the seasonal aspect, the ageku often acts as a counterpart to the hokku. If the first verse is charged with providing a greeting, now it is time for leave-taking and augury. Even when there is no strictly interpersonal subtext, ageku is expected to generate a sense of completion—not just to the closing section of the poem—but to the piece as a whole. Ageku—*at last*—is a summary. Albeit at the figurative level.

In order to meet these rigorous demands, ageku is exempt from the general conventions that condition what a verse may or may not reprise. It is even possible for ageku to return to some aspect of the hokku or wakiku in order to generate a strong sense of circularity—a practice which is otherwise condemned.

The composition of the ageku is, like that of the hokku, a special honour. The same poet would not be expected to figure in both.

Turning the page

The hokku is the first verse of a sequence and ageku the last. But there may be several other beginnings and endings in a poem.

The concept of *movements* that characterises many compositions is derived from the number of writing sheets traditionally used to set down a piece. The lengthy hyakuin of medieval courtly renga required four sheets—a total of eight sides. The first and last sides needed room to record ancillary information, so fewer actual verses were placed there. Accordingly the hyakuin's 100 verses were recorded as 8/14 – 14/14 – 14/14 – 14/8. Likewise Basho's radically shortened Kasen—at only 36 verses—required two sheets, four sides: 6/12 – 12/6.

Clearly the beginning or the ending of a side is a way-marker in any composition. We are *turning the page* after all, and, though it is impractical to list them all here, there are specific names in Japanese for all the relevant verses.

It is important to emphasise that these verses are not directly comparable to the hokku or the ageku. Those on opposing sides of a writing sheet or movement boundary are still considered to be contiguous. The same principles of cohesion and progression apply as would if they were physically adjacent. Nonetheless poets often add overtones of re-launch to the start of a side, and a countervailing shade of completion to the last verse on a side.

Haiku and low ku

The particular compositional characteristics of hokku, wakiku, daisan and ageku are respected in the majority of modern renku sequences, though the social formalities of verse allocation and their associated subtexts are more likely to be seen in ceremonial composition.

In recent times some shorter sequences such as the twelve verse junicho have created the impression that every verse must be a 'break away' verse in order to maximise variety over the limited course of the poem. Often wakiku and daisan get ignored as a state of permanent revolution reigns from the outset.

This is unfortunate as it tends towards strident writing. But it is not a lethal problem. For that we must recapitulate a point made above.

A hokku may have a subplot. But, other than that, it is indistinguishable from a haiku. However. This is true *only* of the hokku. No other verse in a renku sequence can be usefully described as being *haiku-like*. They are not. They are fundamentally different.

A haiku is an independent verse. It doesn't need to bounce off anything else. By contrast, other than for the hokku, a good renku verse depends for its effect on the place it flows from. The dynamic forces which animate haiku are not found *within* renku verses. They are found *between* them. So, far from being any sort of stand-alone verses, they are can-only-stand-together verses.

And is there a *ku* name for this type of lowly, plain or planar verse too? Well of course there is! In renku theory books they are called *hiraku*.

A Dynamic Pattern
pacing with jo–ha–kyu

Introduction

The phrase *jo–ha–kyu* describes an ideal dynamic pattern or pacing paradigm that can be applied to the martial arts, music, drama, flower arranging, the tea ceremony or linked verse. It has three parts: *jo*, which may be given as *introduction*; *ha*, as *scattering*; and *kyu*, as *finale*.

Originating in *gagaku*, a form of 7th century Chinese court music, the concept of jo–ha–kyu was brought to Japanese theatre by the great Noh master Zeami in the late 14th century. Though poets subsequently discussed its application, such talk was largely speculative until the Edo period and the advent of the Basho school. In part the impetus which drove Basho to favour the shorter thirty-six verse kasen over the traditional one hundred verse hyakuin was the appreciation that jo–ha–kyu might be most effectively employed in a more compact sequence.

With the establishment of the Basho-style kasen as the standard vehicle, the notion of jo–ha–kyu became a core element of renku theory. The following comments are made in this context only. Other art forms apply the idea in a broadly similar way, but with differences of nuance.

The preface—jo

The initial movement of a poem is *jo*: the preface or introduction. Tonally the preface is relatively restrained. It is polite and pleasant, perhaps exploratory, never challenging. Overt humour is light rather than crude, wry but never sarcastic.

There are restrictions on choice of topic which complement the tonal constraints. Heavy or unfortunate subjects are avoided. In the Edo period this included all mention of death, war, illness, impermanence, religion and sex, not forgetting long distance travel, an indicator of how gruelling it could be. *Foreign*, in this case meaning *Chinese*, reference was also frowned on, as were all person and place names.

Though war and pestilence are obvious enough, these latter exclusions bear closer examination. The bar on all things Chinese looks like an assertion of identity in the face of a looming neighbour—exactly such sentiments as are found in Wales with respect to England, or Canada with respect to the United States. And it is true that the history of Japanese literature is not one of *if* but rather *when* a particular aspect of Chinese language and culture will predominate. But, as with the injunction against the use of proper nouns, the principal intention was to limit the scope for extra-textual direction.

A reference to a person or a place points the reader away from the immediate poem. In the preface the intention is to keep the readers' response within the range of sentiments evoked directly by the poet. Tu Fu, James Dean, Stonehenge and Area 51 are volatile quantities, the associations they elicit unpredictable. This kind of emotive probing of co-authors and readers alike is best left until later in the poem. Likewise the potentially fraught issue of familiarity with all things foreign.

The use of complex or extravagant diction was also seen as a distraction. Or worse, as a misdirection. For centuries much linkage in courtly renga had relied on a forensic knowledge of a limited number of core texts like the imperial poetry collections and the Tale of Genji. Links and references often lifted a section of narrative, reworked the wording of some famous passage, or otherwise demanded immediate recognition of the most tedious of minutiae.

Sogi had already argued that such techniques should be toned down, especially in the opening movement of a poem, and his less ostentatious approach was reinforced by the Basho school who were keen to avoid superficiality at all times. The contemporary understanding of *jo* is unchanged.

The avoidance of proper nouns and exotic diction helps to ensure that it is a relatively quiet place where poets may establish their presence without feeling the need to wave trophies or bray. The reader is likewise eased in. Cordiality prevails.

In theory the first verse, the hokku, is exempt from constraint. However, given the tenor of the rest of the preface and the tendency to code the hokku for greeting or augury, very harsh treatments at the head of the poem are rare. Renku does not avoid difficult or unpleasant topics—the best writing embraces all aspects of the human condition—but the less fragrant facets are the stuff of *ha*, not the stuff of *jo*.

The development—ha

The second movement of a poem is *ha*: the *development* or *intensification*. In the kasen, and associated four part poems such as the nijuin and tankako, *ha* is split between the folios to appear as equal halves.

Where the preface is restrained and circumscribed, in *ha* just about anything goes. It is unusual for poets of the Basho school to be extremely vulgar, crassly insulting or gratuitous in their portrayal of violence. Nonetheless sex, sarcasm and civil strife find their way into *ha* as readily as do high religion and low farce. The widespread belief that haikai always tries to be *nice* is pure misapprehension.

This is not to suggest that *ha* is composed of ever more strident attempts to shock or that it is uniformly blaring. The poem certainly develops, but, in the absence of the contrivance and lexical flummery typical of earlier renga, it does so in ways that are carefully modulated.

The requirement on each verse to shift comprehensively from the verse before last means that any direct narrative or thematic extension is only possible between a given pair, but this does not preclude subtle concatenations of tonal and emotional evocation that can extend over a range of five or six verses. The introduction of *nioizuke*—scent linking—and the consequent accentuation of the resonant space between verses, allows both rapid forward movement and the perseveration of non-cognitive effects in the mind of the reader. The twelve verses of a single face of *ha* in a kasen, or the ten central verses of the triparshva, can be made to swell between peaks and troughs of impact in a way some call *the renku wave*. Good renku is a sinuous beast, not a swarm of gnats.

The extra-textual direction and inter-textual reference avoided in the preface may now be used, albeit sparingly by comparison to classical renga. Poets will take more risk with the way the reader responds. Known quantities are subverted. Cultural icons recast—not in the search for novelty at all cost, but to comb and recombine them for fresh insight.

Some writers show a tendency to become more heterodox as the movement progresses, both in terms of content, verse structure and prosody. The latter portions of *ha* in some Basho kasen contain stanzas so irregular that later editors assumed them to be transcription errors and duly corrected them. In contemporary Japanese renku also, conventional metre is sometimes dropped for a limited number of stanzas. The rokku, one of the more recent forms of sequence, dedicates its penultimate phase to experimental prosody.

The development movement is the place for speculation and innovation. But only the crudest writing thrashes in pursuit of effect. The Basho school sought *makoto*—truth. They found that loud is not the same thing as profound.

The finale—kyu

Master Zeami reputedly likened jo–ha–kyu to the course of a mountain river: *jo* is the tributary's gentle rill; *ha* the river in spate as it cuts back and forth between mountain peaks; and *kyu* the plunge of a mighty waterfall into a deep and silent pool.

The metaphor is important, for, though *jo* and *ha* have been reasonably well understood in western renku, the closing movement—*kyu*—has tended to be taken as simply a mirror of *jo*. As a result the 6/12/12/6 verses of a kasen are often seen as quiet/loud/loud/quiet. There is nothing catastrophic in this proposal, but it neither respects Zeami's clearly stated paradigm nor accords with the evidence from Basho's own writing. Perhaps more to to the point, the sequence fizzles out.

The 6/12/12/6 division of the kasen is better understood as quiet/varied/intense/rush and stop. *Kyu* is the *rush and stop* or, as it is commonly but less accurately given, the *rapid close*. At the risk of over simplification: we might expect the first three verses of the closing movement to be striking, whilst the final three move to a happy and tranquil state. More often than not they are set in spring—a season that turns towards the light.

Given that the latter part of the development movement is *intense*, and the first part of the closing movement *rapid*, the two may easily blend. Indeed some authorities argue that in Basho's own work the rapid close often effectively begins around verse position #27 or #28. But there is a distinction to be drawn between the aims of the two passages. *Ha* encourages diversity of content and style whereas the early stage of *kyu* requires compaction and irresistibility. So whilst content might remain brash the prosody will now be unchallenging, the metres more conventional, and inter-verse linkage tight. Extra-textual direction is limited too, the reader held close once more. We want our audience to experience the waterfall, not fly off in some random direction.

Kyu is therefore drum roll and cymbal strike, its reverberation coloured by the final exchange. Far from being a succession of anodyne verses, *kyu* is the crash of the breaker on the beach, followed by the hiss of foam and the growl of the undertow.

Beyond jo–ha–kyu

The 6/12/12/6 division of the kasen is optimised for jo–ha–kyu. And vice versa. The length of each movement is bound up with how the pattern unfolds. Likewise, though at first sight odd for being tripartite, the 6/10/6 of the triparshva will permit the full range of expressive effects.

Handled with skill the tankako's 4/8/8/4 or the nijuin's 4/6/6/4 can also be made to suffice, though the nijuin can feel rather tight. Whether it is possible to go any lower is moot. The suggestion that the 3/3/3/3 of the shisan enables jo–ha–kyu is optimistic at best.

However, the work of Basho does not demonstrate that a poem must necessarily employ the jo–ha–kyu pacing paradigm. It demonstrates that a poem needs *a* pacing paradigm of some sort. Whatever its style or length, a renku sequence requires more than haphazard assembly. It demands a more enduring sensitivity to tone, not to simply switch from one instant to the next. The analogy is to music. We are not obliged to stick to the concerto. We can improvise and be free form. But even a very short piece, if it is wholly amorphous, is not very likely to be good.

The invitation to the contemporary poet is clear. There is absolutely no reason why you should not form your own structures and pace your sequences as you will. The only requirement for high quality writing is that it is both structured and orchestrated rather than shapeless and haphazard.

Link: Making the Connection
manners and methods of linkage

Introduction

As befits a wandering saint-cum-prestidigitator Matsuo Basho was rarely at a loss for the odd *bon mot*. It was not unknown for two or three *bons mots* to gain him a free hermitage, banana tree, or other such handy asset.

But if, as reputed, he did indeed express the hope that, even if his hokku didn't stand the test, he would at least be remembered as a master of link, he may have been thinking beyond lunchtime.

Basho was indeed a master of link. In fact Basho was The Master of Link—capitals and florid font— changing the face of linked verse forever.

Elsewhere in this learned tome an overview of link, and its partner shift, is given in the cunningly titled chapter *Link & Shift: An Overview*. Here we lift the lid on the pickled corpse that is *link* alone.

So button up collars please, straighten ties, and don a respectful face.

Laying down the lore

Unlike many of the celebrated renga masters before him, Basho didn't really do *rules*, resisting the temptation to publish endless volumes of theory. His preference was to lead by face-to-face dialogue and example. Unlike the weasel faced man in my bathroom mirror, Basho let his poetry do the talking.

Such of his overt theorising as does remain can appear elliptical and contradictory as it is gleaned from the memoirs and commentaries of his followers, poets who quite naturally had interests of their own, and who, when push came to shove, needed a tale to tell on the after dinner circuit.

But, when it comes to Basho's attitude to linkage, there is enough correlation between reliable sources to be unequivocal about the old boy's bent. Kyorai had it most succinctly. Per the quotation carried in our *White Space* chapter, Basho clearly identified all prior approaches to linkage as old hat. His own, he placed firmly in the van of things to come:

> *In the distant past, poets valued word links. In the more recent past, poets have stressed content links.*

It is often argued that Basho was speaking in code—that by *distant past* he was referring to Matsunaga Teitoku's *Teimon* school of haikai, and by *more recent past* to Nishiyama Soin's *Danrin* school. This is possible; Basho had studied both styles in his early years and they continued to exert a competitive claim on some of his patrons, *des bons mots* or no.

However the critical distinction between word links and content links had been drawn more than three centuries earlier by Nijo Yoshimoto, and the poet Sogi, revered by Basho, was strongly identified with content links. Further, despite the obsessive attention lavished on them by the Teimon school, baroque lexical devices had been a mainstay of linking technique from the earliest times. So it is equally possible that Basho was speaking literally, and considered his own approach to be the culmination of a thousand years' worth of literary development.

And if that doesn't look particularly modest... it was probably time for another tonsure.

Three tiers of technique

Whatever the precise historical reference, and the degree of his attachment to the wheel, Basho was clearly making a qualitative distinction which is held just as strongly by modern followers. Basho identified not three types but three *tiers* of technique which he placed in ascending order of artistry.

Kotobazuke—word links—and *monozuke*—object links—occupy the lowest rank. These are forms of linkage predicated on the word choice or primary content of a verse. We are dealing with everything from crass puns to abstruse flummery, from the simple association of one object with another, to an intimate knowledge of the contents of a shrine maiden's portmanteau.

The middle rank is composed of *kokorozuke*—core or content links—and *imizuke*—meaning links. Under this regime an added verse most often reads as an extension of the action or setting of its preceding verse, so forming a distinct pair. Despite some potentially ingenious twist, there is a narrative connection between them. Even where the link is more subtle and indirect, it remains amenable to understanding. The poets lay the story on the page before us. The reader has merely to read.

Basho places his own contribution to the development of linking technique uppermost. This he calls *nioizuke*—scent linkage. Nioizuke evokes a much more tenuous set of associations which are nowhere specified in the text itself. Linkage is by implication. The reader is obliged to engage with the poem as an active interpreter. With the advent of scent linkage the space around the words is opened out.

Kotobazuke: Bits of text

The very reasons for which word and object linkage had been so highly regarded in the past were, for the Basho school, grounds for them to be all but dismissed. Early linked verse had prized *engo*, inventive word play relying heavily on cognates and homophones, or *yoriai*—linking via fixed associations between groups of words or objects. In almost all cases these set affiliations stemmed from their having featured in some classic verse or tale that was subsequently cited in a critical treatise or royal anthology.

Thus *engo* and *yoriai* were the preserve of the educated and leisured classes requiring high levels of verbal dexterity, a flair for etymology, a comprehensive knowledge of the approved Japanese and Chinese literary canon, and a thorough grounding in the normative concepts of category arising therefrom. It was all frightfully clever.

Rooted in the more plebeian haikai tradition Basho and his followers had little time for this. Erudition for its own sake had little value. Ostentation was simply tiresome. Conventional associations were the route to atrophy. The common language and common experience could be the stuff of artistic excellence just as readily as the royal courts and the endless reworking of centuries old waka.

As with modern Shofu renku, the occasional word or object link did still find its way into a poem, very often as a wry or throw-away aside. But a sequence composed mainly of such links, for all that it might be striking or droll, could hardly have any substance, coherence or evocative depth. The essential character of word and object links is that they are hopelessly superficial.

Kokorozuke: The whole text

These deficits had been identified well before the Edo period, and, though wit remained a prominent feature amongst those who considered it a pastime only, many poets had sought to broaden and deepen the expressive power of linked verse. So we arrive as Basho's *recent past* and the techniques grouped under the rubric *kokorozuke*—linkage via content, core or meaning.

For many persons new to renku this approach remains the linking technique of choice. The attraction is self evident: one simply studies the setting, the protagonists, or the action of the preceding verse and extends them in some way—perhaps adding a clever or novel twist—so that the added verse and preceding verse work to form a new scene.

Unlike *kotobazuke's* focus on snippets, the sense of each verse is now considered as a whole. The added verse links in a rational, relational or narrative manner. It furnishes corroborative detail, describes consequent events, delves into a protagonist's background; or shifts the scene to another place or time. Just occasionally it may pursue an abstract idea from the preceding verse.

In theory at least the obligation to *shift* from the verse before last ensures that a run of verses linked in this manner do not become thematic. Each pair of verses forms a fresh vignette, only for this to be deconstructed by the introduction of the next added verse as a new combination is offered to the reader.

In practice, particularly in the one hundred verse plus sequences of the medieval period in which topics such as travel, lamentation and Buddhism could persist for a run of verses, something approaching a conducting strand often builds up. The more pedestrian of Basho's own kasen demonstrate something similar where four or five spring, autumn or love verses appear in a row. But, by the standards of the best Shomon sequences, and in all modern Shofu renku, this is simply evidence of poor writing. There is nothing in kokorozuke that inhibits change per se. The very fact that linkage is via stated content allows *shift* to be easily judged. A defining characteristic of kokorozuke is that the forces of relation and disassociation which govern the momentum of a poem are entirely within the purview of the poet.

During the course of the last century the continuous recombination of pairs of verses characteristic of this style of linkage persuaded some scholars in the English speaking world to present the text of sequences as though each perceived cameo had indeed been composed as a separate waka or tanka—as a separate poem. We are therefore treated to verses reprinted as **AB**, **BC**, **CD**, **DE** etc—the more adventurous of our experts going so far as to retranslate the text of each combination in order to highlight their intimacy.

It may just be possible to defend this approach in the case of medieval linked verse, and other forms of haikai no renga that employ kotobazuke throughout, where the principal scope is the continual construction and deconstruction of matching pairs. The stop/start nature of the reading is a hideous distortion of the musicality of the source text, but the general standard of translation is anyway so execrable that any euphony was long since lost. But to present the work of the Basho school in this manner is frankly unforgivable, betokening an utter failure to understand the depth of innovation it embodies.

In the best Shomon renku the relationship between verses has undergone a transformation, and the question of coherence over extended passages of verse is now very much to the fore. The focus has moved to the dynamics of the poem as a whole.

Nioizuke: Beyond the text

Those with the money to fill their bookshelves will discover that there are an infinity of terms to describe the various gradations of the Basho-style link. The one thing they have in common is that they are vague, overlapping and variable—highly dependent on the author's view of the protagonist's intentions. It does not help that so few commentators have written linked verse.

The differences of usage in the historical sources are frequently attributed to confusion. The poets of the Shomon school did not really know what they were doing, the argument goes, because they failed to employ terms consistently. In fact the reverse is true. The poets knew exactly what they were doing, and so had no need to resort to the index of somebody's doctoral thesis for guidance. The art comes first, and the analysis second. Unless one is an academic.

Despite the scholarly obfuscation it is perfectly possible to make a clear distinction between *kokorozuke* and *nioizuke*. Whereas *kokorozuke* employs a form of dependency in which the relationship of each added verse to the preceding verse is apprehensible—amenable to intellectual scrutiny—*nioizuke* is supratextual. It does not seek to make sense, relying instead on the interplay of mood, tone and dynamic intensity.

Nioizuke goes beyond the primary sense of the words, decoupling the expectation that there must be a plausible connection between the content of the added verse and that of the preceding verse. The space between them is broadened as evocation, figurative exchange and tonal synergy replace narrative, descriptive or logical extension.

Although the reading experience remains sequential, the moment of the added verse becomes synchronous with, rather than consequent to, that of the preceding verse. The relationship is now more akin to exchange or dialogue (*kakeai*) than to addition (*tsukeai*)—a crucial distinction as it produces relationships typical of the matching of intangibles (*awase*) that is the essential characteristic of modern styles of juxtaposition (*toriawase*). Basho has opened *between* his renku verses the same generative space that modern poets place at the heart of their haiku.

This white space becomes the main locus of expressive force—one into which the reader must enter as active interpreter. The continual process of synthesis and reconciliation generates its own conducting strand woven from the emotional tones and colours evoked. With sufficient skill, entire passages of verse may be generated which unfold with power and grace despite the fact that the content of their verses moves at a continual tangent.

The range of content is greatly increased too. The abandonment of realism or naturalism as the basis of linkage allows heterogeneous subjects to be juxtaposed without automatically generating incongruity. Commonplace themes and language may appear alongside icons of high culture. Humour and profundity can mix. The permanent glimpsed within the churn of the transient. Basho has freed haikai no renga from the gutter, without obliging it to spend the rest of its life primping in the salon.

Layering, proximity and pace

As ever with the poetics of the Basho school the relationship between theory and practice is fluid—its precepts offered as advice rather than direction.

Nioizuke permits great subtlety and offers extended dynamic control, but it is best understood as the highest order of linkage available to the poet, rather than the sole technique appropriate to all occasions. Even in sequences led by the Master himself there are many instances of basic word play, as there are of content linking so direct as to be little more than narrative extension.

Perhaps most interesting to the practicing poet are those links which layer their relational devices. A word link might be used as a throw-away joke whilst a deep-level suggestion is infiltrated behind. An allusion which may be too obscure for some is mediated by a more obvious connection between events. If all else fails the sheer beauty of language may be just enough to pull the reader through to the next step.

Just as each verse of a sequence is not of uniform intensity, neither is each tie between them uniformly pitched. The earliest linked verse treatises drew a distinction between tight links (*shinku*) and loose links (*soku*) which remains a useful tool for the writer. Blends of word and meaning linkage will tend to produce tight links whereas scent linkage, by its nature, directs us outwards. Used in combination with sensitivity to cadence, both within and between verses, the poet can exercise fine degrees of control on the proximity between verses as an element in the orchestration of the poem's wider movement.

The avid student will find that there is a superabundance of terminology to describe the various manners, methods and schools of linkage both in the Japanese and occidental critical literature. A term will be cited, and an example or two given. Case proven—we have just witnessed *mikomi* or *ominashi* etc. This is all well and good in so far as it gives food for thought and points the aspiring poet in a general direction. But it can be misleading if it is taken to indicate that a set and static range of techniques exist which, if only they can be learnt accurately enough, will of themselves produce the required result.

Such terms are indicative only. In every instance they have been retrofitted—settled on, either by the poets of the day or by latter commentators, in an attempt to describe an approach which had already been pioneered in practice.

A willingness to break with the past, and to experiment with new concepts, was a core tenet of Basho's quiet revolution which obtains to the present day. This is not the slash and burn nihilism of the self proclaimed radical but rather the calm reappraisal of those whose maxim it is to first learn from the work of past masters.

In the Basho style, sensitivity to the proximity of linkage is a key component of overall pacing, and carefully judged pacing is central to ideas of wider coherence. But it is not necessary to have an encyclopaedic knowledge of terminology in order to be effective in linkage. The art of linked verse is in the doing, not the naming, and an awareness of Basho's three tiers of association is grounding enough for a worthwhile understanding to develop.

Merely dealing with snips of text will yield a frustrating read. Looking at linkage through a rational lens is worthy, but tends to the staid. Going for the merest waft of association, if done badly, will lose the reader. If done well, it will let him loose.

The practicing poet should do just that. And make of this what they will.

An afterword: The Mozhukhin Experiment

More than two centuries after the emergence of nioizuke, renku theorists in the 1920s such as Torahiko Terada were excited by the radical montage techniques of the Soviet cineastes Pudovkin, Kuleshov and Eisenstein which they saw as the visual equivalent of Basho's style of linkage. Nowhere was this parallel more intriguing than in the famous Mozhukhin Experiment.

Fascinated by the work of Pavlov on conditioning, Lev Kuleshov devised a short sequence of film which cut back and forth between close-ups of the famous actor Mozhukhin, a bowl of soup, a woman's corpse, and a child playing. This he showed to an invited audience of cognoscenti in one of the better halls of culture. According to one contemporary report the audience...

> ...raved about the acting of the artist. They pointed out the heavy pensiveness of his mood over the forgotten soup, were touched and moved by the deep sorrow with which he looked on the dead woman, and admired the light, happy smile with which he surveyed the girl at play.

In fact there was only one, carefully neutral, shot of Mozhukhin, repeated severally. The reading of emotion—the links, the response—existed only in the mind of the viewer.

It would seem that the technique of nioizuke was on the cutting edge of what we currently call cognitive psychology. Which is really quite impressive, for a bunch of men in skirts.

More About Shift
some practicalities

Introit

If the notes haven't been shredded and used to line the hamster cage, elsewhere in this august tome is an overview of the core generative mechanism of linked verse known as link and shift. It is best to read that first.

The present chapter examines the practical implications of the imperative to *shift*—in Japanese: tenji. The word is intended in the narrow sense of the avoidance of reversion to any aspect of the content or execution of the verse before last. Shift, in this context, does not refer to the more generic notion that every verse in a sequence must introduce a degree of newness.

Because of the persistence of high concentrations of lead in the water supply of many developed economies the word *renku* is sometimes used to describe thematic haikai no renga and other pathetic trivia. For the avoidance of doubt: people who promulgate such nonsense are usually Professors of Tying Their Own Shoelaces and should be treated with sympathy. But otherwise ignored. *Renku Reckoner* deals with haikai no renga as written by the Basho school. In this style of writing the degree of shift is graduated to ensure that thematic development is impossible. There is no such thing as thematic Shofu renku.

So, ushering the Professor gently out the door, let's recapitulate by taking a look at a group of verses **A**, **B**, **C** and **D**.

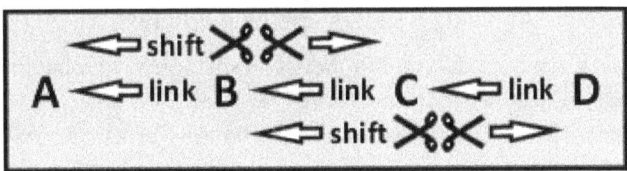

The basic mechanism is straightforward enough. Each time we add a verse it links to the preceding verse, whilst purposefully disassociating itself from the verse before last. **C** links to **B**, but breaks from **A**, just as **D** then links to **C** but breaks from **B**.

It is the nature of the disassociation from the verse before last that is the stuff of *shift*.

The same topic

At its simplest Shofu renku can be seen as a strand of poetry which opens continuously outward. The subject treated by any given verse develops via the link into the following verse, and the poem moves on. The new verse in turn treats a fresh subject, and the poem is ready to step forward via the next link. **A** develops into **B**, so that **B** may then develop into **C**.

So powerful is the creative potential of the white space between verses that it is surprisingly easy, as one develops the transition from **B** into **C**, to flip back directly to a principle aspect of **A**. The poem has already moved on so substantially that **A** can feel like a long time ago. Its actual verse content, always of less importance than the transitions created by the intervening links, may have been forgotten as the writers direct their attention towards progressing the poem.

For all that it may seem blindingly obvious therefore, it is good counsel to check back to the verse before last to ensure that a wholesale reversion has not accidentally occurred. This is best done at the point of composition of each added verse. If the process of composition involves extracts of the wider text being posted back and forth, it is always helpful to copy over the current working *trio* of verses rather than simply the verse to which one is linking. The imperative is unequivocal: each new verse, and the verse before last, must be about different things.

Of course this begs the question of how different is *different?* Within the bounds of reason, and remembering that we are involved in the composition of poetry not the investigation of a murder, the answer is easy: *completely different*. Neither the totality of the new verse, nor any prominent part of the new verse, should feel as though it deals with the same subject as the verse before last—a bar which extends to the use of closely associated key words and concepts.

What precisely constitutes *the same subject*, and those attributes which are closely identified with it, will vary from culture to culture. But they are not difficult to identify for any literate person writing in a familiar language. There is no need for a massively complex superstructure of precedent and practice, or a proscriptive list of what may and may not be allowed. The best test is instinct. If something *feels* like a reversion to the verse before last, then it *is* a reversion to the verse before last.

The compulsion to seek out the most tortuous connections between the added verse and the verse before last should be resisted. Beyond that—artists must use their judgement.

Person and place

To take Tachibana Hokushi at his own estimation he was the most important of Basho's ten disciples. Chief amongst his attainments was the elaboration of a practical guide to the balance of *place* and *person* verses in a sequence. A subject on which he proceeded to lecture his Master. Who duly ignored him.

Tempting as it is to giggle, Hokushi did develop a worthwhile set of considerations which amount to a theory of narrative perspective. Applying it flexibly can help ensure shift.

The earliest renga treatises drew a distinction between person and place verses—*ji-ta-ba*—and, in contemporary renku theory, ideas of what constitutes *place* are little changed. In their 1994 paper *Link and Shift: A Practical Guide to Renku Composition* modern scholars Shokan Tadashi Kondo and William J. Higginson gave a succinct definition which could equally have been written in Hokushi's day:

> *Place encompasses everything from geography to the site of a specific activity—virtually any stanza that does not show a person or a group of people. A caterpillar on a leaf, a basket of fruit in the market, a bird in the sky, and so on. Whether its locale is mentioned or not, any object may be construed as implying its setting, thus qualifying it [...] as place.*

With the notion of place already as a given, Hokushi turned his attention to person verses—identifying at first three functional categories to which a fourth was later added. Each category represents the stance from which a verse is recounted, and/or describes its human content. In Japanese Hokushi offered us:

- *ji* – self, first-person experience

- *ta* – other, the experience of another person

- *ji-ta-han* – self & other, the experience of oneself with another or others

- *ashirai* – public or mixed, the experience of a group of people, even if indistinctly drawn

- *ba* – place, an event or scene without human involvement, though artefacts may be included

In some senses Japanese is a more elliptical language than English. Certainly, when it comes to specifying the number and gender of actors in a verse, it is more flexible—a feature which allows for some slippery transitions from verse to verse. But it is not impossible to imagine a set of English categories which model Hokushi closely enough, and which serves as a base from which to judge variety or perspective. One possibility is:

- *ji* – first person (singular or plural)
- *ta* – third person (singular or plural)
- *ji-ta-han* – second person, or an authorial presence in rhetorical mode
- *ashirai* – human affairs, with no clearly discernible protagonists
- *ba* – place, an event or scene without human involvement

Hokushi proposed many and complex ideal combinations of viewpoint over a given trio of verses, some of which are arcane at best. But the core of his work is both simple and valid. It is rarely good writing to use the same narrative perspective in adjoining verses. And it is *always* poor writing to simply alternate with, or revert back to, the same viewpoint that was used in the verse before last.

Hokushi understood the demands of shift and urged his contemporaries to keep a change of narrative perspective in the mix. It is evident from some of Basho's less inspired work that he could have done worse than pay a little more attention to his annoying friend.

Location and angle

For all that it may be given by implication only, according to the earliest authorities, whether a verse deals with a person and emotion (*ninjo*) or place and object (*ba*) it will have a spatial location. A basic distinction would be drawn between indoor (*uchi*) and outdoor (*soto*) settings which was then broken down into various subcategories according to the number of pages available for prognostication.

During the early part of the last century these older perceptions of spatial location were transformed by the identification of a strong creative synergy between the cinematic techniques of filmmakers such as Sergei Eisenstein and the highly imagistic verse to verse juxtapositions typical of the renascent Shofu renku.

Overleaf the chapter *Link: Making the connection* touches on some of the similarities between scent linkage and montage. Here it is sufficient to note that the ability to view verses in terms of shots, angles and clips is a highly useful tool when weighing the variety of visual content. Location, focus, depth, speed of movement—all can be used to specific effect.

As with the speculations of Hokushi on persons and place, it is not that some hard and fast formula must prevail in respect of the spatiotemporal location of a verse, only that a flexible and imaginative cycling between the many options will yield better writing.

The closest thing to a *rule* is that we should not revert to the location, focus and angle of the verse before last. To do so would be a failure of shift.

Phrasing

It is not an unbridled benefit that many persons come to the writing of renku via haiku.

One of the more pernicious effects of the absence of any serious 20th century occidental haiku scholarship is a wholly distorted attitude towards the English language itself. Words are bad. Those who study words are mere pedants, doomed never to experience the eternal now.

History cannot be undone and there is no depth of contempt adequate to the condemnation of the pathetic assortment of addicts and loons who have perpetuated this nonsense, so let us simply observe that, the last time anyone got off the sofa and looked, poetry did indeed involve the use of language. And Shofu renku is poetry.

No literary form is a stranger to ideas of inappropriate usage, artificiality, unimaginative word choice, or careless repetition. A general awareness of the pitfalls of compositional inelegance is the starting point for all forms of creative writing. Just as a renku sequence may use elements of syntax and sound to cement the linkage between adjoining verses, a countervailing emphasis is placed on the avoidance of grammatical and morphological echoes between an added verse and the verse before last. Clearly, if the ear picks up strongly on a phonological or structural reversion, our verse has failed to shift.

Frequently the problem is that both added verse and verse before last share near identical syntax. The reader is directed backwards and the forward momentum lost. Register can also be an issue—the poem inadvertently flicking back and forth between high and low styles of diction or rhetorical mode. Indeed any form of stand-out word choice can be a problem as it will exercise a lingering effect on the verses that follow.

But these pitfalls will be apparent to any person with adequate language skills and a basic grasp of literature. They can be corrected with a minor edit. It is necessary only to review the working text as composition progresses.

More perplexing for many writers is the question of the repetition of articles, conjunctions and prepositions. It is not unknown for the midnight oil to sputter over the re-appearance of an *in* or a *to*—a conundrum which holds true for the content of the preceding verse as much as for the verse before last.

Were we to believe our haiku heroes the solution is simplicity itself—if a word can be omitted, it should be omitted. If this produces a hideously ugly telegraphese devoid of any sense, all the better. It just goes to show how profound it is. Man.

If we turn instead to poets writing poetry, specifically to Japanese poets writing renku, the suggestion is that the mind slips lightly over such minor parts of speech unless the repetition is highlighted by some other deficit of phrasing. The opening and closing syllables of a verse, and those that open or close a line or metrical phrase, do need handling with care as the prominence of the position can make an otherwise insignificant repetition much more apparent. But persons new to renku should be assured that, in other circumstances, the minor parts of speech will look after themselves. It takes something more substantive than the repetition of *the* to constitute a failure of phrasing to shift.

Ground and pattern

Just as the 1920s and 30s saw the language of cinematic montage enter Japanese renku theory, so early renga theorists drew on the dyeing and weaving industries for parallels to their craft. Thanks to the enthusiastic if somewhat dubious advocacy of a number of occidental academics one such analogy remains current and rewards a passing glance.

Ground and pattern are the most common English translations of the Japanese words *ji* and *mon*. Originally these referred to the distinction between an unfigured and a figured part of textile. As the artisans would have it, one is weak and the other is strong. One is quiet whilst the other is striking. The application of such ideas to verse is obvious—*ji* tends to the passive, *mon* to the active.

In so far as the terminology reminds us that not all verses are intended to be of equal intensity the distinction is a boon. But the application of a binary system in respect of medieval renga is already questionable and, when used in the context of either Edo period haikai no renga or modern renku, it becomes something of a distortion.

The greater interest shown by the Basho school in the possibility of wider dynamic control over extended passages of verse means that the impact of each verse in a section or movement may be carefully calculated. This is not a question of the meaning or content of the verse but rather of the depth of response it evokes in the mind of the reader. In the best work there are subtle gradations. Unlike REO Speedwagon, Shofu renku is not uniformly full on. Or indeed full off.

But the notion of ground and pattern is neither bogus or wholly redundant. At least it may remind us not to flip back and forth between strident and anodyne verses. Any such either/or alternation of tone, mood or intensity in a given trio of verses clearly constitutes a failure to shift.

Anomalies and exceptions

The general thrust of the argument is plain. If there are laws in renku, the law of shift brooks no argument: whilst an added verse (*tsukeku*) and the verse to which it links (*maeku*) may share some characteristics, the added verse and verse before last (uchikoshi) may not.

All well and good, except that at this point the Professor—freshly showered, shaved, suited and elastic-panel booted—reappears, complete with cat.

One of the features of the renku revival of the last half century has been the search for ever shorter sequences. Once we get down to the twelve verse junicho or shisan, compared to Basho's beloved thirty-six verse kasen, there is not much space to go around. Even the appearance of spring or autumn—nominally a major event—does not get allotted more than a consecutive pair of verses as the overall piece is so compact. The same holds true for the sole extended *human affairs* topic to have made the transition from renga to renku. In a sequence this tight, *love* does not, cannot, carry on for more than a pair of verses.

This is a happy outcome for the law of shift as nothing has been infringed. Two verses good, three verses bad—a formula so attractive that some modern writers prefer to adopt it across the piece. Haku Asanuma's mould breaking rokku, for instance, may extend to thirty or more verses, but at no time does a given season, or trusty old *love*, occupy more than two verses together. There can be no allegation that shift has been compromised because added verse and verse before last are *never* asked to share the same quality.

At the kasen end of the spectrum matters are different. Spring and autumn may occupy a run of five verses together. Love can take up to four in a row. Even grotty old summer and winter have been known to straddle the magic trio of added verse, preceding verse, and verse before last. Clearly Master Matsuo knew a lot about wabi-sabi, and other spicy seasonings, but didn't have a clue about shift. *Whufaffu*, murmurs the Professor round a mouthful of bright green peanuts. *Thematic*.

Persistence of belief in the face of overwhelming evidence to the contrary is a virtue, otherwise Dawkins could not imagine himself to be sentient, so somewhere in this dyslexic haystack of a typescript *Renku Reckoner* dedicates a short chapter to the distinction between thematic and non-thematic linked verse. It is the one with the red pencil through the expletives. For the moment, two observations will suffice. One is purely technical, the other relates to our ability as poets.

In a renku sequence neither autumn, to draw an example from the seasons, nor love, are static. Though the seasons themselves may appear in random order, within the bounds of run of verses taking the same season, time moves chronologically. We start off in early autumn, we progress through mid autumn, and we end up in late autumn.

So constant is this aspect of renku that those unfortunate enough to resort to lexicons of season words to aid composition will find the majority of the benighted *kigo* tagged with an appropriate temporal locator. The occasional *all autumn* verse might be infiltrated at some point, but in a run of season verses time never runs backwards. The moment of the added verse will always have moved on substantially from the moment of the verse before last.

Love is similarly associated with an unfolding pattern which, in classical renga at least, tended to follow a particular pattern of development, echoes of which are strong in Edo period haikai no renga and may still be found in modern writing. As every star-crossed lover knows, we start out young and optimistic, develop a little grittily, albeit perhaps with a degree of humour, only for it to end in despair and misery.

At a technical level therefore, with love, as with a season, an added verse and verse before last do not share precisely the same background, the point of time or of being has altered.

The key phrase here might appear to be *precisely the same*. But in fact, when it comes to our ability as poets, the word *background* is far more important.

Only in the most inadequate writing does a link between season verses, or between love verses, rely on that shared aspect for its principal relational quality. An autumn verse is not *about* autumn. Love is the *context* of a love verse not the totality of its subject. For all that our schematic layouts may feature ideograms, pictograms or acronyms boldly proclaiming *haru* or *koi* these are indicative qualities only. They represent an invitation. They are the starting point of a verse *not* descriptors of an aspect that is sufficient of itself for a verse to be seen as adequate. If you find that you have elevated *spring* to the level of a conducting strand between otherwise unrelated verses it is best to pack up your brushes and go home.

It is tempting therefore to cock a snook at the Professor, dash the cat from his arms, and advance some frightfully recondite argument about the multiplex nature of shift. But to do so is to complicate matters unnecessarily. It is simplest to acknowledge that the obligation to shift comprehensively from every aspect of the verse before last, in all other circumstance, does indeed extend to the purely contextual elements of a verse.

The extended season and love runs of longer Shofu renku sequences are an anomaly, an exception.

Two verses good, three verses bad, is indeed the rule.

Uchikoshi no kirai, kannonbiraki, and reversion

Given that we are now in the territory of rules it is hardly surprising that certain crimes have been identified and named.

Originally the word *kannonbiraki* referred to the pair of doors on a portable Buddhist altar. These open outwards to either side, their inner surfaces carrying matching pictorial motifs which frame the centerpiece. In Japanese renku circles, when verse **A** and **C** display an unfortunate degree of similarity, they are viewed as forming a symmetrical frame around **B**. The failure of **C** to shift in respect of **A** has generated a clear case of kannonbiraki, the erstwhile *double doors*.

As we have seen above, *uchikoshi* is the name applied in Japanese to the verse before last. A literal translation is something like *leap-over verse*. But it is equally used as a contraction of *uchikoshi no kirai*—to *smack of the leap-over verse*. Uchikoshi may therefore refer the verse position before last, or to an unwelcome similarity between the added verse and the verse before last. Context will clarify usage.

There is little agreement amongst English renku poets on how to describe a failure to shift—otherwise known as too little movement from the verse before last—so the Japanese words uchikoshi and kannonbiraki are often used as terms of preference. But the Professor would like to point out, in the spirit of amity, that his peanuts are wasabi flavour, not wabi-sabi, and that he agrees with my suitably humble proposal that the best specialist English term to describe a failure to shift sufficiently, and hence revisit some aspect of the verse before last, is *reversion*.

That's OK Professor—I'll untie you from the radiator shortly.

No. Sorry. The cat is lost to us.

Thematic Renku
reasons to join the circus

Because it's there

A fatuous, stupid, waste of time and resources. Or a triumph of the human spirit?

In the days of Rae and Amundsen we could probably answer the latter. Someone needed to find the North West Passage, and brave men rose to the challenge. But by the time we reach 2013 and the spectacle of a crazed dilettante shedding digits here and there as he single handedly (sic) drags 3,000 bottles of Lucozade across a wasteland so unknown that it is only remapped to an accuracy of 2 nanometers every 24 hours from space...

People are strange creatures. Some collect Soviet postage stamps. Others think thematic renku is worthwhile.

The stamp collector wins.

Having fun

The history of linked verse is littered with blind alleys, each with a big name charlatan or two pointing the way to nowhere. Here we have the 1,000 verse sequence. Any good? Dunno. We only bothered to keep the first few verses of each page.

Well, over there's the 10,000 verse recitation. That's impressive! Yeah, probably. But he was speaking so fast we couldn't write anything down.

What about some point-scoring renku then? Ooooh, ok, we like those. You only have to read the verses that got the big money. Money? Well, prizes then. They give out prizes for good verses.

Isn't that a bit like a verse-capping competition? Yeah. But that's best of all because you don't have to bother with the sequence in the first place.

Oh but I like sequences. As long as they're about something—you know *real*. Tell you what—why don't we write some thematic renku? Aardvarks. No one's done them yet. It'd be fun. And we'd be bound to get first spot in the anthology.

Shofu

Alternatively you could take up sword swallowing.

There is no such thing as thematic Basho-style linked verse. There is a very good reason for this. Basho didn't write any. And there's a very good reason for that. Every instinct took him in the opposite direction. Basho and his followers had some lofty ideas—they sought *fuga no makoto* for instance. And there's not much *poetry as truth and art* to be had by stringing together a gazillion verses about cherry blossom. Or cats.

That thematic haikai no renga has existed in the past, and that there are contemporary instances of thematic renku, is beyond question. It is for others to make the case that such writing has merit. The purpose of this chapter is to illustrate why any idea of thematic Shofu renku is a contradiction in terms.

Uchikoshi no kirai

Uchikoshi no kirai is a straightforward idea. It means *return to the verse before last*. Which is bad. A snappier name for it is *reversion*. But that doesn't stop it being bad. The chapter *Link & Shift: An Overview* gives the basics. I left it around here somewhere, along with *More About Shift*. Please have a look and see what they say, if you manage to track them down.

Proponents of thematic renku believe they can validate the genre because shift between added verse and verse before last is not absolute even in Basho's own work. Ergo: there are *degrees* of shift. Five spring verses in a row. Four love verses ditto. And all those times Basho and Co get stuck on some aspect of the floating world. These hardly support the claim that uchikoshi no kirai is in all ways ascendant. Therefore, as long as there is an inventive degree of forward momentum in the poem, and no really gross return to the verse before last, we can tease out the manifold aspects of our chosen theme and still be writing in the style of Basho. Or at least still be writing perfectly respectable haikai no renga.

One way to counter this argument is to conjure a distinction. These alleged instances of failure to shift do not constitute thematic writing. They are *para-thematic*. Neither a run of season verses nor of love verses are static. Their chronology moves on. Crucially, to mistake the season or the fixed topic of the verse for the substance of the verse is just poor artistry. Such considerations are supposed to be the context of the verse, not the totality of the verse itself. And the para-thematic element is not in place for the whole poem. Even in a kasen five verses maximum is all you get.

There is a degree of truth in this rebuttal. The temptation to elevate the contextual element of a verse to a theme—to a conducting strand—is a powerful one, especially for writers whose development has been blighted by tick-box notions of correctness. And a glance at our handy kasen schematic will confirm that autumn etc never do persist for more than five verses.

Yet as we bat the argument back and forth we fail to notice the elephants, one of which has entered the room whilst the other has left in disgust.

The first elephant admits that, yes, it is true, there *are indeed* degrees of shift. No element of a Shofu renku sequence demonstrates fixed quantities. Just as the proximity and style of linkage varies from one passage of verse to another, so does the extent of shift. The entire point of a Basho style poem is that it flexes. Or fails to. Edo period kasen often do display a bit of hangover from ushin renga wherein a long sequence would treat human affairs topics such as travel, illness or religion etc for three or four verses at a time.

It is only modern renku which demonstrates a wholly uninflected approach to shift. The shorter, highly imagistic, sequences of contemporary renku move at great speed. Juxtaposition after juxtaposition rapidly obliterates old ground. In the most modern writing, shift is maximised almost by default.

But as the departing elephant said, we're completely missing the point. Fortunately it left a deposition: Shofu renku and thematic renku are indeed mutually exclusive. But the reasons have nothing whatsoever to do with shift. Degrees of, or otherwise.

Everything under the sun

Perhaps the most swivel-eyed conflation of the hippie haikuists was that between Shiki's radical revisionism and Zen Buddhism. So we do well to tread lightly on the complex religious and philosophical beliefs of others for fear of offensive tokenism. The interested reader will find any number of carefully considered resources dealing with the area we touch on here. They will repay attention.

What we can say, without fear of distortion, is that the development of the aesthetics of linked verse in Japan incorporated many metaphysical principles drawn from both Shinto and Buddhism. One such, familiar to many, is the idea of *za*—the intense creative dynamic generated during the course of multi-authorial composition by the emergence of what the occidental might more readily term the *group mind*.

The great Zen master Dogen remarked that to forget the self is to be enlightened by the ten thousand things. For all that the more prosaic amongst us might favour phrases such as *all of creation*, or *everything under the sun*, the idea is plain. When we write in the absence of an overweening ego our awareness opens out to embrace the totality of existence. Every aspect of man and nature. All are drawn into the furnace of the creative now as the group becomes more than the sum of its parts.

Shingon Buddhism furnishes a complementary interpretation. A linked verse sequence as an instance of mandala. This is not offered as an analogy. It describes an occurrence. The poem is an iteration of the cosmic gestalt. As each verse slots into place, the wider state of being is identified. By assembling a pattern that is not predetermined, a transcendental symmetry is achieved.

The slightest familiarity with Basho's espousal of principles such as *fueki ryuko* and *kogo kizoku* is enough for the most reluctant amongst us to realise how fundamentally his aesthetics spring from the mainstream of both philosophical and esoteric Buddhism. Factor in a mystical appreciation of the unique sanctity of one's surroundings, courtesy of Shinto, and it becomes clear that any suggestion of a pre-selective channelling designed to embody or express a purpose in a Basho style linked verse sequence is an absolute nonsense. It runs counter to belief.

A Shofu renku sequence cannot be *about* something. It has meaning only because it turns. Anyone who wishes to suggest that such turn may nonetheless be achieved within the confines of a theme really should go and join the weasels. They're good with words. Smelly too.

A little technical difficulty

Of course we don't all spend our time fretting about when to get our heads shaved or which particular young man to go gallivanting off with. So we might want to shelve the talk of metaphysics for a bit and just go back to being poets. This is actually quite a good idea because there's a slight technical problem with the thematic proposal when it comes to the nuts and bolts of writing Shofu renku. You can't do it.

The Basho school is renowned for many things. But it would be hard to point to a feature more significant than the elevation of nioizuke to the linking technique of choice with its consequent heightening of the importance of the white space between verses and the subsequent facilitation of a sinuous, linear, development. The Basho school were so far ahead of the pack they didn't actually leave much for modern renku to do. Other than ramp up the intensity of verse to verse juxtaposition.

But for any of these technical aspects to work the organizational and relational qualities of *sequence* have to come from the verse to verse movement. And from the verse to verse movement alone. The poem reveals as it unrolls. Not because each verse delivers a new angle on a known topic but because, with each transition of the white space, the superpositions of potential direction collapse down in the mind of the reader to form a single, unique and previously unknowable moment of rightness.

Thematic linked verse cannot do this. Too much is already on the table. The reader is instead presented with something more akin to a series rather than a sequence. Given that a core part of the organizational principle is external, the significance of the movement between verses is no longer prime. In which case, if the writer is to engage the reader, the content and structure of the constituent verses must take more of the strain. Each must be more novel. More remarkable. More stand-alone.

For Shofu renku the greatest artistry lies in the verse to verse movement. In thematic linked verse the reader's attention is drawn instead to the component parts. And quite right too. Who would want to waste time on a load of not very memorable stuff designed just to make the piece flow? What we want is fire and brimstone. And lots of individual verses that are nearly as good as reading my latest haiku.

RENKU THEORY AND PRACTICE

The Mechanics of the White Space
in the void between verses

Good god

In 1793 the politico-religious establishment decided to garner a bit of popularity with philosopher and fishmonger alike. Basho was deified. For a while anything other than the most fulsome praise of his poetry was blasphemy. The mere possession of this book—heresy.

As if that wasn't enough, he has since been credited with everything from the discovery of penicillin to being the first man in space. His literary exploits are legion. He is the father of haiku. Grandfather of travel blogs. He single-handedly turned comedic linked verse into high art thanks to the miracle of scent linking. Or something.

As ever the truth is different. The word *haiku* never crossed Basho's lips. The collection and publication of independent hokku predates him. *Oku no Hosomichi* was an idealization. And linked verse had scaled the heights of artistry a good few times before.

However Basho did indeed perform miracles on the mechanics of linked verse in such a way that changed its nature irrevocably. Without his tinkering the short imagistic sequences of recent years would be unthinkable. There is a direct line running from the kasen to the junicho. And scent linking is the key. If not something of a wrench.

Good riddance

If the Rationalists are to be believed there's nothing new under the sun. Some commentators argue that a precursor to Basho's revolutionary thinking can be found in the guise of *yosei*—a method of linking verses through indirect or uncontained feeling that had been around for years. A less convincing case is also made for *uzumiku*—buried linking—but that technique does little more than lionise the obscure.

Basho went far beyond yosei. He was not so much concerned with the shape of a particular socket as with the entire box of aesthetic tools that governed verse to verse linking. These he saw as converging on a single node—*nioizuke*—that he put front and centre of his rapidly evolving style. *Nioizuke*, he asserted, was quite simply superior. And universally applicable. As such, it superseded all prior approaches which must henceforth be consigned to the dustbin of history.

An overstatement? An exaggeration on my part? Haruo Shirane's essential *Traces of Dreams* has Basho's most reliable disciple, Kyorai, doing his best to quote the old goat verbatim:

> *The hokku has changed repeatedly since the distant past, but there have been only three changes in the nature of the haikai link. In the distant past, poets valued word links. In the more recent past, poets have stressed content links. Today, it is best to link by transference, reverberation, scent, or status.*

For a man who liked to think of himself as humble this is strong stuff. Not least because, as some would have it, that *distant past* and *recent past* are code for the rival Teimon and Danrin schools. So Basho isn't just lauding his own style here, he is dissing the current opposition.

But what *is* this nioizuke? What exactly does it do? And what have transference, reverberation and status got to do with it?

Good vibrations

Part mistranslation, part missed opportunity, the generally accepted English rendering—scent linking—is not particularly helpful. *Zuke*, we can pretty much agree, means *linking*. And, when spelled with the correct characters, the word *nioi* does indeed mean *scent* or *fragrance* in both the real and figurative sense. The phrase *odour of sanctity* comes to mind.

More simply though, *nioizuke* also means *radiance, insinuation, attraction* and *to have the sense of something*. It therefore describes a form of linking that draws on the subtle emanations and emotions that permeate a situation. Perhaps a more fitting term would have been *aura linking*. The ageing hippies amongst us mumbling that, hey, it's just *vibe-link*, man.

As to the operation of the technique itself—frankly it has been described to within an inch of its life. There are any number of chapters, articles, dissertations, and blogs which set out in mind numbing detail the (alleged) divisions and degrees of scent linking.

Barely had Basho's body cooled than his acolytes were at it like knives: *hibiki, utsuri, hashiri, kurai, omokage, keiki*—echo, reflection, run-on, rank, nostalgia, setting. *Etc.* Etc. People dined out for years on this stuff—*Oh yes, the Master agreed with me that* insert-your-zuke-here *was the over arching category of scent linking. More sake? Thank you, just a little.*

Any search engine or index will furnish details. Mostly conflicting. Even *nioi* turns up—as a specific subdivision of *nioi the greater*. Arrgghhh.

At some point this perpetual grind of detail begins to look like a displacement activity designed to prevent understanding. *Transference, reverberation, scent, status*—if Basho and Co were being a little loose with words that's because they already knew what they meant. Scent (aura, emanation) linkage. We use it to write poems. Man.

So let's leave the learned to rehash each other's studies and look instead at what scent linking does on the page. In fact let's look first at what it doesn't do…

This schema represents the conceptual structure of linking pre-Basho. Each added verse generates a new pairing, whilst breaking the previous pair-bond. So, with the introduction of **C**, the relationship between **A** and **B** is disrupted as the reader is invited to consider instead the scene presented by **B** and **C**. With the introduction of **D**, the spell is broken. **B** becomes redundant as the focus is drawn to **C** and **D**. The spotlight for our next golden pair falling on **D** and **E**.

To master this technique was to achieve a series of fleeting cameos. The reader is presented with a staggered set of scenarios, each new inter-verse tie serving to synchronise and concretise the present pairing whilst disrupting the previous pair-bond.

Various types of linking technique were employed ranging from the bald and often crass use of puns, through abstruse extra-textual reference, to narrative, scenic, logical or topical extension. Common to all was that the pairings they yielded were apprehensible. The reader needed to *get* them in order for the poem to work. They had to *make sense*.

In general the types of linking based on single words or objects tend to be grouped under the rubric *kotobazuke*, and those that rely on overall sense or meaning under that of *kokorozuke*. But both these terms can now be forgotten as *nioizuke* does something completely different.

Good as gold

Nioizuke generates associations based on scent, emanation, aura or vibe. Relationships are evoked. They are indirect and implied. Scent links are not just open to interpretation, they *require* interpretation. Not only do they *not* tie verses together in such a way that the poets' intention is intellectually amenable, scent links deliberately generate uncertainties that can only be reconciled in the mind of the reader. By intuition.

With the advent of scent linkage, a white space is opened between the verses that the reader must navigate at will.

In this model the purpose of each added verse is not to create a new pairing. Instead we have a form of dynamic apposition in which each new verse recasts the content of the previous verse as the poem moves ever onwards.

The reconciliation of the tensions between a pair of verses is now an act of synthesis so far removed from the comfortable two-step of medieval linked verse that it looks more like syncresis. But it is in this white space that the principal expressive power of the poem resides. And suddenly it has gained great force.

The staggered effect of earlier linking styles is gone. We have instead a much more direct and compelling impetus. As each white space is traversed by the reader, the intangibles that power its resolution endure in the mind. Whilst the content—the stated text itself—obeys the dictates of link & shift, the emotive tenor of the white space may evolve more fluidly, and over an entire passage of verse.

In the world of *nioizuke*, meaning has become more fragmentary, but empathy has gained consequence. The poet may orchestrate extended dynamic effects from a completely non-linear strand of verse.

Good on paper

There are few Basho texts that employ scent linking throughout. Some participants are of a conservative bent. Others just lack the skill. And often one encounters a kind of layered link in which an obvious conventional technique masks a more profound metaphysical association. But with his proclamation of *nioizuke* as the overarching principle the great man had well and truly let the cat out of the tool box—at a stroke ramping up the speed, cohesion and emotive power of haikai no renga whilst engaging the reader as participant not consumer.

In so doing he prepared the ground for the highly contracted and imagistic sequences typical of much contemporary Shofu renku—sequences which employ outright juxtaposition between a flurry of consecutive verses.

Tangential they may be, but the best achieve more. In the hands of the truly skilled artist *nioizuke* can generate that oddest of paradoxes: a text which makes almost no sense at all, but is somehow more enduring, and *right*.

Occurrence and Recurrence
variety and change in a renku sequence

Introduction: The lore of rules

One of renku's less palatable truths is that the forces governing variety and change in a sequence are mostly seen as negative—they deal exclusively with what we may not do. The impression is given that participants spend an inordinate amount of time looking over their collective shoulder at what has gone before. There is little time to think freely about what can be added.

The hideous chimera of *backlink* stalks English renku circles (see *On Backlink*), its protean intangibility generating a collective psychosis characterized by the paranoid and forensic parsing of a text for deviation from criteria so occluded as to be unknowable. It beats Orwell. And Kafka. It even beats the grammar of that sentence.

The historic sources aren't much help. Treatises from the Muromachi period onward mince ever more finely the circumstances in which this or that must be disavowed. Unlike the backlink fetish there was clarity of sorts. But rather too much of it.

So complex was the mass of codification that correct composition required not just the presence of a master—*sosho*—to lead the poem, but also that of a scribe—*shuhitsu*—to act as a kind of clerk of the court, advising the master of any potential infringement of the mountain of rules—*shikimoku*—thus allowing the great man to concentrate on more important matters. Like getting drunk with his cronies.

Not that the rules were universal, or consistent. Differing authorities placed different degrees of emphasis on this or that creaking timber, all the while seeking to make a bit of heavy weather themselves. For those seeking fame, their chances of success were directly proportional to the number of barnacles they bequeathed to the good ship haikai.

By this reckoning Basho was rubbish. Not only did he fail to publish a rule-book of any sort, he held the strange idea that poetry could speak for itself. Fortunately some of his most pithy insights were recorded for posterity by one or other of his many acolytes. Less fortunately, said acolytes, though good men and true in the general sense, also had a living to make as master poets in their own right. Like all ambitious people, they tended to remember what they wanted to hear.

But nowhere in a recorded discourse does Basho advance a theory of forbidden subjects, pursue the categorization of suspect combinations, or proscribe certain classes of word. Instead he focuses on holism, instinctive linkage, and the creative aesthetics that power all forms of haikai.

It is notable that Kyorai, one of Basho's closest disciples, was able to boast: *From the time of my earliest studies I did not find it necessary to know the rules of haikai. Therefore I did not memorize the sarikirai, or the seasons and such.*

But perhaps more to the point is Kyorai's comment on Basho's own approach to the shikimoku: *He used them when possible, but was not bound by them. On occasion he broke the old rules, when something came to his mind, but he seldom broke them at random.*

Clearly, for all Kyorai's revolutionary posturing, if one wishes to appreciate Shofu renku, it is necessary to have a general understanding of those rules. Otherwise how can we know what we are breaking?

The piece which follows draws on the liberal attitudes of the Basho school and attempts to show how they might be understood in a contemporary international context, stripped of their culturally specific accretions, and devoid of the imbecility attendant on over-simplification.

This rough thesis repeatedly uses the word *locus*. It looks ugly. And sounds ugly. Damn it—it *is* ugly. But it's the only one that means *place, intersection, source* and *vector* all at the same time. So locus it is. As an aide memoire—unlike lotus or locust, it's the one you can't eat. If at any point the whole thing gets too much, the chapter *The Three Rs* is locus-lite.

Thesis: Four loci of change

Irrespective of the nature of the sequence, the language of composition, or the cultural background of the participants, in a Shofu renku sequence the occurrence or recurrence of topics and tones depends on an array of factors that converge on one of four loci.

Each locus has a temporal relationship to the moment of composition—immediate, intermediate, remote, and overarching.

The first locus of change: The immediate

At its simplest, Shofu renku is driven by the tensions that exist within any trio of verses. So important is this primary locus that minimalist definitions of renku go no further. They are mistaken. But for understandable reasons. This first locus is the sine qua non.

Early renga treatises refer to it as *sanku no watari*—the *arc of three verses*—or *sankume no utsuri*—the *three verse transition*. Though renga is frequently portrayed as a purely Japanese literary innovation, the nature of the core relationships within a given trio were almost certainly influenced by the Tang Dynasty poetic form the *jueju*, familiar to early Japanese literati as the *zekku* (see *Yotsumono: Description*).

The zekku divides into four short stanzas or lines, each with a specific function. The first stanza is known as the *disposition* or *introduction*, the second as the *continuation* or *extension*, the third is the *dislocation* or *break*, whilst the fourth draws the strands together to offer an *outcome* or *determination*. It is the break and turn between the second and third stanzas that is crucial to the emergence of Japanese linked verse.

In many of the Chinese originals the alleged dislocation between #2 and #3 adds up to little more than a mild conceptual twist or a whimsical excursion—the whole affair then neatly stitched up by the closing verse that follows. The genius of renga is that, rather than supply a resolution after a single instance of turn, it sets in train a rolling superposition of the initial relationships—**A•B•C** becomes **B•C•D** becomes **C•D•E**. In so doing the balance of forces at work within each trio becomes more taut, and the degree of turn, by the Edo period, has begun to approach the tangential.

The initial verses of the jueju may be represented as **A+B¬C** where **A** and **B** are a pair, and **C** turns from them. Apply this mechanism to a longer sequence and we have (**A+B¬C**) (**B+C¬D**) (**C+D¬E**) etc.

At first sight, with the extension of the chain, nothing has changed. Indeed that **A+B¬C** of the starting combination exactly captures the way the relationships between the hokku, wakiku and daisan of a renga or renku sequence are described to this day. The hokku and the wakiku form a more or less tight pair. The daisan breaks away.

But if we examine the next combination there is an unsatisfactory paradox. **B** and **C** are transformed into the tightly linked pair from which **D** must diverge, only for **C** and **D** to become the best of friends and **E** walk off in a huff.

Over time, the defining characteristics of the immediate locus came to be understood differently therefore—each added verse must generate a new pairing, whilst breaking the bond between the previous pair. So **A+B**, with the introduction of **C**, becomes **A¬B+C**, only for **B+C**, with the introduction of **D**, to become **B¬C+D**—a series which may be represented as (**A¬B+C**) (**B¬C+D**) (**C¬D+E**).

To master these forces was to achieve an ever evolving series of fleeting pairs—a quality described as *yukiyou*—a *balance of transitions*. Conversely, the failure to recast the previous pair, and to generate instead a sequence such as **F+G+H**, was referred to as *sanku garami*—a *knot of three verses*.

With the advent of the Basho school, the relational dynamics of linked verse—in the less studious guise of haikai no renga—underwent further change. In part the impetus lay with the shorter kasen's ability to reflect the jo–ha–kyu pacing paradigm, and the attendant interest in extended dynamic control. But by far the most important factor was Basho's advocacy of a new and indirect style of linking.

The significance of *nioi*—scent linking—is that it dispenses with the creation of a tight, tangible, pair-bond as the principle scope of each added verse. Instead we move towards the position where the primary creative tension of a sequence is understood to lie in the nature of the relationship between each added verse and that immediately preceding.

The key concept is *between*. With the advent of nioi we see the emergence of linking techniques based on forms of apposition that prefigure the outright juxtaposition typical of modern haiku (see *The Mechanics of the White Space*) and which have since fed back into shorter renku.

So it is that in Shofu renku we have **A<>B<>C<>D**, a series of relationships that favour both a rapid forward momentum and a degree of linear control as the space between verses gains a powerful reverberation of its own.

But the need to avoid thematic development remains as important as ever. This is achieved by the deliberate divergence of each added verse from the verse before last. The erroneous **F+G+H** is no longer described as *sanku no garami*—a knot of three verses—but as *uchikoshi no kirai*—return to the verse before last.

Thus we arrive at the formulation proposed by Higashi-sensei in the latter part of the last century which defines the immediate locus of change in contemporary renku: *The linking verse is deduced from the preceding verse but it has no other logical connection with the leap-over verse.*

The phrase given here as *leap-over verse* is a direct translation of the Japanese *uchikoshi no ku*. For the sake of consistency this book uses the expression *verse before last* throughout. Likewise, as there is little agreement between the English sources, the chapter *The Three Rs* argues that the failure to heed Master Higashi's advice, and so return the reader's attention to verse before last, should be known as *reversion*.

Whilst the first locus of change might appear to be purely retrospective—occupied solely with the avoidance of reversion—it is well to remember that the forces at play run forwards as well as backwards in time. The principal topics and tones that make up verse **C** will themselves be found to stand in the leap-over relationship to verse **E**.

This might seem rather abstruse. But practice proves otherwise. If we know that the moon is due to rise in #13, for example, a good dose of starlight at #11 can put the proverbial cat amongst the pigeons, if not actually to the sword.

Some of Basho's wittier sequences have entire sections in which the participants try to make each other's lives as difficult as possible by deliberately fouling in advance the chances of a clean moon, love or blossom verse where it would otherwise be due.

There is more than one way of putting good technique to use. Be it in skinning onions. Or cats.

The second locus of change: The intermediate

The intermediate locus occupies a span of several verses either side of the verse under consideration. The main forces at play here are *sarikirai* and *kukazu*.

Sarikirai translates roughly as *clear-cut space* and determines the number of verses that must separate the appearance of closely related subjects. The term is sometimes given in English as *avoidance* or *minimum separation*, but is perhaps more universally understood as *intermission*.

Kukazu is more or less accurately given as *verse count*. It defines the number of verses for which a group of related topics may, or should, persist once the subject has been introduced. The term is sometimes given in English as *seriation* or *appearance* but is most easily understood as *duration*.

As the first line of the figure below illustrates, mathematically speaking the minimum value of intermission is one. A subject is treated at **A**, dropped for **B**, and resumed at **C**. But, in modern renku theory, this describes reversion—uchikoshi no kirai—an insufficiency of shift, and belongs to the immediate locus of change. Sarikirai therefore deals with intermission values greater than one. The second and third lines of the figure below show separations of two and three verses respectively.

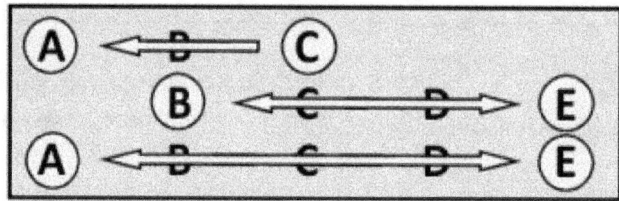

In medieval renga theory intermission values varied between two and seven. Then as now, the more prime the category of topic the greater the separation needed. A breach of these rules—and *rules* they were—with the attendant premature reappearance of a particular category of topic, was a blatant case of *rinne*. Literally meaning *reincarnation*, this book uses the more neutral term *regression* (see *The Three Rs*).

Such intermission values of two, three, five and seven are to be found in the earliest theoretical treatises. The subject areas they governed were specified in great, and ever increasing, detail. When we learn that Sogi's disciple Shohaku called his 1501 opus *The New Rules of Linked-verse, With Additions, Suggestions for a New Day, and Other Comments* it will come as no particular surprise that a minor portion of his five verse intermission regime included: *instances of the following words and subcategories—Day, Wind, Cloud, Smoke, Field, Mountain, Bay, Wave, Water, Path, Night, Trees, Grasses, Birds, Beasts, Insects*. Anyone for tennis?

Shohaku was wrestling with the hyakuin and therefore sought to optimise the occurrence and recurrence of topics over a span of one hundred verses. Once we reach 1678 and *The Enlarged Sneeze Grass*, a treatise by Teitoku's follower Ryuho, interest in the kasen was already widespread and the seven verse intermission had largely disappeared—five being the new maximum thought suitable for the shorter form.

In his 2006 dissertation *Haikai Poetics: Buson, Kito and the Interpretation of Renku Poetry* the Swedish academic and poet Herbert Jonsson offers a particularly useful representation of Ryuho's approach to intermission and duration which allows us to see the two forces working in tandem. Publication of *The Enlarged Sneeze Grass* coincided with the establishment of the Basho school and though Teitoku, who had also been Basho's mentor for a while, ran a thoroughly conservative establishment, his faithful pupil's book indicates the type of thinking of which even Kyorai would have been aware.

Kyorai was the chap we heard boasting about his lack of knowledge of just about everything at the beginning of this chapter. The following table is after Jonsson, with thanks.

OCCURRENCE AND RECURRENCE

		INTERMISSION		
		2 two verse intermission	3 three verse intermission	5 five verse intermission
D U R A T I O N	1 — one verse duration	sky phenomena: (*moon, sun, stars*)	the same character occurring in any sky phenomenon	the same character occurring in any of: moon; rice paddy; smoke; dream; bamboo; boat; dress; tears; pine
	1–2 — one to two verse duration	falling things: (*rain, dew, frost, snow, hail*) rising things (*haze, mist, clouds*) human relations; art; food; famous places; name of country; name of person	clothing; animals; plants; time—and the same character occurring in any of falling things; rising things	summer winter
	1–3 — one to three verse duration		Shinto; Buddhism; travel; reminiscence; night; mountain things; water's edge; dwellings	
	2–5 — two to five verse duration		love	
	3–5 — three to five verse duration			spring autumn

It is immediately apparent that the values Ryuho associates with the seasons and with love are substantially the same as those evidenced by Basho's own work. Summer and winter have a one or two verse duration and a five verse intermission. Spring and autumn may last for up to five, but are also separated by five. Love, meanwhile, occupies either two or three verses, but may return after a further three have elapsed.

The table shows that the most common value of duration is now two whilst *Shinto; Buddhism; travel; reminiscence; night; mountain things; water's edge* and *dwellings*—the group of subject areas that may be pursued for up to three verses at a time—are caught in a moment of transition. Previously substantial categories in their own right, with the demise of the hundred verse sequence and the rise of the Basho school, they are about to be absorbed into the bloc of subjects which may occupy no more than a successive pair. In effect we will shortly be left with only spring, autumn and love which may last for three or more verses and in so doing provide a de jure breach of the obligation to shift comprehensively from the verse before last (see *More About Shift*).

In recent years, until Haku Asanuma's controversial intervention (see *Rokku*), the advent of ever more compact sequences had all but removed issues of duration from the agenda. But it would be a mistake to assume that notions of intermission have been similarly peripheral. As with Kyorai, so with Kito, there has never been a shortage of people who claim to have torn up the rules. Yet all the evidence is that, in the matter of intermission at least, they have simply internalised them. Either that or, in the case of our contemporary *backlink* friends, made an utter nonsense of them. In any event, to understand this better, we need to take a closer look at what it is that sarikirai separates.

The non-italicised items in the table above do not indicate single subjects. They are category headings, each of which will embrace a number of sub-topics. By way of example, some of the constituent topics of the categories *sky phenomena, falling things* and *rising things* appear in parentheses after their respective headings.

If we examine the category *falling things* we gather that a verse featuring *rain* may very well be linked directly to one featuring *dew*, as the category has a two verse duration value. But thereafter two clear verses must elapse before *frost*, *snow*, or *hail* may appear—unless the same Chinese character is used in writing both words, in which case the required intermission goes up to three.

To 21st century occidental eyes these category headings, and the sub-topics they group, may seem somewhat arbitrary. But they are not. For the major part they represent the thematic and lexical categories of the imperial waka anthologies, court poetry contests, medieval word matching games and so on. As such they would have come as second nature to any reasonably literate person. Even to the present day—for the educated Japanese reader—there is nothing mysterious involved. The categories do no more than bring together topics that are automatically seen as related. We may take Kito at his word therefore when he, like Kyorai, assures us that he has no recourse to this or that reference book in respect of sarikirai. He would not need to—his poetic sensibilities would automatically do the job for him.

Several implications flow from this. One is that sarikirai—intermission—does not set out to govern the separation of individual words, but rather of closely associated cultural emblems. Further, these iconic elements are considered to cluster naturally into categories—categories which in turn are seen as having differing degrees of primacy. Though one or two sub-topics may be linked in successive verses, thereafter the greater the primacy of the overall category, the greater the intermission necessary before any further sub-topics may appear. Otherwise we might risk going backwards.

Whilst the nature of any category, the number of its constituents, and their collective primacy, will be culturally dependent, the way in which sarikirai operates is not. It is universal. Closely related things, in close proximity, tend to get easily noticed. Loosely related things, when further apart, slip quietly under the radar.

It would seem that the constant proliferation of rules based on categories that bedevilled the evolution of medieval renga theory—all those sub-topics, durations, and intermissions—is evidence not so much of an autistic tendency brought on by too much rice, as of a determined striving after a principle glimpsed but never wholly grasped. The theorists understood right from the outset that Chinese characters played a part. If it is not all Greek to you, the word *ideogram* gives the game away.

The conclusion is obvious enough. The intermediate locus of change is concerned with the language of signs—both signifier and signified—in what Charles S. Pierce, the founder of modern semiotics, described as the *primary mode* i.e. at the level of raw individual concepts.

The impetus for variety and change going forward—the flip side of the desire to avoid regression—means that when we use a sign, unless it is in the express context of our immediate linkage, we should wait for a sufficient interval before any closely associated sign is employed. The perceived forcefulness of the sign, and the intermission needed, will depend upon the shared non-cognitive vocabulary of author and reader alike, but elements that are seen as particularly prominent may in fact be best left standing on their own.

And therein lies a problem which has led to much bating of breath. As the genre has spread beyond Japan—and in the absence of any understanding of the vectors that underpin variety and change—the claim has frequently been made that people of whatever culture, when writing renku, must necessarily use the original canon of duration and intermission if they are to properly adhere to form. Some sensibilities are more refined than others. And after all, there is only one system for which we have a thousand years' worth of lists, charts and mnemonic chants.

To do so as a learning exercise is surely worthwhile. Anyone who has read a little Japanese literature will already have absorbed many iconic associations as readily as they would those from Russia or the Punjab. But the general proposition is fraught with danger. The likelihood of parody is deeply unwelcome. Yet this pales into insignificance when faced with the principal difficulty. If the writer's norms are Japanese, and the reader's norms are English, communication between the two becomes impossible. Shofu renku isn't supposed to be arcane. The Basho school weren't just good, they were *popular*.

One solution is for poets from the world's different linguistic and cultural settings to articulate their own category headings, each with its list of sub-topics and an associated intermission value. But when viewed from the perspective of semiotics it is not clear why such elaborations of sarikirai are necessary. The underlying concept is simple—a primary sign, or one closely associated with it, equals a longer intermission. A minor sign, or one loosely associated with it, equals a shorter intermission. There is no reason why the precise values ascribed to these variables should not be a matter of artistic judgement.

There is no need for anguish—or the consultation of runes or lists. It is not difficult to go forward with an open mind, or avoid a careless return to the sort of thing we were talking about just two or three verses ago.

The third locus of change: The remote

The Kasen progresses by thirty-six steps. It is not desirable to retrace a single footfall —Matsuo Basho, as recalled by his disciple Hattori Doho in *Sanzoshi*, The Three Booklets.

Basho's followers were not averse to a spot of selective reporting but there is no reason to doubt the essential accuracy of Doho's recollection of this particular nugget. Unfortunately in recent times its significance has been so comprehensively misunderstood that it is often advanced, suitably de-contextualised, as a validation of the more simplistic approaches to variety and change in what is alleged to be modern Basho-style renku. Of one thing we may be certain—when Basho warned against the temptation to revisit previous steps he was not in the vanguard of those warning against *backlink*, nor was he making the radical suggestion that the intermission values of sarikirai should be indefinitely extended. He was simply making reference to the centuries old notion of *torinne*, albeit with a Shofu twist.

Torinne is an expression borrowed from Buddhism meaning *distant reincarnation*—sometimes secularised in translation as *remote repetition*. The element *to*—which gives us *distant* or *remote*—is vital as *torinne* is entirely distinct from *rinne*, the breach of intermission values that pertain to the second locus of change. The similarity of the Japanese words, coupled with the inconsistent use of equivalent terms in English, has tended to muddy the waters. Here we give *rinne* as *regression*, and *torinne* as *reiteration* throughout (see *The Three Rs*).

Modern Japanese dictionaries give the literary definition of torinne as the situation in which phrases and/or verses are connected by an identical or near-identical link. If we go back to 1372 and Yoshimoto's *New Rules of the Oan Era* we find an recondite but extensive examination of precisely which combinations of words might constitute such a breach of good style—principally in respect of inter-verse linkage. The question is also raised as to whether a given instance should be disbarred for the duration of the full hundred verses, or if a recurrence of so-and-so, in association with so-and-so, might not be permissible once on each writing sheet – a full sheet being twenty-eight verses, fourteen verses a side.

By the time we reach Shohaku's *New Rules of Linked Verse* in 1501 the internal phrasing of verses commands greater attention to the extent that, in the section on historic renga technique of Jin'ichi Kinishi's seminal 1972 study *Sogi*, puns and tropes are bracketed with inter-verse links as falling under the purview of torinne.

Onwards then to Basho who, in the context of his thirty-six steps, cautioned against the repetition of devices employing identical synonyms and homonyms before going on to include the sense *implicit* in preceding links. For all that might seem to complicate matters, one thing at least had been simplified—with the advent of the shorter Kasen, exclusions based on torinne would henceforth be viewed as absolute. For the duration.

All well and good. But, remembering that the literal translation of torinne is *distant reincarnation*, if the span of *distant* is tractable enough, how are we to understand *reincarnation*?

At its simplest it could be argued that *torinne* has broadened its scope over time to embrace all aspects of poetic sensibility that guard against gross repetition. Though superficially attractive, such definitions are of limited use. All we are really being told is not to be bad poets. In this case it is also unnecessarily generic. There is an underlying principle at stake that holds true from the early mediaeval period onwards. For this we need to return to the USA and Pierce's *science* of semiotics.

Whereas sarikirai operates at the primary level, governing the degree of intermission needed before the recurrence of individual signs and their close associates, *torinne* describes an unwelcome recurrence of signs at the secondary level of communication, at what Pierce refers to as a *proposition*. Here we are no longer concerned with the attributes of single signs but with the *dependencies* both writer and reader impute between two or more signs.

Irrespective of the classes or categories of the elements themselves, whether it be expressed as an inter-verse link, an internal juxtaposition, or a trope articulating some form of comparison or correlation, any recurrence of an identical or near identical dependency between two or more signs is a case of reiteration—torinne.

When Basho referred to the thirty-six steps he was not therefore suggesting that the kasen should have only one moon verse, but that there should not be two verses in which moonlight is presented as the source of the poet's inspiration. Equally there should be no more than one inter-verse transition between moon and ocean, and no more than one instance of a play on *tsuki*—moon—and a homonym such as *tsuku*—to start out on a journey.

Far from being so arcane as to be redundant, the forces that impelled the old school poets to wrestle with the precise nature of torinne—reiteration—were real and still demand our consideration. Thanks to Pierce and Co we now have better tools for the job.

But what of that Shofu twist? As the earlier discussion of the first locus of change indicates, at the time of the emergence of the Basho school, progression in a renga sequence was understood to reside in the continual creation of fresh pairs of verses—individual cameos—with the consequent sundering of the previous pair bond. Basho by contrast offers the analogy of one footfall after another. A distinctly linear process.

The fourth locus of change: The overarching

The Kasen progresses by thirty-six steps. It is not desirable to retrace a single footfall. As the sequence advances it renews our spirits, due entirely to the consciousness that impels it —Matsuo Basho, as recalled by his disciple Hattori Doho in *Sanzoshi*, The Three Booklets.

As is clear from the more extended quotation, not only was Basho referring to something other than the most rudimentary prohibitions in order to ensure variety in a renku sequence, he was stating a negative only in order to emphasise a positive. But whose is that *consciousness* to which he refers?

Masaoka Shiki might have been more tolerant of what he called *renpai*—linked fiascos—if the guiding ego of a linked verse session was thought to be that of the master—*sosho*—or poem leader—*sabaki*. But the reverse is true.

Renga arose in a society whose artistic and spiritual life was permeated by the metaphysics of the many strands of Buddhism. It is in this context that we must understand the idea of a guiding consciousness, and of the world which this consciousness was believed to mediate.

Addressing issues of permanence, mutability, and the modelling of reality, Yoshimoto, though more of a secularist than many of his peers, put it thus: *Renga does not bring together past and future thoughts […] The poet thinks of yesterday yet already today arrives. He thinks of spring and lo: it is autumn. He thinks of the blossom yet already the leaves are changing. Is this any different from the way the blossom scatters and leaves fall in life itself?* —Tsukuba Mondo, 1372.

In his 15th century primer for the potentially uncouth bourgeoisie, the warrior-poet Nitta Shojun enjoined participants to prepare for composition *as though for meditation* —Rules for the Linked Verse Meeting. This was desirable, he explained, because *the way of poetry conforms to the Buddhist truth of ultimate reality*.

Directly prefiguring Sogi, Shojun was keen to underline the importance of the creative flux generated by the meeting not just of people, but of minds, suggesting that the best renga demands the surrender of the individual consciousness in order to access the multiplex nature of reality. As Dogen, the founder of the Soto school, had put it: *to forget the self is to be enlightened by the ten thousand things.*

Sogi, an ordained Zen monk, was a great influence on Basho. But although he is also popularly portrayed in the west as a devotee of Zen, Basho's own belief system was in fact more nuanced, embracing Shinto's native spirituality and incorporating elements of the esoteric Buddhism—Shingon—beloved of his other great hero Saigyo. Indeed the founder of Shingon, Kukai, was himself a considerable poet and over the centuries Shingon temples had fostered the writing of linked verse not least because a renga sequence was seen as a direct reification of the totality of being—a mandala both from and of the cosmos.

The Meiji Period. Step forward Masaoka Shiki, freshly armed with European notions of romantic individualism and a futurist ire. Mandala?!! Disembodied consciousness?!! Such effete drivel was to be swept away—cleansed by the twin fires of progress and realism. Henceforth it would be the job of the poet to sketch the truth—*shasei*—with essential honesty—*makoto*. And he would do it the way the modern world demanded. Alone.

That Shiki's unlovely attentions were nearly fatal is proof that linked verse had indeed become corrupt and sclerotic. In railing against regressive and baroque conventions, Shiki was pushing at an open door. The nation had set its face against the past, turning instead to the clatter of machine tools and the promise of its own *black ships*. It would be some years before interest in renku began to rekindle. But when it did so it would be with renewed vigour. It would also tap old roots.

One of the first to publish was Torahiko Terada who, with his teacher Soseki, had visited Shiki on his deathbed. Terada's essays of 1931 drew comparisons between renku and the deep level emotive power of music. He further considered renku as montage—combining Eisenstein's ideas of cinematography with Freudian psychology and proto-semiotics.

By 1943 Tomoji Nose, with *The Nature of Renku Arts*, had re-entered the realm of metaphysics: *In renku we transcend an individual's thoughts, and a group of poets co-operate to construct a small cosmos.* He also observed that each verse other than the hokku was insufficient in nature, but that this quality inferred an awareness of the whole.

The concept of a verse's essential insufficiency was central to Juju Ogasawara's 1965 work, *What is Called Renku*, which once more made its case in terms of Shingon theology. Complementary arguments are to be found in Tsutomu Ogata's 1986 classic *The World of Kasen*. Ogata identified the well-spring of renku as the community mind. Like Shojun and Sogi before him, Ogata saw this as emerging in the crucible of *za*—the meeting of hearts and minds under the creative pressure of the moment of composition. Elsewhere Makoto Ooka was proposing that the Japanese psyche, when not in solitary mode, was particularly adept at operating in the commonality of *banquet*.

Ogata's *community mind* is taken up by Shokan Kondo in his 1992 English paper, *Link and Shift*, a shorter version of which, published in association with William J. Higginson, was one of the first renku resources on the internet. Here the community mind is a core principle of unity. Kondo goes on to use the word *mandala* in a variety of contexts before concluding: *When we find our position in relation to the whole world mandalic awareness is attained.*

1992 also saw publication of the essay *Renku Fantasy* by Sono Uchida—an essentially religious view of renku as a vehicle for human salvation. Uchida observes that, by annihilating individual consciousness, the group mind arrives naturally at those iterations that mark out the cosmic mandala.

In essence Kondo and Uchida return us to the 12th century and Saigyo. That they should do so exactly 100 years after Shiki had set out to purge the past of its embarrassing illogicality is a fitting tribute.

It may be that some English poets have difficulty accessing the more hermetic aspects of these arguments. They do after all stand the Enlightenment on its head. But as we have seen with other elements of variety and change, there are universal truths at play. After all, holism is now such a ubiquitous idea in the west that it is used to sell everything from tablet computers to toothpaste. And it is common knowledge that, suitably prefaced with the letter *w*, it has long since been greater than the sum of its parts.

If that's too silly, Reuven Tsur's 2003 work, *On The Shore of Nothingness*, a study of cognitive poetics undertaken without any specific reference to Japanese literature, makes interesting reading. When considering the close relationship between meditative states, the orientation processes of the brain, and their similarity to emotional experiences Tsur observes: *The switch from ordinary consciousness to meditative consciousness involves replacing the analytic and sequential information-processing mode with a holistic, relational, and more simultaneous one.*

Beautiful Lotuses, Beautiful Roses, a 2011 essay by the information scientist and aestheticist Masaru Yoneyama takes us further still: *The small individual worlds into which we were locked open up, worlds meet worlds, and they overlap and become an immensely rich, open, qualitative space [...] It is my belief, therefore, that such a polyphonic, monadological creative space can be the basis for the arising of a true transcultural aesthetics.*

So it is that Shiki was both right and wrong. Renku, like renga before it, does indeed require the surrender of the authority of the lone poet's voice whilst proposing the validity of relationships which are both acausal and atemporal. But there is more than one way of modelling reality, Horatio. There are more things in heaven and earth.

Whereas the immediate, intermediate and remote loci of change appear as facets of recurrence, the fourth locus deals with occurrence itself. It is overarching, treating the poem's creation as both an instant and an instance. This is reductionism in reverse. When a group of poets achieve group consciousness—*za*—the subjects that emerge undirected are glimpses of a wider and undifferentiated gestalt, fragments of the greater entelechy.

To describe Shofu renku as non-thematic is therefore so inadequate as to be false. It is anti-thematic. The fourth locus casts the *sosho* or *sabaki* not as guiding ego but as a facilitator of potential. In the territory of the multiplex mind, renku is an uncharted journey.

Conclusion

Perhaps the most misogynistic axiom of all is the one that has female prostitution as *the world's oldest profession*. Not only is it profoundly insulting, it is also a lie. The world's oldest profession is shamanism. An almost exclusively male pursuit.

One way in which a Shaman exerts power is by deliberately clouding understanding. This is particularly useful when he himself has no effective understanding of any sort. As long as he shouts loudly enough, he us unlikely to be found out. Certainly not by those who enjoy being bullied.

But let's turn to renku—specifically to Shofu renku—and the last half century. Whatever the motives of our various experts, a constant refrain has been that renku is complex. It has such a lot of rules.

The lack of scholarship evidenced by these assertions is stunning. Especially when it comes from academics who were paid well for their time. Be in no doubt—those immense rule books belong to high-style renga. Principally to its exercise as *ushin renga* during the medieval period. There are still a few standard bearers who compose verse of that style. All power to them. They, at least, understand the difference.

It is a defining characteristic of Shofu renku—Basho-style haikai no renga—that it is not, and never was, formal. Just because the old goat ended up deified, and his likeness now appears on everything from packet soup to postcards, we forget at our peril just how revolutionary the Basho school was. Their approach to variety and change in a sequence was informed by a general sense of the strictures that had hitherto obtained, not a slavish adherence their minutiae.

> *He used them when possible, but was not bound by them. On occasion he broke the old rules [...] but he seldom broke them at random.*

This same spirit animates modern renku—necessarily—otherwise we cannot claim to be writing the same form of literature. Just as the immediate Basho school had to tease the essential from the trivial, our task is to unpick contemporary practice and discard the culturally specific.

Variety and change in a renku sequence is not a complex issue. But it *is* multiplex. At any one time there are a number of variables in play, the effects of which may be manifest immediately, or at quite some distance from the verse we are working on.

The four loci of change described in this chapter are neither arcane nor plucked from the air. The first—the immediate—is well understood by anyone with a passing knowledge of the genre. We wish to guarantee change and avoid reversion—the careless return to the verse before last, known in Japanese as *uchikoshi no kirai*.

The second—the intermediate—reminds us that the human mind tends to pigeon hole things and will always group what it sees as like with like. Failure to heed this causes regression—an equivalent term to *rinne*.

The third locus—the remote—is occupied with the constructions the writers themselves have built. The reader will always be disappointed if we offer them the same assemblage of ideas twice. Do this and we have *torinne*—literally, *distant reincarnation*—but better described by the less freighted term reiteration.

Admittedly, the fourth is sensitive to the advent of very short sequences. It is debatable how low we can go and still contain Dogen's *ten thousand things*. Yet at a minimum we may readily embrace the injunction to resist the lens of predestination when sequencing those things at hand. If in doubt, remember *fueki ryuko*. It seemed to work for Basho.

With these criteria in mind we can write any type of Shofu renku, in any language, with persons drawn from any culture. There is no need to posit an irrevocable dichotomy between past and present, or between Japanese and non-Japanese poetry.

> *Is this any different from the way the blossom scatters and leaves fall in life itself?*

RENKU THEORY AND PRACTICE

The Three Rs
how to avoid going backwards

The author bites back

> *Linked verse technique has developed over time thanks to the thoughtful engagement of poets and commentators. It is neither necessary nor desirable for those in the English speaking world to propound facile hypotheses that distance us from our source. If renku is indeed literature any worthwhile theory will hold for all forms of the genre, in all languages, and in all cultural contexts. There is no such thing as* backlink.

Oh dear, I must have been having a bad week. Or month. Or year. In fact a bad lifetime, by the look of it. And as for the Japanese speaking world:

> *During the latter part of the last century [...] interest in Basho-style linked verse had begun to spread beyond the native language and culture. These novel circumstances raised [...] the need to distinguish between the culturally specific facets of renku and those which were universal—a mode of analysis largely alien to the Japanese literary tradition which in the case of haiku had yielded little of value.*

At least I am even handed in my unpleasantness. And by way of atonement I have gone on to write the chapter *Occurrence and Recurrence*—variety and change in a renku sequence—which tries to take the thing a bit more seriously and, if you add those helpful diagrams, has got to be at least a million words long. Albeit totally impenetrable words. For anyone in a hurry at least.

So the challenge is clear. If backlink is a load of bulldust (which it is, and not just in Australia) and Japanese renku theory is rammed to the gunnels with word-level injunctions about what not to say on a Tuesday in Osaka (double ditto) how on earth are we to judge when element *a* or *b* of our otherwise perfect verse is in danger of taking us backwards? And can a set of criteria that work for Moses in Ouagadougou also make sense to Kimmo in Finland?

Feel the lerv

At less than a metre tall, and weighing in at nearly half a tonne, it is a wonder that Barry White could feel anything at all. But The Walrus was right to put lerv so high up on the agenda, second only to (woh, oh oh) *feeeeeeeling*.

If it feels wrong it is wrong—the old axiom will get you quite a long way in renku. For a very short sequence it will serve as a measure of unwanted similarity or a lack of forward momentum when faced with a choice of verse—always remembering that we're talking about artistic judgement here, not about wringing a tearful admission from the text after hanging it up by its feet. We leave that to foreigners.

But for longer sequences we need something a bit more sophisticated. Ideally something with a passing resemblance to the wisdom of our forbears. So I'm going to describe a triple-lock that will stop us from going backwards in a poem. And I hope to show that the who or the where of its application matters not a jot.

A single caution: the best renku faces forwards and opens outwards. It's not all about looking nervously at one's shadow for fear of making mistakes. Back in the day a young lad called a *shuhitsu* (scribe) was employed to do the mundane task of checking for conflict. The big men were too busy swilling strong drinks and trying to work out how to stitch each other up. Nowadays the ladies are all at it too. But you get the general gist—you're supposed to enjoy writing renku, not be intimidated.

Right. Each step of the triple-lock starts with an **R**. So let's take a look at reversion, regression, and reiteration—always remembering that, though there is a good deal of agreement in the *serious* literature about these issues, the use of terms does tend to vary.

Reversion

Easy peasy. If you've ever written renku you'll know this one already as it's not really possible to write a sequence otherwise. But it's helpful to agree on a word for something. That way we're less likely to keep slipping on *thingie* skins. Yellow. Fruit. Curvy.

Write verse **A**. Add verse **B** to it. Now add **C**.

If the writing is any good, verse **C** will be seen to flow from **B**, just as **B** could be seen to flow from **A**.

You can call that a sequence. But you can't call it renku. For it to be renku our verse **C** must do two things: it has to flow from **B** whilst at the same time being comprehensively different to **A**.

What makes renku unique in the history of literature (earth, human) is that this dual pressure is then exerted on the following verses in turn. So (in the sequence **B–C–D**) **D** must now both link naturally to C whilst moving well away from **B**. And **E** must etc. Etc.

Put another way—each time we add a verse, we want to get a synergy going with the verse we're linking to, without reverting straight back to some aspect of the verse before that.

So reversion itself is very straightforward. But what exactly does that *some aspect* mean? The chapter *More About Shift* explains in detail while anyone prompted by Satan to write yet another verse about cats is politely advised to memorise the chapter *Thematic Renku*. Otherwise the quick answer is (**a**) just about any aspect that's obvious (what, who, where, how), and (**b**) trust your inner Walrus.

Note—in some longer renku sequences a given season can persist over three, four, even five verses. And a passage of love verses can last for three, conceivably four. But even there you don't go from early spring, to late spring, then just revert to early spring. Or happy as Larry, miserable as sin, and straight back to hap-hap-happy.

No alternation of topics, tones or phrasing. No repeats from the verse before last. No Reversion.

Regression

Regression sounds like the kind of thing the idle rich and their psychiatrists get up to. So, given that renku loves the scientific method, let's falsify some data and invent a case study too. Let's examine why, if you use the word *crab-apple*, you need to wait for a while before you can use the words *goat* or *pliers*. But only if you are from Bogushetia. Or writing with (and for) people of Bogush extraction...

One of the more fictitious nations of the Caucasus, Bogushetia boasts a particularly grim (and anatomically impossible) national creation myth featuring a goat, a crab-apple, and pair of pliers. Whilst too disgusting to fully explain, in the minds of some these three elements are irrevocably wedded to one another, taking pride of place in the sanguinary corpus of Bogush cultural iconography. The mention of two, let alone all three, in close proximity will guarantee a cheerful riot.

Done.

The key words in our study are *minds*, *some*, and *wedded*. We are dealing with ideas. Perhaps specific to a culture. But tightly associated.

The second stage of our lock is therefore tuned to the tendency to categorise or pigeon-hole things. An American will probably group *Mom*, *Rockwell*, and *apple pie* together in a way that a Sumatran will not. And most people, when confronted with the image of *tiger* too soon after the mention of *lion*— even if the contexts are radically different—will tend to respond with, *Hang on, haven't we just been there?*

In that flicker of partial recognition, our forward momentum is gone.

So the question is: unless we are deliberately using them in a verse to verse link, how many clear verses do there need to be between things our minds put in the same bracket? How much distance between associated ideas does it take to avoid regression? And the answer, as before, is twofold: (**a**) it depends on how powerful the bracket, and (**b**) not as many as you think. Well, threefold really because there is always (**c**) don't forget the Walrus.

Regression. The more significant the icons—and the more tightly they are associated with each other—the greater is the distance needed between related ideas. Things which we hold dear will need four or five clear verses. More loosely grouped things, which aren't exactly stand-out, will barely need a couple or three. A well written sequence moves relentlessly on. It is surprising how swiftly what has gone before moves beyond the lens of now.

And please, I implore you, we must avoid the temptation to be overly literal. Our text is not a crime scene where the mention of **up**stairs six verses after **down**town points to the murderer. Regression exists at the semantic level rather than in the words per se. So *vermillion* and *cerise* will take a bit of separation not because they are both colours but because, for anyone with taste, both belong to that sub-set of tints known as *dodgy types of reddy pink which are neither one thing nor the other but always push the price tag up*. Were they good old green and brown, regression wouldn't apply. And anyone attempting to refer to *puce* is banned from poetry anyway.

Reiteration

Why would a person who regularly mocks the spray-on Buddhists spend ages agonising over whether to call this third tumbler of the lock *reincarnation* or *reiteration*? Obsessive personality? Or a genuinely difficult choice? The search terms at the end of the chapter might illuminate the dilemma. But in the end *reiteration* won out. It's more accurate.

Semantics. Semiology. Semiotics. Only Daniel Dennet is clever enough to tell them apart. But it doesn't really matter because with reiteration—as with the early stages of incarnation—all that matters is that it takes two to tango. Signs, that is. Two words or phrases. Each flagging up a core idea. Two prime elements compounding away at each other. And then doing it again later on. The dirty swine!

Time was, the men in skirts spent forever on this problem, knowing intuitively that there must be some principle at stake but getting stuck instead with endless lists of what could go with what if what had gone with what before, and when. If you follow. No, I don't either. In fact so few people did that nowadays all that's left of the theory is a bulge under the occasional carpet. Which is either dust. Or a poet. Slowly turning to dust.

But, for all they used brushes instead of ball points, those oddly dressed fellows were 100% correct. If we need to be aware of things like *tiger* being too close to *lion* (the second stage of our lock) how on earth do we deal with full-on repetitions? How come no-one slapped Matsuo Basho's wrists for putting three moon verses in a single poem? And even if we stake the lazy claim that *moon* and *blossom* are special cases, why is it that poem ***A*** can twice refer to a mountain landscape without staggering to a halt whereas poem ***B***, which does the same, goes round and round in circles shouting, *We've already mentioned that*!

The answer is what clever people call a *proposition*. And it does involve lots of tangoing, but not in seedy bars. Now we've moved beyond the mention of things which our minds might associate with one another. Instead we are talking about the direct specification or the strong implication of similar *relationships*. Relationships between two or more ideas. Like the dependency of elements within this or that phrase. Or replaying the transition from an item in one stanza to an item in the next. If you repeat them, no matter how many verses have elapsed, the reader's mind flits back faster than a photon. And hey, we've been here before—*reiteration*.

So the problem is not that there are two moon verses. But that in one the moon shines on a poor man writing a poem, and in the other it shines on an empty fridge. We've repeated a tie-in between moonlight and poverty. *Reiteration*! One blossom verse has petals stuck in the salad, whilst the next has petals falling on a flute. *Reiteration*! Happy man is linked to holy mountain, only for holy man, later on, to be linked to alpine breeze. *Reiteration*! Possibly. That last one might depend on the exact phrasing. Certainly, if you also make the breeze out to be happy, you lose.

Reiteration is therefore to do with the way two things combine or are juxtaposed. Either within a verse. Or in the link between verses. It is the repetition of the *connection* which sinks the boat.

There are admittedly a few exceptions. On the face of it these come across as just a single thing. But they only occur where the mind factors in an extra tag shouting *unique*. So if your poem has an early mention of the (unique) ascension of Lord Jesus, don't expect to get away with a verse later on that cites the (unique) ascension of the Prophet Mohammed. And naturally a mention of Armageddon (unique) will preclude a later reference to Ragnarök (unique), not because they're both about the twilight of the gods, but because the same guy played bass in both bands.

To sum up

There's no need to resort to bogus guff like *backlink* or play *spoon feed the foreigner* when looking for a reliable way to assess impediments to forward movement in renku. And while intuition is invaluable in any artistic judgement there are some explicit considerations that keep us on the same page. In this case on the same page as those old school poets who spent forever thinking about this stuff. We are not morons. And neither were they. We don't need their ideas simplified to the point of cretinism and packaged up as laws.

To be clear—immediate verse to verse linkage is not at issue here. If you are sharp enough to link *albatross* directly to *ancient mariner* without making it seem hackneyed or ludicrous then good luck to you. The triple lock starts with the verse before last as we guard against obvious reversion. It then keeps an eye on closely associated ideas inadvertently popping up in the last four or five verses via regression. And it goes on to stop us from casually nailing the same two ideas together from anywhere else in the poem by careless reiteration.

Reversion – topics, tones and phrasing. Don't flip back directly to the verse before last.

Regression – for an Englishman, other than when used as an immediate link, *clotted cream* and *Auntie* might need a bit of distance as both are redolent of Edwardian high tea.

Reiteration – once you've associated *elephant* with *circus* in the same verse or inter-verse link, you won't get away with joining *ball-skills* to *seal*—even if it's a dozen verses down the line.

Oh yes... those search terms. There should be quite a lot online for the first two. The last will take a bit of page turning:

Reversion – tenji, uchikoshi, uchikoshi no kirai, kannonbiraki, yukiyo, sankume no utsuri, sanku no watari, sanku no garami.

Regression – sarikirai, kukazu, rinne, sashiai, renku (renga) + intermission, renku (renga) + avoidance, renku (renga) + seriation, renku (renga) + topics, renku (renga) + materials, renku (renga) + category.

Reiteration – torinne, shikimoku, ikkumono, 'remote repetition', 'distant reincarnation', renku (renga) + occurrence, renku (renga) + checklist, renku (renga) + smartypants.

On Backlink
no better way to waste your time

I was in a renku session once where the leader said, "I'm sorry, Gary, you can't have hubcap *in this stanza because it is a backlink to* beer". *I said, "WHAT?!?!?!". And they said* beer *was obviously in a can, which is round, and* hubcap *is another man-made round metal thing, which obviously could not be allowed.* —Gary Warner

The usual suspects

There's a postgraduate thesis to be written somewhere down the line that traces the exact origin of the word *backlink* in the sense that it has come to be used in English-language renku. The researcher could do worse than examine the sources before, during and after the Renku North America tour of 1992. Whatever the outcome, one thing is certain: the theory of *backlink* is useful only to the extent that anyone urging its application should be shunned.

To be fair, in so far as it can refer to the intention to move forward in a renku sequence, to avoid thematic development, and to ensure as much variety as possible, the term *backlink* almost passes muster. But in the minds of many, rather than describing a hazy principle, it has come to be viewed as a precise stricture—doubtless a translation of some Japanese term or other—which has, since time immemorial, illuminated a vital aspect of renku theory. As such it is seriously misguided. In fact it is just plain wrong.

Elsewhere in this assemblage of diatribe the chapter *Occurrence and Recurrence* examines in greater detail the pursuit of variety in renku whilst a practical and rapid alternative can be found in the chapter *The Three Rs*. The current maunderings survey, more in sadness than in anger, the ubiquitous fallacy that is *backlink*.

Early adoption

Like all the best delusions *backlink* starts from a good place: a recognition of the importance of category to Japanese perceptions of topic. For centuries Japanese poetry collections, treatises and competition criteria have been organised on the assumption that certain subjects fall into natural groupings. This has been as true for classical styles as for haikai. Poet and reader alike know that *smoke* and *clouds* fit into the category of *Rising Phenomena*, whilst *rain* and *frost* belong to the category of *Falling Phenomena*. Artistic choices, and critical appreciations, rely on a common understanding.

When renku began its spread into English there was some debate as to whether poets should come up with a fresh set of categories of their own or simply adopt the established system. But it was generally held that, even though a given category might be culturally specific, the issue of category itself was vital. The notion of *category* or *topic group* lay at the heart of Japanese theory, not least because it told what should be banned.

Regrettably the lustre of this essential truth was tarnished by a simple, but ghastly, mistake.

By way of illustration let's look at the historic Japanese category *Nocturnal Phenomena*; it contains such things as *dawn, lightning, fireflies,* and *fishing with cormorants*. This category has an associated intermission value. All categories have one, which varies according to their perceived primacy—according to the prominence or importance of the topics they contain.

The notion of intermission—*sarikirai*—dictates that, other than when used in an immediate verse to verse link, there should be a minimum number of clear verses before topics from a particular category may reoccur. The more prime the category, the greater the degree of separation. In the case of

Nocturnal Phenomena the required degree of intermission is three. Therefore, when a verse refers to *fireflies*, at least three clear verses should elapse before *dawn*, *lightning*, or *fishing with cormorants* may appear, for all are from the same category. By the same token, when any given verse refers to *fishing with cormorants*, at least three verses should elapse before *fireflies*, *dawn* or *lightning* may appear. Please note: not only is repetition of the named topic barred. The repetition of *any* topic from the same category is barred. And this for the *x* number of verses. For renku—a value somewhere between two and five.

So far so nearly good. But not. Let's return to the nub of Mr Warner's account.

It is possible to imagine a category for English renku called *Urban Litter* which contains, amongst other things, *beer can*, *cigarette butt*, *polystyrene tray* and *hubcap*. But any application of category-driven exclusion theory drawn on precedent would merely say that a given number of verses must elapse before it is wise to mention *cigarette butt* after *polystyrene tray*, or *beer can* after *hubcap*. And so on. What renku theory does not say, and has never said, is that if *beer can* is mentioned then *hubcap* cannot appear at all, or *cigarette butt*, or *polystyrene tray*, or any other topic included in the category *Urban Litter*.

The mere fact that one item is mentioned does not mean that all other items from the same category are now barred from the entirety of the poem, forever, totally, for the duration. Renku is more subtle than that.

Sadly our early adopters didn't really run to *subtle*. Or *informed*.

Suburban garbage

It is not difficult to understand the implications of such a fundamental error. Those who favoured shouting over knowledge were in the ascendant. Pigs in—well, many things really—few of which were clover. Paper thin? If so, then no one could mention *sycamore* or *sessile oak* thereafter as paper is made out of trees.

With this ingenious logic each time a verse is added entire swathes of allegedly related topics and tones are suddenly rendered inadmissible. Or until next week at least. And whilst it could be argued that such blanket injunctions were not always what was meant by *barakarinkuu* that in itself is a part of the problem. If *backlink* does not mean *beer-can-no-hubcap-forever* then what does it mean? And in the absence of any such agreement, how can it mean anything at all?

We few survivors can attest to the Kafkaesque effects of such uncertainties in practice. Sleepless nights spent forensically combing previous verses for God knows what kind of correspondence. The mad-eyed certainty of a cornered sabaki. The arguments. Frustrations. The sheer randomness of it all. Little wonder many gifted writers have looked at the genre, scratched their heads, and walked away. They've been presented not so much with *Urban Litter*, as *Suburban Garbage* pure and simple.

Linked verse theory will of course evolve over time. But the mere assertion of this or that axiom looks rather more like creationism. At best. And at worst—like the clutching of straws. Most galling of all is the suggestion that simplification is necessary because full-on reasons are beyond the ken of the barbarians at the gate. This is nonsense. Renku theory is only a complex field because it is full of cabbages claiming to be artichokes. Global ones.

Justified and ancient?

The renku revival of the last several decades has been characterised by the search for ever shorter sequences. A negative consequence of this otherwise interesting trend is that it appears to validate some of the *backlink* baloney whose baleful eye might just permit a twelve verse sequence wherein the only word repeated is the definite article *the*.

But far more misleading is that half remembered article about medieval renga one read in French—or maybe a machine translation from Mongolian? — anyway, quite long ago…

It is certainly true that, back in the good old days when sequences spanned several thousand verses, and poets dashed them off before breakfast, subjects drawn from the more prime categories had intermission values as high as seven. Sometimes more. There were also a small number of individual words and topics limited to a single appearance per side—fourteen verses, or per page—twenty-eight. In truly exceptional cases the gavel came down on once only per poem. Opinions varied from expert to expert, but most agreed on a once-in-a-lifetime limit on *bear, tiger, dragon, demon* and, naturally enough, *woman*.

In linked verse theory, the idea of comprehensive disbarring therefore has previous—as the comedy policeman would say. But the key word in all this is *exceptional*. Not to mention *medieval* and *renga*. What constitutes the exceptional may change from place to place, but the notion itself does not. Some things are just too heavy to handle more than once. If in doubt try putting *Bergen-Belsen* twice in your poem.

More confusion has arisen from the fact that, for centuries, some strands of aesthetic theory based on Shingon Buddhism have treated renku as an instance of *mandala*. If a poem is supposed to contain everything in the known universe—and renku does indeed demonstrate an astonishing appetite for ever more topics and tones—the temptation is to feed the furnace willy-nilly, to just throw materials in at random.

Yet any theory based on continuous and absolute novelty can clearly be seen to be false. Basho championed the Kasen. This has a handful of love verses, three moon verses—a pair of them in autumn (mostly)—and two blossom verses—both in spring. Would the advocates of *backlink* please stand up and explain what Basho did wrong.

Linked verse technique has developed over time thanks to the thoughtful engagement of poets and commentators. It is neither necessary nor desirable for those in the English speaking world to propound facile hypotheses that distance us from our source. If renku is indeed literature, any worthwhile theory will hold for all forms of the genre, in all languages, and in all cultural contexts.

Talking of falsehoods—*barakarinkuu* is offered in the text above as a romaji transliteration of the katakana rendering of *backlink* as a loan word in Japanese. It doesn't exist. Sorry.

There is no such thing as *backlink*.

Cut or Uncut?
haiku, hokku, and hopping mad

Something mything

At the turn of the century, in the English speaking world, it was almost axiomatic that the most commonly repeated assertions concerning renku were false. Nowhere was this more true than in the murky world of cut and uncut verses.

Stage left stood expert *A*. This man had once visited a Korean supermarket. He therefore knew that renku verses were just the same as haiku. Erm well... the ones on three lines anyway. Because that's the way the Japanese write their haiku. Isn't it?

Stage right, renku editor *B*. This man rejected our best work outright after finding an internal verse that used a break in syntax. And it is well known that only haiku should do that. And only the first verse, the hokku, may look like a haiku. So I'm tearing up your SASE. Hah!

Given that these positions seem diametrically opposed, surely one of them is right. In fact both are wrong. The good news is that my wristwatch now says 2013. The bad news—we're not much further on.

From hokku to haiku

Even miserable Masaoka Shiki acknowledged that the *haiku*, in form at least, springs from the first verse of a renku sequence, the *hokku*. And, if poked with a stick, he would also admit that Basho had a bit to do with it. Particularly on the how and why of juxtaposition.

Elsewhere in these pages the piece *Beginnings and Endings* looks at the subplots that may lurk beneath the surface of a hokku. But that's a question of content, of phrasing, and intention. In terms of prosody, of typical syntax, and overall structure, there is absolutely no difference in the way a haiku and a hokku go about their business.

The defining quality of both is that the verse is internally sufficient. Independent of context, it will bear consideration as a complete work. A haiku, like a hokku, is a poem in itself—a quality sometimes described as *free-standing*.

The cut and the cutting word: Kire and kireji

It is beyond the scope of this chapter to examine Japanese haikai prosody in any depth. Some fool is doing that elsewhere in the book. But we need to look at two terms if we are to engage with the question of the haikuness or otherwise of renku verses. Those terms are *kire* and *kireji*. They describe key features of the structure of a typical haiku or hokku.

The word *kire* translates more or less directly as *cut-off point* or *break*. The element *ji* means *character* or *glyph*. A *kireji* is therefore a *character which cuts-off*. Otherwise known as a *cutting word*.

The kire—the break—is the point at which a poem pauses and the meaning turns. The kireji—the cutting word—is a kind of verbal punctuation mark that emphasises the pause, and colours the nature of the turn. This colouration is possible because, in Japanese at least, there are a number of cutting words to hand, each with a different emphasis.

Building the verse

The long verse of Japanese haikai poetry is written as a single unbroken line or column. It contains three metrical feet—the famous 5/7/5 syllables. Strictly speaking we are counting *morae*—a more narrow type of timing unit. But for the moment *syllable* will do.

Within the overall 5/7/5, a haiku, or a hokku, typically juxtaposes a pair of images. The most obvious point to switch over is at the end of a metrical foot. So the development of the images will be asymmetrical. One occupies a single metrical foot, while the other straddles the remaining pair. In these circumstances the cutting word appears as a monosyllabic utterance immediately before the moment of juxtaposition. It is the last syllable of its associated metrical foot.

This this type of construction is so common that it has gained the useful tag of *fragment and phrase*. Always remembering we will also encounter *phrase and fragment*.

We can represent the first as: 4+1¬ 7/5

The fragment is sketched into the first metrical foot. It takes up four syllables, followed by the monosyllabic cutting word. The sense now turns. And the juxtaposed image is developed over the remaining two metrical feet. Which contain seven and five syllables respectively.

We can represent the second as: 5/6+1¬ 5

An image is developed over the first two metrical feet, the last syllable of which is a cutting word. The sense now turns. And the juxtaposed image is sketched into the five syllables of the final metrical foot.

Minor quibbles

Leaving aside deliberately irregular work, not all Japanese haiku or hokku use this construction. If the words can't be made to fit sometimes the cutting word is omitted. Sometimes the cutting word does not mark a strong internal divide at all but appears as the very last word of the poem—as a kind of closing sigh or shrug. And sometimes the text, at least at first sight, is nothing but a single sentence. More rare yet is the poem that does break with a cutting word, but slap bang in the middle of the central metrical foot.

However the asymmetrical two part poem, complete with cutting word, is by far the most common structure encountered and has served as the model, or the justification, for the three line stanza typical of English haiku and hokku in which either line one or line two is end-stopped.

Haikai prosody has developed over the centuries. During this time the list of cutting words has changed. As have ideas of where they might be used. In classical or courtly renga you will find the odd one embellishing an internal verse. And, just to be difficult, Basho liked to flourish the odd wild card too.

But by the end of the Edo period the debate had essentially been settled. And for modern renku in the Basho style the question of *kireji* is perfectly straightforward: cutting words are the preserve of the haiku or the hokku. Only.

Nagekomi: A major caveat

So far so dandy. If the scalpel reveals a cutting word, we know we are looking at a haiku or a hokku. But the problem that pits our noodle expert against our bull-headed editor lies elsewhere. Not with the first verse of a sequence at all, but with those that follow.

In renku, the internal verses do not seek to juxtapose otherwise unrelated images. Only the hokku does that. But they *do* use apposition. Not all the time. Sometimes. It is simply ill-informed to claim that no internal verse will use a break in syntax or a degree of turn. If in doubt, please go away and read some renku. Not by the Okefenokee Seniors Writing Circle, but by someone who knew what they were doing. In Japanese. A while ago.

Japanese renku writers borrow the term *nagekomi* (throwing-in) from flower arranging to describe the way space may be teased out to good effect. The space in question may be syntactic, semantic, or both.

At first sight, other than for the fact that it does not use a cutting word, such a verse may indeed look like a haiku or a hokku. And, as noted above, not all haiku or hokku use a cutting word anyway. Sigh. But, on closer examination, the break in syntax is often just a function of the phrasing, the diction, and there is no semantic turn at all. Or, where a degree of turn *is* present, it is far less marked than than in the case of a true stand-alone verse. We find that one element simply gives the setting in which the action of the other element takes place. Or one element cites a general state of some sort, whilst the other gives a specific instance of that same state.

The fact that such a description adequately characterises very many verses purporting to be haiku in English is unfortunate. But this has everything to do with the poor artistry and worse scholarship of those who self-identify as *haiku poets*, and nothing whatsoever to do with a deficiency in renku theory.

It should be noted that nagekomi is not employed in the majority of renku verses, nor would it feature in a succession of verses other than as a deliberate attempt to create a particularly jagged passage. A renku sequence is not made up of uniformly loud or uniformly quiet verses. And nagekomi is most likely to be used to create moments of high impact.

Emulation or equivocation?

A large part of the confusion surrounding the structure of internal verses in renku therefore springs not from renku at all, but from questions of form in English haiku. Particularly from the vexed issue of how to emulate the effect of the Japanese cutting word—the kireji.

Perhaps because of the ludicrous, but personally vicious, excesses of the Haiku Wars, English haiku prosody has been little debated for too long. It is not that the vital questions of form have been answered. Inertia has simply won the day.

One such comfy default is the assumption that the, or rather *all*, Japanese cutting words might be emulated by the use of an em dash, or similar, at the end of line one or two.

More maximal yet is the fashionable suggestion that a break in syntax of any sort, when allied to a line ending, is exactly the same as a cut. And that must be the same as using a cutting word. Because there aren't any cutting words in English.

These highly equivocal standards are then projected back onto renku, with the result that the simple use of parataxis in a renku verse is held up as a *kire* or, stranger yet, a *kireji*.

Thus renku competition judge C (the real target of this diatribe) and his haiku cronies talk themselves into the frankly absurd conclusion that the internal verses of an English renku sequence must, and can only, display unitary phrasing. Because otherwise they are the same as haiku. Genius!

Beware haikurashii

Clearly a break in syntax alone cannot be the final arbiter of what is or is not a cut verse in English haikai. It is not the *pause* which creates juxtaposition, it is the nature and degree of the *turn*.

A verse which successfully uses strong internal juxtaposition via a marked break and turn is almost certain to have the characteristics of a free-standing poem. Japanese renku theorists describe such a verse as *haikurashii*—which translates directly as *haiku-like*. When used in the context of an internal verse it is a criticism. There are very good reasons why free-standing qualities really only suit the hokku.

The expressive force of a renku sequence lies in the space between the verses, not in the content of the verses themselves. Each verse derives its primary resonance from its position in series, not from its internal dynamics. The hokku is of course the exception for, as the starting verse, it has no other verse to which it is subordinate and must generate its own effect.

In English renku, as in Japanese renku, or Pomeranian renku, an internal verse may indeed use various types of breaks in phrasing. And even a degree of semantic turn. The question of how frequently such techniques are employed, and how marked their intensity might be, is a matter of artistic judgement. If anyone remembers what that is. The only *rule* here is that a renku sequence is better understood as a sinuous whole rather than as a succession of individual, autonomous, verses.

As to my friend, the renku competition judge—I keep sticking pins in the ju-ju dolly. But his dark and corrupted soul is protected by something yet more malign.

Know Your Enemy
haikai stanzas in Japanese

Bliss

You are a Malaysian entrepreneur about to invest in high-performance motorcycle manufacturing. Do you (a) check that your engineers have a thorough grounding in the history of Italian racing power-train design, or (b) claim that noodles are better than spaghetti?

You are a British percussionist fascinated with Egyptian darbuka playing. Do you (a) learn everything you can about Egyptian darbuka playing, or (b) boast that Egypt was once part of your empire?

Shofu renku is a literary genre which arose in Japan. Some of its aesthetics and techniques date from time immemorial. But, just as the theory of relativity holds true for those other than German Jews, this does not mean that an Englishman or a Kenyan cannot write renku for want of the correct nationality. Nor does it mean that they must write their renku in Japanese. It simply means that certain features of the Japanese language must have influenced the development of the genre, so an awareness of these features may influence how one chooses to write the genre in English or Kiswahili.

Could anything be more obvious? And wasn't all this resolved years ago with the advent of haiku? Well, no, actually that was a disaster. The repercussions of which reverberate still.

September 1999 saw the publication of perhaps the most abject testament to cultural incomprehension since Capra's wartime *Know Your Enemy*. The Matsuyama Declaration purported to examine the prospects for international haiku in the 21st century. But it reads more like a surrender. Or a washing of hands. A shrug of the shoulders of the badly cut suit of inter-lingual literary discourse.

In other words teikei means to find out the inner order of the language and for the poetry, that could be universal.

Yeah right. In other words—*We neither know nor care. Go forth and multiply.*

But the Declaration served its purpose. All sides were happy. The dialogue of the deaf that had endured for fifty years was given carte blanche to continue. Better still, to entrench. As I type, in 2013, there remain in Japan many authorities who will not accept the existence of haiku in a language other than Japanese. Whilst on the other side of the Pacific there is an equally large number of self styled *haijin* unable to distinguish a caesura from a caesar salad.

Inauspicious? Not really. Just unacceptable.

The difference

A haiku is by definition a short single verse which exists in isolation. If it is to succeed it may do so purely on its own terms. It is independent. It is spontaneous. It is free. Unfettered by norms of prosody, English haiku poets can declare a blank sheet of paper to be genius, for, in the absence of any comparator, each work is literally peerless.

Not so renku. The verses do not stand alone. In a sequence where each takes a different form, the wider movement of the poem is easily lost. Self-referencing structures crash and stutter against each other as each attempts to validate its identity.

In such circumstances it takes great artistry to establish any form of sequence at all. Too readily we are presented with what is in effect a series: a succession of highly variable and quasi-autonomous verses whose very amorphousness requires us to study their shape.

So what? comes the retort. All that has happened here is that the bean counters don't like it. The tidy-minds have been offended. The 5/7/5 insect wants to crawl round in circles again.

No, that's not the case. We'll come to the insect later. For the moment let's just make two observations. One is that Shofu renku, when written in Japanese, does indeed make extensive use of phonic correspondence, both within and between verses—often to cement relationships, sometimes to generate distance.

The second is that, whilst it is untrue that some form of regular prosody is necessary for renku to work at all, it certainly is the case that, when renku is written in English, the adoption of purely free verse has specific consequences.

When the phonic properties of a sequence are absent or marginalised, inter-verse linkage is pushed towards the rational and the tangible. Poets naturally reach for meaning-links and object-links to ensure that their transitions make sense. In the absence of the pulse of long after short after long after short, the deep-level evocative potential of scent linkage becomes problematic. Stripped of the conducting cadences, the relationships between verses may be too tenuous for the more refined cognitive effects to function.

The risk of a purely free verse approach is that, as we focus on the structural rationale and hard content of individual stanzas, the creative power of the white space between them is lost. And it is the power of that white space, far more than any issue of form, that is the defining characteristic of Shofu renku.

To reiterate: this book does not seek to dragoon anyone into anything. It is for the poet to decide how to write their poetry. The proposal is simply that we base our decisions on a little bit of fact rather than on a lottle bit of lie.

So let's take a look at some aspects of haikai prosody in Japanese. *Haikai*, by the way, means both haiku and renku, plus related genres like haiga and haibun.

Some phonic tools

One of the weirder claims of the beardy brigade is that haiku, and by extension all haikai: *don't do poetics*. Perhaps the cat was having a haiku moment at the time, because apart from the fact that very short stanzas do not readily support complex tropes, this much chanted mantra holds true only for *Loon*. The sheer abundance of vowel sounds in Japanese does make nonsense of the idea of end rhyme, but the word *poetics* embraces more subtle sins than that, and poets of all periods have happily succumbed.

Japanese haikai makes extensive use of assonance and alliteration to animate diction. Onomatopoeia is common both in its literal form and in the more abstract sense that certain sounds are understood to evoke particular emotional palettes. This technique in turn is related to that of *vowel harmony* in which heterogeneous sounds are subordinated to the repetition of a given vowel.

Phonetic and syntactic parallelism are standard. Great play is made of cognates and homonyms—the flexible orthography favouring both fine shading and creative ambiguity. Sorry, let's try that last bit in English—the availability of both ideograms and phonetic characters allowing extra scope and subtlety when playing with related, or related sounding, words and ideas.

Symbolism, metaphor, oxymoron and hyperbole are everywhere. Extra-textual allusion are meat and drink. In short, the Japanese haikai poet works with words and skeins of words. Crass writers do it crassly. Good writers do it well.

To suggest that the writer of English should always and only employ the most utilitarian vocabulary is an instance not so much of misunderstanding as of self-hatred. True, we are dealing with the poetry of evocation, so any technique which draws attention to the surface of the text must count as a failure. But that is a question of poor artistry, not evidence of a mistaken philosophy.

Only an octopus would want to wave eight phonic devices at any one time, Basho eventually outgrowing the temptation when he renounced the Danrin school, but anyone with a wish to add penitential privation to their beardiness should go off and join the Taleban. We poor Sufis are at the mercy of the muse. We must make nuanced decisions about which linguistic devices are appropriate, and when. Always we must quake before the power of words.

On the page

Whereas discussion of the linguistic devices appropriate to English haikai has been scant, and heavily skewed by the baseless fabrications of the cat fondlers, issues of form have at least been on the agenda. Until recently. What shape should a stanza be? Should it have a shape at all? How long should it be? Measured in terms of what? And how do we decide?

These are excellent questions. So let's put our natural interest in the English Vorticists to one side for a moment and take a look at how the stanzas are set down in Japanese. If anyone has actually brought a 5/7/5 insect into class, would they please keep it in their matchbox for now.

Traditionally, a typical stanza is written as a single unbroken column of characters. Additional verses, or other text, appear as successive columns, the whole page arranged right to left.

In recent times a typeset stanza is just as likely to present as a horizontal line reading left to right—additional verses, or other text, set out on the lines below. The modern arrangement is therefore more familiar to the European eye.

In either case, there are no gaps or punctuation marks to indicate the boundaries of a particular phrase or segment. Nor are there additional blank character spaces to separate one word from another. Over the course of the last several decades functional prose has started to use the period (full stop), a somewhat haphazard comma, and a rather blocky set of quotation marks. But poetry does not.

Poetry of all styles employs a comprehensive range of traditional inflection markers that have secondary effects of punctuation. Nowhere is this more apparent than in the case of a haiku or a hokku whose much mystified *cutting words* are no more than a subset of the wider array of inflection/punctuation indicators. Note though that these markers are not glyphs or symbols after the fashion of a European query or dash. They are brief utterances—words in their own right—which are pronounced when a poem is read aloud, and whose scansion value is therefore taken into account when a poem is parsed.

Except when treated as an exercise in calligraphy, a haikai stanza gives very little away visually. The eye is presented with an undifferentiated string of characters. The individuation of words, phrases, pulses and pauses takes place entirely within the mind of the reader. Not on the page.

Syllables and morae

Taking care, please, not to let them run around the room—you can now let your insects out.

It is immediately apparent that the 5/7/5 insect is a dubious thought experiment. Most puzzling of all are the metaphorical legs, which are not syllables, but morae. In fact, given that it takes a number of these legs to make up a single metrical foot, it might be best to despatch our mixed-metaphoric insects without delay.

Krink!

How many syllables was that? And any more for morae?

The word mora—Japanese using the terms *on* (single sound) or *haku* (beat)—is a technical term drawn from the prosody of Latin. The plural is moras or morae. *Mora* describes a timing unit more precise, and regular, than the notoriously elastic *syllable*. This distinction is important because Japanese is not written using an alphabet. And its words are not made up of syllables but of phonetic units.

Much Japanese core vocabulary may be written using *kanji*—ideograms—but all words, including those normally represented by ideograms, may be written using one or more phonetic characters. In phonetic writing each character represents a single phonetic unit which may be parsed as a single mora.

There are two separate phonetic character-sets. *Hiragana* are used in most circumstances. *Katakana* are reserved for foreign words, or for spelling out some sounds and meanings.

It is a feature of Japanese phonetic units that, since the earliest days of proto-linguistics, they have been held up as the perfect example of a language whose core sounds are of very similar duration (length) and amplitude (loudness). This type of language came to be described as a *syllable timea* language (sic) and was thought to be in total contrast to the other class of world languages—the *stress timed* languages—which exhibit wild fluctuations. Almost inevitably, chief amongst the stress timed languages is English. In theory anyway.

The fact that this proposal asks us to judge Japanese in terms of attributes it does not possess—syllables—is a mere detail. The beard and sandal lovers who bestrode late 20th century haiku gleefully seized on it as scientific proof that Japanese is a very regular language—and therefore uniquely suited to a very regular prosody—whereas English, or Cryptosporidium, are not. Cue a sudden rash of *My Verse—Keepin' it Free!* bumper stickers, while back in Matsuyama the men in shiny suits read as far as the word *uniquely*, bowed to each other, and went home for tea.

Any recent and half-way serious exploration of the supposedly absolute divide between syllable-timed and stress-timed languages doesn't just shoot the particular fox, it rapidly precedes to run the SUV over it several times. But never let the truth stand in the way of a good stipend, as they say in academia. So let's return to the real world and look a little more at the way phonetic units are written, and how they are then transliterated.

With the exception of a number of free-standing vowels and a nasalised *n* similar to that found in French, each Japanese phonetic unit is the equivalent of a consonant followed by short vowel—an arrangement known to occidental linguists as *onset plus nucleus*.

Typical Japanese phonetic units therefore follow the pattern *a, i, u-ka, ki, ku-ma, mi, mu* etc. These may be words in their own right, or they may be combined to make words. Looking at the assortment above for example—a *kami* is a native spirit. The word is made up of *ka* and *mi*. Written phonetically it requires two characters. Parsed as poetry it counts two morae.

It is important to note that, in literary circles at least, the use of a Latinate alphabet to give a rough equivalent to pronunciation—the system known as romaji—is most certainly *not* a further alternative to using ideograms (kanji) or phonetic character-sets (hiragana, katakana) in order to write a word. For all that exactly such usage has begun to be seen as cool in metropolitan Japan—in branding, sloganising, and graffiti—romaji is not treated as a mainstream Japanese writing system. In effect it is not Japanese at all.

But neither is romaji English. Reading Japanese transliterations in romaji can be misleading. Take for instance the word *onji*—once believed to be the correct translation of *mora*. Every literate English person can see that it has two syllables: *on* and *ji*. But Japanese is not made up of syllables. It is made up of morae. And here there are three: the free-standing *o*, the nasalised *n* and the onset plus nucleus *ji*.

Take the name *Chiou*. A single syllable on any civil tongue. But in Japanese, three morae: *Chi, o,* and *u*. As a general rule, when several vowels follow a consonant in a romaji rendering, only the first is a part of the onset plus nucleus pair which make up a phonetic unit. The others are free-standing vowels, and therefore phonetic units, and consequently separate morae, in their own right.

Clearly we need to read romaji renderings with care if we are to gain any insight into the structure of a source text. The more so if we are looking for paradigms for our own writing.

Kurinku!

Ahhh, someone seems to have stepped on the neck of the sole surviving 5/7/5 insect. It has met its last. And in Japanese too (courtesy of a romaji rendering). Had the notional beast expired in English it would have plinked apart with a repeat of the monosyllabic *krink* made by our earlier victim. But Japanese sound effects simply won't do a consonant-clustered *kri*, nor a hard closing *k*- opting instead for *kuri* and the less guttural *ku* respectively. Hence *kurinku*. Three syllables, but four morae: the onset plus nucleus *ku*, then *ri*, the free standing *n*, and the terminal *ku*.

A syllable is not a mora. Morae are shorter and less variable. If morae count time differently, a mora based time signature will not support syllabic music. And if a mora is shorter than a syllable, a poem which uses the same number of syllables as morae will go on for longer—both in terms of the length of tape it takes up on the cassette recorder, and the number of things it says.

Attempts to make the 5/7/5 insect run on English fuel are a waste of time. But that does not mean that the internal structures of the Japanese original are irrelevant to the writing of haikai in other languages.

Making the Whole

Unless they are deliberately experimental, Japanese haikai stanzas are composed of metrical units of five or seven morae. These divisions are found everywhere from the earliest poetic forms to the public information slogans on the Tokyo underground. Their permutations, and the interplay of their cadences, are profoundly familiar to their audience.

The emphasis here is on the word *metrical*. The occidental reader is used to seeing representations such as 7/7/5/7/5 in discussions of early waka or whatever. These are excellent shorthand, but the oblique slash is easily taken to represent some sort of division on the page: a dash perhaps, an indent, or a line break. Such assumptions are as misleading as they are natural. Dashes, indents and line breaks modify syntax, and therefore modify meaning. But the boundaries between the fives and sevens of Japanese prosody are, of themselves, neutral. They no more automatically modify the sense of what is being said than does the transition from one foot to another in a passage of anapaestic tetrameter in English.

Nor should we imagine that the fives and sevens represent the totality of the music of a verse. Were it so, any old combination of the requisite number of morae would be great poetry. The fives and sevens are *metrical* divisions. They are a coarse measure, a dosage of sound. They are a starting point only, the basis from which poets use their phonological sensitivity to develop the broader music of the piece.

Somewhere in the waste bin are the notes for a chapter on cut and uncut verses which, amongst other things, looks at how bi-partite juxtaposition is most frequently achieved in a Japanese haiku or hokku. Hopefully Nurse will rescue it before we all revert to our component atoms. But the fact that an exclamatory punctuation word must be introduced in order to fully end-stop a metrical boundary is a powerful indication of quite how semantically neutral that boundary otherwise is. We must resist the temptation to construe the oblique slashes and suchlike of metrical descriptors as being the automatic equivalent of a break, an indent or a pause of some sort.

So how *is* the content of a Japanese verse organised? What *does* occur at a metrical boundary beyond the tallying of an appropriate number of morae?

It is not unknown for the component parts of a word to straddle a metrical boundary but such instances are rare. In almost all cases a metrical boundary is also a word boundary. Frequently, though by no means invariably, the metrical boundary also works in conjunction with elements of syntax to become a phrasal boundary. And, as we have seen, this phrasal boundary may be end-stopped to generate what is in effect a sentence boundary.

Leaving aside the haiku and hokku (thank you, Nurse), the 5/7/5 long verse may read through as a single complete sentence. Just as readily it will pause at one or other of the metrical boundaries via some form of discontinuity of syntax. The pause may be purely a matter of phrasing and diction going no further than parataxis. Alternatively the discontinuity may be allied to a degree of semantic turn so that the pause functions as a pivot—as a form of soft juxtaposition. The one thing a long verse *will not* do is stop and break at each metrical boundary in order to generate a three item list. This has always been regarded as deeply ugly and would only be done to shock.

Naturally the 7/7 short verse demonstrates a corresponding degree of flexibility. Its single metrical boundary is never fully end stopped via a cutting word but otherwise the same range of constructions occur—from run-on syntax, through a pause in diction, to a degree of semantic turn. Given the symmetry of the metrical pair, ideas of syntactic parallelism drawn from Chinese poetics readily come into play.

So what?

So there is nothing massively unknowable about the basic features of Japanese haikai prosody. Quite why there should be so much obfuscation is worrying as it seems to speak of constructive ignorance.

No matter. In a moment we'll swap new ground for old. Let's just recap some of the things we've learnt.

The expressive language used in all forms of Japanese haikai is far broader, varied and flexible than has been admitted by the out-dated agenda-driven approaches to haiku in English. This has particular significance for renku as a sensitivity to phonics is integral to both successful verse construction and inter-verse linkage.

The Japanese stanza does not fall back on visual quantities for its proportions and breaks. It relies on movement within the text. The famously elusive haiku and hokku cutting words, the *kireji*, are no more rare nor strange than any other set of punctuation and inflection markers.

The difference between syllables and morae is not arcane. They simply measure different things. The one-for-one correspondence between written phonetic characters, spoken phonetic units, and morae makes a verse easy to parse in Japanese. But representations of the verse in romaji can be misleading.

There is nothing uniquely restrictive or pattern-specific about Japanese that makes it more demanding of, or suited to, formal structures.

The metrical boundaries of Japanese prosody are not analogous to English line breaks. The latter always inflect meaning, the former *may* inflect meaning.

In sum: Japanese haikai prosody, including stanza structure, is far more flexible and varied than is generally believed. Paradoxically, despite the ubiquity of free verse, English poets have been painting with a restricted palette for too long.

It is time to move on. To 8/8/8 for example.

The meaning of eight eight eight

In 2000, a year after the debacle at Matsuyama, Kumamoto University published *From 5-7-5 to 8-8-8 (An Investigation of Japanese Haiku Metrics and Implications for English Haiku)* by researchers Richard Gilbert and Judy Yoneoka. The paper raises issues so central to our understanding of the metre and rhythm of haikai stanzas, in any language, that the significance has barely begun to sink in.

Gilbert and Yoneoka's method had the lucidity of genius. They simply borrowed some white coats, strapped a few native speakers to a lab chair, wired in a measuring device or two, and politely asked their victims to read out a random assortment of haiku. Their findings were recorded *scientifically*, and stipend be damned.

The results are clear. When uttered aloud the 5/7/5 morae of a typical Japanese haiku are remapped by the speaker onto a constant substructure composed of a rolling eight pulse. 5/7/5 or no, the reader adds pauses, extends the allegedly inviolate morae, and generally deforms the words in response to the pull of a more fundamental set of underpinnings. Linguists and neuroscientists call this unconscious adjustment to a hidden attractor *entrainment*. And there's that word again—*science*.

That we should be so surprised is itself instructive. Gilbert and Yoneoka have really only demonstrated in respect of poetry what every musician or dancer has always known—the timing and extent of the expressive phrase or gesture is conditioned by, but goes beyond, a one-to-one correspondence with the underlying pulse.

This then is the new ground. We learn that 5/7/5 describes the coarse metre only—a rough measure of the dosage of sound units. The actual rhythm of the piece arises from the musicality of the constituent phonetic units—skilfully selected so as to acquire the slips, drags and pauses that chime with the undertow. Once again we find that, as with the more elusive cognitive properties of scent linkage, the most subtle phonic effects of our poetry reside not on the page but in a subliminal hinterland shared by writer and reader alike.

From 5-7-5 to 8-8-8 ends with the invitation to take the work forward into other languages in order to further explore the relationship between metre, rhythm and bass beat. The prospects are intriguing. There are indications from neurolinguistics, for instance, that certain aural processing periodicities may be universal—that some poetic timings are simply a function of being human.

Yet in the case of English, for the moment, the call seems to have gone unanswered. Which is unfortunate. But not entirely unexpected. It is almost as though the search for a cross-cultural and inter-lingual understanding of haikai prosody has been characterised by a pressing need *not to* know. We have two opposing camps whose only shared desire is to find the most polite way to say: *Your language is not my language. Goodnight.*

This state of affairs is intolerable. It is high time for otherwise rational Japanese commentators to stop citing *kotodama* and understand that people of other nations have a feeling for words too. As for the Commodore Perry's of this world: would you please go somewhere else and turn your guns on yourselves. When it comes to knowing your enemy—that's what mirrors are for.

Know Yourself
haikai stanzas in English

A Delphic maxim

This chapter is the counterpart to the ill-tempered *Know Your Enemy*. It does not recant.

The supposedly unbridgeable chasms of difference between Japanese and other languages are nothing of the sort. They are chimeras conjured by chauvinism and sloth on the part of insecure people trying to boost their fragile self esteem via the deliberate obfuscation of perfectly straightforward issues of linguistics.

It follows that both the general nature and the specific features of Japanese haikai prosody, far from being arcane and unknowable, are easily understood. And that this understanding may influence the development of haikai prosody in English or any other language.

The key phrase here is *may influence*. A case can be made for the origination of completely novel forms of English language haikai prosody which are valid as long as they facilitate the exploration of the meaning and intent of Japanese haikai whilst, their proponents would argue, holding true to the essential spirit of that haikai. A brief review of some of the subsequent experiments, digressions and alternatives follows. It includes an idea advanced some years ago by the present author—the *zip*.

But a central contention of the present rambling manifesto is that, in the case of renku at least, there are distinct limits on how self-referencing an English haikai prosody might be because the source genre relies directly on features of language in order to achieve a significant part of its effect. The implication is that, if English language poets are to have a sufficient range of techniques available to them, the English prosody of renku must closely emulate or otherwise parallel the effects permitted by Japanese in respect of verse construction, inter-verse linkage, and the impact of proportional cadences over extended passages of verse.

This chapter closes with the proposal of a style of English haikai prosody which is intended to do precisely that. It is neither exactly fixed form, nor entirely free verse. Done well, it looks unforced and familiar, but is more considered than it seems. If it succeeds, it does so because it is *supple*.

If you have yet to fight your way through *Know Your Enemy* either the idiot editor has put the chapters in the wrong order or the idiot author's oh-so clever sniping proved unbearable. In any event, please take a deep breath and read it through as, in amongst the chaff, there is the germ of truth needed to contextualise what follows.

So, without further ado, let's lighten the mood and have a glance at some of the ways people down the years have responded to issues of form when seeking to convey the essence of Japanese haikai. In the main we are dealing with haiku or hokku here, as linked verse was mostly off the radar until recently.

Short prose

One of the earliest translators of haiku, Lafcadio Hearn, pioneered this approach.

Unkindly characterised by later critics as a mere *dribble of prose* the snippets of text he proposed use capitalisation and standard punctuation, sometimes with the addition of a line break or extra spaces to highlight parataxis.

With so few constraints the technique is highly flexible. It is relaxed and discursive. The main objection is that, by its very openness, it bears little resemblance to the tight structure of the source genre.

But at least it does not pretend otherwise. Contrast the very large number of academic renderings one encounters which are nothing other than dribbles of prose boasting that most pathetic fig leaf of legitimacy—a random pair of line breaks.

Concrete poems and the variable use of space

Striking effects engineered by the concrete arrangement of text and the variable use of space have been of particular interest to English-language haiku poets since the 1970s, the techniques having been co-opted from the wider experimental movements of the 50s and 60s.

The active juxtaposition of text against blank space is supposed by some to echo Buddhist aesthetics, drawing on the tension between presence and absence. There is also a belief that to concentrate on visual presentation is to reflect the importance of brushwork in earlier times.

But whilst excellence in calligraphy may indeed be associated with the presentation of a poem in Japanese it remains a separate art form. A Japanese verse is an undifferentiated string of characters. Its internal movement relies on word choice and the conceptual, not concrete, use of space.

In the light of this, even the staggered indents so beloved of the 80s and 90s English *haijin* seem little more than baseless affectation. Rather like the florid font and the centering of text, they are unlikely to enhance a poor poem.

The one-liner or monostich

Perhaps the most demanding of all the English stanza forms, the one-liner (generally an unpunctuated monostich) lends itself to complex disjunctive and agglutinative effects. In skilled hands the results range from the subtle to the profoundly disconcerting. Though there are character spaces between words, the stanza looks at first sight very much like its Japanese counterpart.

Yet this apparent similarity is the source of its difference. The single bloc of the Japanese stanza is natural to its reader, as is the ability to regenerate both sense and sound from an agglomeration of text.

The English audience, by contrast, is trained to expect the presence of some or all of capitalisation, punctuation, spaces, indents and line breaks in order to fully decipher a poem. The unbroken line is therefore somewhat alien.

Be that as it may, there has been truly excellent linked verse written using this style of prosody. It is highly adaptable and responsive.

The two-liner

In theory a two line construction—one long, one short—might seem the most suitable to emulate a typically bi-partite Japanese haiku or hokku. It would allow the line break to function as the point of juxtaposition whilst respecting the roughly one third to two thirds proportions of the opposed images/phrases.

But such an arrangement—an asymmetrical distich—is not what most people think of as a two-liner. Automatically poet and audience alike reach for familiar ideas of *couplet* with their strong implications of syntactic and metrical parallelism.

A pair of evenly matched long lines using familiar poetic devices may be pleasing to the English eye and ear, but it has very little in common with the structure and function of the source material.

The quatrain

For the general reader the quatrain, the four line stanza, is perhaps the most familiar of the short forms. Unlike the couplet it looks and feels complete. However, though it may easily accommodate the run-on syntax or light parataxis of a Japanese internal verse, it does not easily lend itself to handling the roughly one third to two thirds proportions of the typical haiku or hokku where one or other asymmetrical phrase is end-stopped.

The number of lines is a problem too. If they are not to seem too compressed, there is a tendency for each to carry a complete phrase. Cumulatively this generates a more extensive treatment of a subject than is typical of the source genre.

The quatrain can feel elegant, engaging and appropriately whole. But it tends to be over long and promote questionable binary symmetries.

The zip

First proposed in 1999 by the present author the zip attracted a great deal of initial interest for its unlikely combination of high flexibility with a recognisably fixed form—this latter quality still considered a minimum condition by some of the more conservative Japanese commentators for a poem to qualify as *haiku* in the first place.

The zip can accommodate a wide range of semantic structures, adapt to any style of phrasing, and enable all sorts of comparative devices from soft pivots to harsh syntactic disjuncture. However the stanza is difficult to type-set correctly, particularly as html, and many social media platforms suppress its formatting altogether.

It may be that the zip also looks a little odd to its audience. But perhaps the most significant criticism is that, whereas the format of the long verse has been shown to have merit as a vehicle for stand-alone poems, it does not so readily deliver the plain internal verses of a renku sequence. Some writers also report that the format of the short verse feels contrived.

The three-liner then—obviously

Or not, as the case may be.

The three line stanza has the advantage of ubiquity. It is nothing if not familiar. Haiku: seventeen syllables, 5/7/5. Three lines: short/long/short. The last time I went for a haircut, Gianni knew more about it than me.

One of the most intriguing things about this universal myth is that it appears to have concretised entirely by default. B. H. Chamberlain's 1888 *Handbook of Colloquial Japanese* contained a number of examples of hokku in translation along with the observation that, *This particular kind of stanza [...] consists of three lines of respectively five, seven, and five syllables.* His more or less off the cuff remark set a standard that was to go unchallenged for decades.

The problem lies in the characterisation of the Japanese metrical foot as a *line*, and of a mora as a *syllable*. As shorthand the terms are fine. As linguistic axioms they are false. Had anyone given the subject much thought the deficiencies would have been apparent from the outset. Unfortunately Chamberlain, and other early sources such as W. G. Aston, had scant regard for the genre in the first place and treated it in passing only, whilst those immediately following such as Yone Noguchi and Sadakichi Hartmann who straddled the Japanese and European literary camps were far more taken with the aesthetics and intent of all sorts of nascent minimalist poetry than the lengthy explication of an historic form.

It was not until the middle of the last century and the arrival of the big three—Blyth, Henderson and Yasuda—that we find anything resembling serious consideration of how and why an English haiku or hokku might be written in a particular way. By this time two truths were already so established in occidental thought as to be self evident. One, that 5/7/5 syllables on three lines was formally correct. The other, that free verse was more conducive to unforced sentiment—and hence more in accordance with the spirit of the genre if not the letter.

Whilst it would be stretching credibility to accuse any of the triumvirate of indulging in a truly thoroughgoing analysis of relative prosody they did at least begin to ask some of the important questions. What type of expressive language should be used? How about rhyme and other common English poetic devices? How strict should *strict form* be? Was 5/7/5 syllables actually correct? Always? If not, how many syllables were correct? Approximately? Should translations be as tightly structured? How important was image order—in translation—and in original work?

The answers varied between the three, and over time, Blyth and Henderson also realising that syllabics, if not a blind alley, might not perhaps hold all the cards. Both found themselves drawn to the proposition that accentual metre might better constitute the basis of form.

It is no wonder that Blyth, Henderson and Yasuda are still held in such esteem. This was a fertile period in which a great many of the previous assumptions were finally held up to the light. The only vital element that escaped serious scrutiny was the conflation of the metrical foot with the line.

How disconcerting then to realise that, since the 1960s, there has been so little added to the theoretical work of these three men, not least in the field of linguistics which, having been born as a discipline in the intervening period, can bring a new perspective to bear. Creative writing itself has moved on apace. There has been so much experimentation with cross-overs between haikai and other types of minimalist verse that the very idea of English *haiku* has become extremely fluid even in the minds of those who specialise in the genre. But discussion of form has languished or been notable only in the most negative of contexts.

Towards the end of the last century the mother of all battles between those voicing the strict-form meme and others proselytising for free verse resulted in a great deal of outrage and ill will on all sides. Many protagonists invested a great deal of personal capital in stances so ill considered as to seem, at a distance, absurd. Most unfortunately of all the conflict drew in aspects of cultural identification so clumsily framed as to verge on xenophobia.

The pernicious effects of this bloodletting persist to this day. It is unpopular, if not actively unwelcome, in many ambits to raise issues of form at all. Persons new to haikai soon learn that to ask too many questions is to be labelled a pedant or trouble maker. A corollary is that there must be some form of esoteric auto-awareness associated with the haikai arts that comes with simply *doing*. This presumably has something to do with a mystical bogosity such as Kenneth Yasuda's *haiku moment*. Or perhaps the worship of cats.

Such mumbo jumbo remains a blight on the haikai arts. There is every reason why a poet should choose to just write. There can be no doubt that the creative urge must always take precedence over the analytic, and for some authors critical exegesis is an irrelevance if not an actual impediment to freedom from constraint. But it is also true that for others questions of form, linguistics, literary history and the like have a direct bearing on their understanding of their art. The only problem is when one assumes superiority over the other.

Seventeen syllables

So let's revisit Chamberlain's casual definition in the light of more recent thinking. Firstly, how many English syllables actually do equate to seventeen morae in Japanese? For instance, what do translations tell us?

The answer is *nothing*. Or almost nothing. Not about syllables and morae anyway.

An elegant translation of the world's most famous haiku—Basho's frog into a pond poem—dates from the 1960s. Noboyuki Yuasa adopts the quatrain and takes twenty-two syllables to deliver a memorable verse. Elsewhere the ever imaginative James Kirkup, first president of the British Haiku Society, duly published a tragicomic tercet comprising a single monosyllable per line purporting to be a version of the same poem—a travesty which can only have seen print after being peer reviewed by one or more persons, presumably with a straight face.

At least we have a range then. A typical haiku or hokku will translate to somewhere between twenty-two and three syllables. We also have a warning: styles of translation are agenda driven. They may tell us a great deal about the translator and the spirit of their times, but they do not necessarily convey anything about the source text beyond a passing acquaintance with the most superficial aspect of its content. If you are lucky. And avoid Kirkup. The idea that we can gain paradigms for our own writing by engaging with the work of a renowned translator or two is fraught with ill founded assumptions.

There are however some issues on which a consensus has emerged. The ability of English to code more densely than Japanese has been overstated, particularly by advocates of ultra-minimalist haikai, but the accumulated weight of evidence based on sheer trial and error in the decades since Blyth, Henderson and Yasuda first opened the issue to scrutiny suggests that their suspicions were well founded. When writing a long verse in English, seventeen syllables will almost invariably over-extend the semantic content, the sense, the directly stated meaning of a verse. Clearly if this is the case for the seventeen syllables of the long verse, fourteen syllables for an English short verse will be over-abundant too. We need fewer.

Not unreasonably the first instinct is to establish a new fixed quantity. The commendably moderate William J. Higginson in his *Haiku Handbook* of 1985 suggested somewhere around twelve syllables for a haiku or hokku. Many of his contemporaries agreed. In the 1990s, despite the many talking heads lauding minimalism, a frequent recommendation amongst practitioners was thirteen or fourteen—a number one still sees repeated in perfectly respectable sources.

But irrespective of such theoretical targets the lure of free verse could not be denied. Statistical analysis carried out in 1997 by the poet and editor George Swede into haiku published in the influential journals Modern Haiku and Frogpond confirmed that over 90 percent of poems were written on three lines, with more than two thirds rejecting a fixed syllable count of any sort. Three lines—long/short/long, if only as visual quantities—had become firmly entrenched, with the rest of the conversation, such as it was, revolving around syllabics.

The problem with this impressive uniformity is that, irrespective of the number of syllables involved, Japanese moraic metres and their associated cadences, are more readily accessible and familiar to their audience than are syllabic metres to those who use English. In so far as any active comparison was taking place, apples were being offered as oranges—some protagonists going so far as to argue that the relative impenetrability of contemporary English haiku to the non-specialist audience was an essential part of the art.

At a conceptual level this last point is moot. It may run counter to the source tradition, but there is no absolute reason why a school of haikai should not pursue paradox, oblique inference, or any other form of hermeneutic soliloquizing. So wishing.

But language use is different. Though some Edo period stanzas may be slightly hard to access because a particular aspect of diction is now archaic, haikai as a movement has always been defined by its use of the vernacular rather than the refined. It avoids the recherché. It is closer to the common man. It is familiar. It slips in unremarked.

As Blyth and Henderson had already recognised, this is not really the case with English poetry based on syllabics. The natural cadences of English prose, poetry and the spoken word have always been more readily understood in terms of accentual patterns. So whilst attention must be paid to the total length of the verse, and here the raw number of syllables might have a part to play, its execution is an entirely different matter.

Amongst the few who gave the subject much house room, towards the end of the last century a minority position had therefore developed. Given that the lines must go short/long/short, the 5/7/5 morae of the Japanese haiku, hokku or chouku might be best emulated by a pattern of 2/3/2 stresses—unaccented syllables filling in at will.

Feet and lines

This proposal—2/3/2 stresses—is certainly an advance on the 5/7/5 syllables of popular mythology. But it remains flawed. It is predicated on Chamberlain's other, crucial, misidentification—that of the metrical foot with the line.

As the chapters *Cut or Uncut?* and *Know Your Enemy* go on about until they are blue in the face, the one thing a Japanese long verse *does not* do is split into three lines, images or phrases—short/long/short or otherwise. The only thing there are three of in the Japanese long verse are metrical feet—five morae, followed by seven, followed by five. These have everything to do with the length of the stanza and give a rough indication of its scansion, but they do not of themselves dictate the image order or phrasal structure. They do not control the meaning.

In the form of a haiku or hokku the most common phrase structure of the long verse is an asymmetrical divide of roughly 1/3 to 2/3, or else 2/3 to 1/3, in which the syntax is effectively end-stopped at one of the metrical boundaries whilst the wording at the other metrical boundary reads through uninterrupted. These proportions are also very common for the internal long verses of a renku sequence, though in this case neither metrical foot is grammatically end-stopped as the pause is more a matter of diction than of semantic turn.

The single-image verse is more common to the internal verses of renku, but is sometimes used to mask abstract juxtapositions in a haiku or hokku. Here there are no semantic or syntactic pauses at either metrical boundary. The verse is one unit. It reads through from beginning to end without any significant break.

Least common, either as a cut verse or as an internal renku verse, is a stanza which uses powerful syntactic disjuncture to force a phrasal or semantic pause at a point other than a metrical boundary. Where this does occur the halt is most likely to be at the midpoint of the central metrical foot.

In considering how the Japanese verse applies various semantic overlays to the core metrical divisions it is worth remarking that Japanese enjoys a slight advantage in modularity or flexibility over English. The abundance of post-positional tags and modifiers allows the syntax to be less reliant on word order and long chains of dependency. As a consequence the text more readily segments.

Three lines in English therefore present a problem. In the case of a haiku or hokku, they readily accommodate an end-stopped short phrase tied to the first or last line of the verse. But the transition from one line to another in English always involves a colouration of meaning. Even with the skilful use of enjambment, it can be extremely difficult to reproduce the seamless read through that so readily occurs at the other metrical boundary in the case of a Japanese cut verse, or at both metrical boundaries in the case of a single-image verse.

Centuries of precedent train the English eye and ear to expect a line ending to be *strong*—generally to the extent that it marks off a whole phrase—and the demands of a word-order driven syntax mean there's often little wriggle room as to how long the phrase must be. Factor in the demands of short/long/short—even as a visual quantity—and we suddenly find our options dropping past *few* in the direction of *none whatsoever*.

The conclusion is inevitable. In positing 2/3/2 stresses—short/long/short lines—we are asking the English poet to operate in a vastly more constrained space than is the case for the Japanese. There are just too few verbal constructs and constructions possible. Which tends to suggest that the clap-happy hippies were right all along then, doesn't it? Free love, baby. Free verse.

No it doesn't. Not at all. Just hang fire with the headbands while I go and get my scatter gun.

As it turns out neither the Californian unwashed nor those poetic Edo chaps were the only people to exhibit questionable dress sense. In his day the actor Errol Flynn was famed for an almost unwholesome affinity with doublets and green tights, but no hunk with a pencil moustache more compellingly captured the metamorphosis from purple prose to silver screen. Even as I type I see the insouciant grin. *With one bound he was free!*

So let's stage a bit of theatrics of our own. The three liner has the advantage of being familiar to us as writers, and closely associated with the genre in the popular mind. As our analysis suggests, its principal drawback lies not in the number of lines per se but in their lack of flexibility. The solution is staring us in the face—pencil moustache and all. Short/long/short belongs to Japanese metrics. We should allow the line endings to float. Gadzooks!

Supple Stanzas: Emulating 5/7/5 morae

The idea of Supple Stanzas—caps and all—is hard won. It is the result of a critical appraisal which has developed over time, through the writing of countless haiku or hokku and, most importantly, the opportunity to write a great deal of collaborative linked verse in the style of Matsuo Basho.

Though offered in my name alone it is therefore the fruit of debate and experimentation with many partners whose patience and forbearance cannot be overstated. In recent years I have sought to apply the method to translations from Japanese be they of haiku, hokku or renku. The arguments advanced here, and in related chapters, come after the fact, not before, though hopefully they amount to more than just a retrospective rationale.

My proposal is that the three liner/tercet and two liner/distich may be employed to good effect for all types of original haikai poetry in English, and considered a fair emulation of their original counterparts in translation, when they are approached not as fixed form in the narrowest sense, nor as purely free verse, but as Supple Stanzas employing an accentual metre of seven stressed syllables for the long verse and five stressed syllables for the short verse.

Unlike earlier accentual paradigms the line endings float. The long verse will therefore readily divide as 2/3/2, 3/2/2 or 2/2/3 accented syllables (where the distinction is simply stressed/unstressed). Occasionally 3/1/3 turns out to be effective. Rarely, 3/3/1 or 1/3/3.

The number of unaccented syllables depends on word choice and pause structure—a heavily cut verse often works out at one syllable less—but the total syllable range per stanza is typically thirteen to fifteen.

Supple Stanzas: Emulating 7/7 morae

Mathematically, if seven accented syllables provide a metrical match for the seventeen morae of the Japanese long verse, the fourteen morae of the short verse would equate to 5.8 accented syllables. Logic tell us to round up to a whole number. Therefore to six.

Yet after hundreds of verses in translation, and thousands of original verses in collaboration, five stresses consistently turns out to be the most effective norm, both in terms of the sense of proportion between the stanzas, and for the structural patterns the disparity enables. There will be a reason for this. But I do not know what it is. Having already hoist the soiled flag of experience, I can only cite the penultimate defence of the scoundrel—instinct.

Rather than advance some bogus reasoning it is more honest to just assert that, in my theory of Supple Stanzas, five accented syllables is the most effective and dynamic model for the English-language tanku—the haikai short verse—when this is written conventionally over two lines. Paralleling the long verse, the most common division is 3/2 or 2/3, with 4/1 and 1/4 making an occasional appearance. The typical syllable range is between nine and eleven in total.

Listening and responding

As with the 5/7/5 and 7/7 morae of the Japanese, the reader is respectfully reminded that variations are possible. Most importantly, simply conforming to this or that stress pattern in English guarantees almost nothing at all beyond the fact that the verse will be roughly the right length. These numbers represent coarse metrical measures. They give some indication of the shape and duration of a verse, but they do not constitute the ideal phrasing of the verse itself. They are a starting point only.

In English the broader rhythm—the full music of the stanza—depends on a felicitous mix of accented and unaccented syllables, their selection based in part on how their relative amplitude and duration interact with the pause structures generated by line breaks, punctuation and phrasal discontinuities. All the while, as Gilbert and Yoneoka suggest (*Know Your Enemy*), there is every likelihood that beneath the stratum of our conscious understanding there is the beat of a different drum.

Why does this matter?

We are writing poetry. How can the sound of the words *not* matter? And given the excesses of the late 20th century surely it is time to move on.

In respect of verse structure it was often stated that elasticity of syllable length, variability of stress, rigidity of syntax or indeed some other quirk or difficulty of language must necessarily preclude the realisation of any tangible sense of form in English haikai. To judge from the depth of thought behind them such claims rarely amounted to anything more than a thinly disguised boast that our language was raw, real and free. Unlike that of less imaginative peoples.

For stand-alone verses, at a practical level at least, such lazy distortions may be of little account. We can ignore the competing agendas and simply get on with our writing. But in linked verse—and in Shofu renku in particular—form cannot be ignored. The regular beat of proportional cadences, the ability to echo, reflect, contrast and otherwise exchange phonological features within and between stanzas is an essential part of the art. These are tools which the poet deploys to support and inflect the more subtle cognitive effects. They enhance grace and cogency. We neglect them at our peril.

It is not my intention to propose that all English renku must use this or any other style of prosody for it to have merit. The Supple Stanzas are there for the reader to make of what they will. Used well, in conjunction with a flair for expressive language, I believe they allow the English poet to access the vast majority of techniques available to Japanese writers. But the most important lesson to be drawn from reading the classics is that in order to write renku one must first listen. And having listened one may then respond. Not just to the meaning of the preceding verse, but to its totality. And that must include the sound of its language—a quality the Imagists knew as *euphony*.

Run that by me again

If you've sneaked directly to the back of this chapter—smoothly done! You can ignore the rest. Here's what it all boils down to:

Long verse: Seven stressed syllables: 2/3/2, 3/2/2, 2/2/3 (3/1/3, 3/3/1, 1/3/3) total range 13:15

Short verse: Five stressed syllables: 3/2, 2/3 (4/1, 1/4) total range 9:11

Use expressive language with confidence. Careful with those lumpy poetic devices. Enjoy.

The Seasons of Renku
what, where, when and why

Widgiki

Season words—the jolly old *kigo*—don't we just love them? If the answer is *yes* you've picked up the wrong book. Here the official policy is that we abhor season words, their lists (*kiyose*) and lexicons (*saijiki*). In fact the correct word is probably *abjure*, as in *Satan and all his works*. Other than that we're pretty much neutral.

If the typescript hasn't all been twisted into paper spillers to light the gas, elsewhere in this unwieldy tome the chapter *What Price Kigo?* deals with the many and various functions of seasonal reference in a renku sequence. Here a thin coat of gloss is applied to the seasons themselves—how they are arrived at, how they are perceived, plus their relative order and duration as core elements of structure.

If we had a little widget-man to log page visits, a pound gets a penny that the schematic diagrams are the only parts of this book that actually get read. This is a shame. They are absolutely whizzo for a quick grapple with this or that type of sequence, but in order to get beyond them it is necessary to understand how and why the seasons appear as they do.

Armed with appropriate knowledge it is possible to arrive at an almost infinite number of permutations, even for something that looks fairly fixed like a kasen or triparshva. Also, if you are unfortunate enough to find yourself closeted with the type of oik who insists on using a widgiki full of sago words—or whatever they're called—as the answer to world peace, you can blind them with your erudition about the why of their limitations, whereas they will be stuck wringing their hands over the what of their nominal locations.

Five to four

Renku Reckoner is all about Shofu renku. But in English, not Japanese. And now, not three hundred years ago. It therefore uses the four seasons of the Northern Temperate Zone: spring, summer, autumn and winter. Conveniently these also appear in the source tradition. Inconveniently, they had a fifth: new year.

As if that wasn't bad enough, Japanese culture has a completely different take on when the seasons start and end. Given that plants and animals tend to get on with things regardless of our wish to conform, this turns out to have some serious ramifications for the trans-national Widgikists.

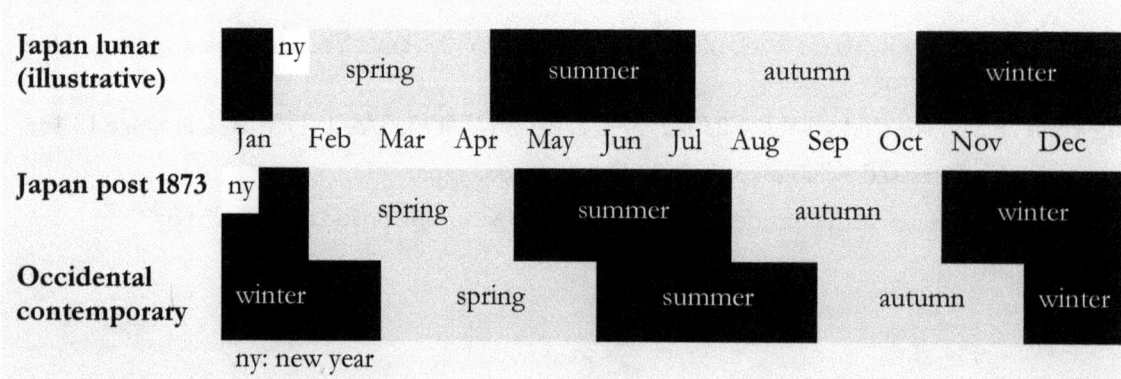

A gawp at the calendar

Row 1 above. Until the late 19th century various types of lunar reckoning held sway in Japan. Because of the vagaries of the lunar cycle any given month could exhibit considerable mobility with respect to the solar year, periodically obliging the intercalation of a leap month in order to realign the calendar with the climate. Winter was reckoned to end along with the calendar year. New Year, as a haikai season in its own right, therefore occupied the first two weeks of what would otherwise be spring.

Row 2 above. With the adoption of the Gregorian calendar in 1873, the new year festivities transferred to the first two weeks of January. However, as the seasons were now deemed to centre on the solstices and equinoxes, new year no longer straddled the cusp between winter and spring, instead being located wholly within the latter part of winter.

Given that the renku seasons need to flow if they are to be effective this official repositioning had the effect of making new year problematic as a separate poetic entity. Most Japanese renku now uses the four regular seasons only, new year being construed as *late winter*. But the lunar calendar still dictates the timing and naming of most cultural and religious festivals, so the many related season words may seem irregular, anomalous or anachronistic.

Row 3 above. In pre-Christian northern Europe the seasons were also considered to take the solstices and equinoxes as their midpoint. However the post-enlightenment consensus throughout the English speaking world has been to revert to the Roman model and reckon the seasons by temperature rather than insolation.

Accordingly, autumn begins in September for a Scotsman, but August for a Japanese. Yet the capercaillie dance to spite them both.

A month is a long time for a growing carrot too. So the urge to ascribe everything to a specific slot in a named season is fraught with difficulty if we all want to use the same list of kigo. At least it is if we want that list to bear some resemblance to what is actually going on in the cabbage patch.

Major and minor seasons

Since as early as the Heian period the Japanese arts have displayed a tendency to associate mood and season. Japan is a mountainous country. Winters can be long and hard. Summers are no less lethal, being hot and extremely humid. So it is not surprising that spring and autumn are viewed in a more positive light, or that they have been mined to a greater depth for emotional overtones.

Spring and autumn are also the seasons of greatest agricultural significance, of planting and harvest, birth and cull. Though recorded literature was initially the preserve of the nobility and the metropolitan elites, rural themes—albeit idealised—were stock subjects, animated by the usual pliant archetypes: the wandering monk, the honest pauper, the stoical farmer etc.

The rise of haikai saw a new and more realistic emphasis placed on the concerns of the common man, culminating in Basho's mature style of *karumi* which advocated the simple depiction of lived experience whilst elevating popular hopes and aspirations to a level of dignity previously reserved for great lovers and heroes. Even today, despite the overwhelmingly urban nature of Japanese society, it is thought completely natural that linked verse should rely heavily on the seasons as elements of structure, that those seasons will tend to have associated tonal palettes, and that spring and autumn will be more present than summer and winter. For many modern Japanese poets a sensitivity to nature is held to be more relevant now than ever as it is essential to our ability to face what is perceived as a global ecological crisis. Paradoxically, advocates of restrictive, culturally specific and archaic systems of seasonal reference are often avowed internationalists.

With the exception of the more radical interpretations of the Rokku, and the controversial speculations of Mr Capes (see *New Junicho*), all formal types of renku are therefore composed of approximately equal numbers of miscellaneous (non-season) and season verses. Of the latter, a larger proportion are ascribed to spring and autumn than to summer and winter. The ratio for the twelve verse shisan being 2:1, for the nijuin 3:2, whilst the kasen is somewhere in between.

It should be noted that within these proportions the two *major* seasons are roughly co-equal, as are the two *minor*. Spring will take a similar number to autumn. Summer will take a similar number to winter, though for longer sequences the season in which a composition is begun may tilt the allotted number of verses slightly in its favour.

Please note that the usage of major and minor in reference to the season is my own suggestion. It is not offered as a translation of Japanese terminology. Neither is it widespread in other English language sources.

Order and duration

So much for the generality. But how do things work out in practice? What are the principles that govern the ordering of the seasons? And their duration—the number of so-and-so that may be strung together at any one time?

Necessarily some of the following bullet points involve a degree of simplification and idealisation. In the case of the kasen they are more reflective of modern theoretical descriptions than Edo period practice. However, with a bit of thought, they will allow the reader to arrive at practical variations to the type of fixed layouts found here and elsewhere.

- all formal renku start with the season in which composition takes place, or, in the case of a very slow paced composition, the season in which a poem is begun

- in all but the most modern and free-form types of renku the wakiku—verse two—takes the same season as the hokku—verse one

- other than for the yotsumono, all the seasons will be represented in a poem, and will appear in the proportions outlined above

- in most types of renku sequence the seasons do not appear in calendar order, the shisan being the only regular exception

- in all types of renku, verses taking the same major season appear in clusters

- in longer renku, verses taking the same minor season also tend to appear in clusters

- in common practice, different seasonal clusters are separated by at least one miscellaneous verse

- after this minimum separation, a major season will tend to follow a minor season, and vice versa

- where two major seasons are obliged to appear in succession they will be separated by at least two non-season verses, generally by three

- particularly in the Edo period, a season will sometimes move directly to another without an intervening clear verse, strong linkage permitting

- two instances of the same season or seasonal cluster will not appear in succession—**wi wi ns ns wi** is avoided

- a season or seasonal cluster will not normally revert after only one other season has intervened—**sp sp ns ns su ns sp sp** is avoided, especially in close succession

- in longer renku major season verses tend to appear in clusters of three, though in the kasen they may extend to four or five in a row
- in longer renku minor season verses tend to appear in pairs, though in the kasen they may extend to three in a row

If you refer to the schematic guides, and have a pencil handy, it should now be possible to sketch in some appropriate variations. The trick is not to panic. These things are guides to a structural outline. They give a bare bones only. No matter how ingeniously arrived at, a seasonal distribution is not a poem in itself.

As to issues of correctness: there will always be people who get a buzz from wearing armbands. You can borrow my *Renku Police* one if you like. But there is waiting list.

The internal chronology of a season run

While the seasons themselves rarely turn up in calendar order the *internal* chronology of a run of season verses is naturalistic. The reason is straightforward. Renku does not cope well with an impediment to flow. Whilst our audience are unlikely to baulk at the introduction of winter as a topic two clear verses after the end of spring—it is surprising how rapidly a well written sequence moves on—nobody burns the very last of the fallen leaves before setting out to harvest their apples, or slogs home through deeply drifted snow only to remark that they have just noticed the first few signs of winter.

As an aid to avoid anachronism, and to the evident relief of all those who like to have the obvious written on their foreheads, the widgikis of sago ascribe one of four positional characteristics to a season word. The deeply stressed poet must therefore choose wisely from *early*, *mid*, *late* and *all*. An *all spring* reference may appear anywhere in a run of spring verses, but the others have to respect some sort of order. If only I could remember what it was.

To be fair, the positional tags are not there because the people using them are too stupid to know that night follows day. It is simply that the precise temporal positioning of a given season word, and sometimes the very season to which it allegedly belongs, may be so arbitrary that it is impossible to judge by any form of natural logic whether it should belong to mid spring, late autumn or early whatever-the-other-one's-called.

For the growing number of poets who reject fixed seasonal association the principle is simplicity itself. Within a run of season verses the natural order of events is respected in order to prevent illogical combinations or loops. For those who feel obliged to use season word lists—have you thought of taking up train spotting?

Whatever next?

Japan is a long archipelago. Climatologists politely refer to it as temperate—a term that covers a multitude of sins. It is cold in the north. Much hotter in the south. But the two great historic centres. Kyoto and Edo (Tokyo), are relatively close together at a mid point in the island chain. For centuries, irrespective of where they were actually based, provincial poets have pretended to come from the big city. For all that it is supposedly an expression of oneness with nature, the depiction of season has often been a simple exercise in conformity—at best an opportunity to frame an aspiration.

Something similar is at work in English. Our literary frame of reference is still largely tied to the British Isles and northern European culture. In the main any decent poet from Adelaide to Barbados is *able* to handle a seasonal iconography typical of Sussex in June, and express the appropriate sentiments. But why would they want to? It is not as if Blake had Florida in mind when he waxed lyrical about his *green and pleasant land*.

What price such commonality? Is it desirable? Is it sustainable? When the man from Burkina Faso writes of snow—is this art, or artifice?

Proponents of a uniform approach to seasonality (i.e. that which obtains in Japan) argue that there is increased expressivity to be had from the many extra-textual layers that the traditional system of reference has encoded over time. And if everyone sings from the same hymn sheet there will at least be a functional degree of harmony. It may be a little forced. But that's true for the Japanese poet too. So it is forced for everybody in more or less equal measure. And there is the added bonus that contemporary writing will synch more readily with the historic corpus of haikai.

For all my cheap point-scoring here and elsewhere, these arguments cannot simply be dismissed out of hand. It is not hard to see how they appear to offer a quick and effective way around a knotty problem. Set against them though is the deeply held conviction, perhaps more typical of English haikai than Japanese, that any form of artificiality is wrong. Fundamentally. Irrevocably. Without exception. If we are serious about our art, even a lightweight pastime like a game of renku (*splutter, choke*) must draw on the artist's true experience. We cannot pretend that we are in Yoshino unless we have actually been there. And that rules out the 1680s altogether.

One solution is to formulate a Kenyan or a North American saijiki—projects which are currently underway with varying degrees of success. Such initiatives offer the prospect of a system of reference that reflects the importance a nation or region invests in their particular seasons and seasonal events. But it also highlights a paradox which lies at the heart of the debate: if seasonal reference *a* or *b* is truly iconic in a given culture, why would it need listing in the first place?

Another solution is to dispense with any formal system of seasonal reference altogether—not just when it comes to the fixed associations which freight the lists of season words but also, in the case of renku, as an element of structure too.

At first sight this is exactly what Ashley Capes proposes with his revolutionary *new junicho*. But in fact Mr Capes is more subtle—and a better poet—than to advocate a wholesale policy of slash and burn. The new junicho raises a more nuanced question: if a verse which is nominally winter may take music as its main subject, why shouldn't a verse which is nominally music have winter as its mainstay?

The essential truth Mr Capes highlights is that a season, as a verse designation, is a matter of context only. Only the most crude of approaches to composition would suggest that to honour an obligation to refer to something or other is a guarantee of success as poetry.

One cannot help feeling that, as with the importance of season words to the wider haikai arts, the entire edifice of seasonal structure in renku has been raised to a level of significance that it does not really merit. This is not to suggest that it is irrelevant. The skilful use of existing conventions can enhance both diversity and cohesion. But, as renku becomes naturalised in many more languages and cultures, we must expect and celebrate the emergence of fresh seasonal structures just as readily as we now welcome the presence of new season words.

Surely it is impossible to write twenty verses in Bengali or Hindi without mentioning the monsoon, its moods and its impact on human affairs. Unless the author was raised in Kyoto. Or Brighton.

What Price Kigo?
the function of seasonal reference in renku

Introduction

Somewhere under my coffee cup are notes for a chapter on *The Seasons of Renku*. Last time I looked this dealt with ideas of what constitutes a season in the historic literature, the way these fed into the macro-structure of a sequence, and some current trends in same.

The present pages do something different. Here we look at the tactical use of seasonal reference at any given point in a sequence, and test the belief that we must do so via *kigo*—season words.

Whilst the generality of the material in *The Seasons* applies to any form of linked verse drawn on the Japanese model, some of the following comments, particularly those on variety, refer more narrowly to the Basho school.

So, with a suitably rhetorical flourish, we ask the question: *what is the function of seasonal reference in Shofu renku?*

Correctness

The formalist answer is that the inclusion of an appropriate season word, at a preordained juncture, is a requirement. It ensures that a verse is correctly composed i.e. that it follows the *rules*. For those of us who like rules this is sufficient in itself. One has only to examine a diagram of a shisan or read a description of a kasen to know that there are enough rules to make Joseph Stalin look like a liberal.

Unfortunately, if we actually read Basho, two things become clear. Firstly he tells us to learn the rules, then break them. Secondly he points out that adherence to requirements of season, topic, structure, and tone guarantee absolutely nothing at all. Such considerations are the starting point for a verse. They do not, and can never, constitute the verse itself.

Will the box-checker please return to the warehouse.

Will the Czech boxer please leave the ring. Ding!

In the Basho school, notions of correctness are at best marginal, and at worst an impediment. If we wish to approach anything resembling *fuga no makoto* (poetry as truth and art) we will not do so with a mindset dominated by rules. In the main Basho did adhere to contemporary seasonal conventions. But in his day there were fewer. He recast them at will. And the word *kigo* did not exist.

Variety

Shofu renku is not thematic. It is quintessentially anti-thematic. Central to the genre are notions of totality and oneness-through-variety inherited from Shingon and Zen Buddhism. Shinto also, at an expressive level at least, supplies an animist element.

Acute sensitivity to the seasons, and their reciprocity with the human condition, is the very stuff of Shofu renku. In both a metaphorical and a metaphysical manner, a poem will embrace all seasons. And all estates. A seasonal context prompts the writer to explore both man and his environment. Taken together, the full span of seasons can better evoke the sum of life's experience, each serving as a figurative representation of the other.

A seasonal reference is therefore not really a constraint at all. It is an invitation. It may nudge the recalcitrant contributor, but it compels no-one. Should any conflict arise between convention and an instinct for the direction of a particular sequence we can simply follow Basho's example and mould the convention to fit. Or, for the moment at least, discard it.

Reality

Any modern poet with an interest in haiku will be familiar with the theories of Masaoka Shiki. In particular with his resolve to be genuine in his writing. To this end, Shiki advocated the technique of *shasei* (to sketch from life). Shasei demands close observation and accurate depiction of the real world, and values lived experience over imagined circumstance—a lack of artificiality readily found by grounding one's work in nature.

Shiki's radical veracity was a reaction to the excesses of a moribund literature crammed with elaborate drivel. By the dawn of the Meiji period, haikai had indeed become a sad and corrupted spectacle. Not unreasonably therefore the perception has since taken hold that natural simplicity is the new style of haikai, and baroque decoration the old.

But the suggestion that the natural world might serve as a foil to artificiality can be found in Nijo Yoshimoto's treatises on courtly renga. That was in the 14th century. It has been repeated many times since. Not least by Basho himself.

Though some of his early writings belong to the fantastical Danrin school, Basho's mature style places great emphasis on the simple depiction of things as they are. One way to convey that reality is to give a strong sense of the natural world and the passage of time.

Axes

It is generally understood that the Basho school's elevation of haikai no renga to the status of high art was achieved against a background of the progressive loosening of the strictures which had hitherto conditioned and constrained so much of linked verse—the sainted *shikimoku*. There have been few literary genres in the history of mankind as densely codified as medieval Japanese renga. In terms of micro management, Basho's approach represented a radical simplification.

It is less commonly remarked that a countervailing dynamic was underway in respect of seasonal reference, specifically in the compilation of lists of topics imbued with a precise, and widely recognised, relevance to a particular time of year.

This process had begun seriously with Sogi in the late 15th century but only started to gather pace in Basho's day. Clearly sensing the direction of travel, he warned against becoming obsessive in such things. By 1800 the 1,000 core seasonal terms his immediate disciples might have recognised had more than trebled to 3,300. At last count a *saijiki*—a dedicated seasonal lexicon—may contain in excess of 15,000 *kigo* (season words). That's enough to write 813 kasen without danger of repeating oneself. Or, for those serious about rules, one must now write 813 kasen before being allowed a repeat.

The term kigo is a relative neologism, and is not necessarily an advance on earlier usages which tended to centre on *kisetsu* (common-to-a-season). When one talks of *season word* the impression is too readily gained that simply by wielding this or that lexeme an appropriate level of poetic insight is on show. Factor in the seemingly endless desire to ascribe every word under the sun not just to a season, but to a particular part of a season, and we have that age old curse: the superficial dressed as the profound.

But despite the downright absurdity of such check-box rectitude, one aspect of the development of recognized seasonal topics (*kidai*) and their associated season words (*kigo*) does bear serious consideration. This is the concept of *hon'i* (poetic essence). It describes the aggregation of common associations, cultural traditions, and artistic references that cleave to a particular bird, plant, agricultural activity, festival etc.

These are the qualities that distinguish the iconic from the generic in any society. Handled with care they add layers of resonance and suggestion. Access to such overtones can provide vital enrichment to verses that are too brief to permit elucidation and would be overpowered by compound metaphors and the like.

Some contemporary English-language critics term this type of transfer by association a *vertical axis* and contrast it with the plain or primary meaning of a word which is its *horizontal axis*. In so far as a season word has tangible hon'i its use may serve not only to ground a verse in the natural world, but also to enhance its range and evocative power through inter-textual and extra-textual reference.

But there is a problem: few things could be more culturally specific than the associations which give something iconic status. Does the mention of *fireworks display* evoke Thanksgiving (USA), Guy Fawkes night (UK), high summer Hanabi (Japan) or Chinese New Year?

To a degree this dilemma has existed for centuries. Japan is a long chain of islands; cherry trees blossom in Kyushu, to the south, months before they do in Hokkaido, to the north. But the centres of metropolitan power, Kyoto and Edo (Tokyo), are relatively central and relatively close. So, from the earliest years, poets have taken their cue from those blessed with a foothold in the capital.

From time to time there are faint stirrings of demand for regional saijiki. But, in renku as in haiku, the vast majority of Japanese writers make reference to a single corpus of seasonal reference as it obtains in a fictional Edo/Kyoto.

True to oneself

So ingrained is the habit of trading in fixed seasonal associations that it is not unusual to encounter otherwise intelligent people who genuinely believe that something in the national psyche makes the Japanese soul uniquely attuned to the relationship between man and creation. It is only logical therefore that all poets, of whatever nationality, should use the Japanese system of seasonal reference. It is the most extensive available, and must necessarily be superior in kind to those which might be elaborated by the more insensate.

The racial stereotyping evidenced by such attitudes is unintentional. But it is gross. Not least for the ghastly prospect of the hordes of occidental orientalists proclaiming their fealty to kelp. Literature is not a charade. The *Oku no Hosomichi* is neither Route 66 nor the Via Appia.

Cohesion and linkage

As seasonal reference has grown ever more systematised, a number of words have remained simply *autumn* or *summer* etc. but the majority have been assigned more precise temporal positions. We therefore encounter *usurai* (thin ice) as *early spring*, *taue* (rice planting) as *midsummer*, *kuri* (chestnuts) as *late autumn* and so on. Many ascriptions are entirely reasonable. Others seem plucked from the air. Why would *watamushi* (bed bugs) be found under *early winter*, for example? Why under *winter* at all? Every Englishman's home is his castle. And in my castle we have bed bugs all year.

The recent fashion for compact forms has obscured the fact that longer sequences may permit a single season to run for as many as five verses. Though the calendar rarely dictates the order in which the seasons appear, their internal chronology is one-way. Renku abhors anything which halts its flow. In a tight-knit group, time's arrow rules. The Beaujolais Nouveau comes *after* the grape harvest, not before. The damp smell of burning leaves presages the end of autumn, not its beginning.

Particularly in longer sequences, this linearity of time-frame can add an element of cohesion to a strand of verses. Even in the shortest forms, where adjacent verses share the same season, the congruence allows other components greater scope to tighten or loosen at will.

But to link solely through shared season is poor writing. A contextual element should not be brought to the fore. Not only is this pedestrian it is profoundly mistaken. If Shofu is anti-thematic, a season cannot function as a theme.

In any event, we do well to remember that a verse may reference the appropriate season with the precision of an atomic clock and still be in every way dreadful.

Cycles and stages

The fashion for shorter sequences has also given rise to the belief that renku demands the headlong pursuit of variety at all cost. Nothing of any sort may be repeated in any fashion, for to do so would be to commit the chimeric crime of backlink.

With a fair wind, and much ill deserved luck, such up-country methods may suffice for a twelve verse sequence. Apply them to anything more demanding and the fruit will wither on the vine.

The macro-structure of the kasen makes it plain that fine renku relies more on modulation and re-contextualisation than on striving for absolute novelty. In the kasen the seasons make a loosely cyclical appearance. But a cycle is not a duplication. Skilful writers know how to balance the meeting and defeating of expectation. And the seeds of expectation can be sown in the cycle.

Whilst longer renku allow for a degree of flexibility in the order and duration of seasonal passages, highly prominent verses such as autumn moon and spring blossom are awaited with anticipation.

Working in combination with the folio divisions these relatively fixed points are staging posts for a poem's development, helping to control the overall sense of shape, and functioning as way markers for the unfolding of the sequence. Paradoxically therefore, a seasonal reference may both evoke the cyclical qualities of the cosmos whilst marking the linear evolution of the poem itself.

In sum

A seasonal reference is often multivalent, and its effect is multiplex. The presence of an authorised word will not improve a verse composed without understanding. And understand comes hardest with alien referents.

Not only is it invidious to suggest that a person should disregard their culture for another's, artistically it is a nonsense. Why else is there so little *dwile flonking* in Basho.

But contrivance can be a problem at the local level too. The well grounded observations of the early Japanese masters have surely met their reductio ad absurdum in the modern saijiki.

Just because a word is touted as a kigo does not mean that it has hon'i. And if something truly has hon'i, why would it need listing in the first place?

Explaining it all Away
strictly need to know

It's not big

and it's not clever—as my Granny used to say—so I've deleted the earlier drafts of this piece and will now try for a version with fewer expletives. Please excuse the authorial I, for once there's no hiding behind the passive.

Some things I feel passionate about. And this is one of them. I want to address the merits and demerits of the participants in a composition explaining, whether briefly or at length, what precisely they intend by advancing *a*, *b* or *c* as a word choice, as a conceptual choice, or as a mode of linkage, when they have proposed, or are about to propose, a candidate verse. Here we go…

Merits? There are none. That's it. You can stop reading now if you like. Demerits? They are legion, and I'll get to them in just a second. But first a touch of clarification. Above I do say *participants in a renku composition*, the key word being *composition*. If it's a renku workshop, or a renku seminar, or a renku demonstration, or a renku fun-session, or any form of structured renku learning situation, then clearly a free dialogue, trialogue or catalogue are absolutely fine. Discuss away—your cat will remain unharmed. Unless it comes in my garden.

A case in pointless

The situation I have in mind is a group of peers—people of equal experience—intending to write to the highest standards. The kind of thing Basho and Co aimed for. None of that *renku is a literary pastime* malarkey. High art. Fuga no makoto. And we're just in time for the hokku. So bring on Vinnie, Minnie and Winnie who, being egalitarians, eschew all notion of leadership.

a mobile phone call
much to my surprise
the April night

Vinnie: I think we should use this one of mine. It's fresh. Modern, thanks to the mobile phone reference, but that *April night* feels like classical kigo too. I thought it was Issa but in fact it's from Donadei: *La Ragazza della Notte d'Aprile*. Full of suspense and romance. Anyway, it's April so it fits. And it flags up where we want to go. Wasn't it Fukuda, who said that everything flows from the hokku?

Winnie: Ooooh I like this Vinnie. But it doesn't really do the cutting thing. Higginson says a haiku can be either way, but a hokku has to have one. At least I think so. My sister's got my copy of the *Handbook*.

Minnie: And here's my come-back Vinnie—*much to my surprise* as the bridge. That's like kokorozuke—heart link. Maybe I've left the season open. But *beer drinking* is definitely spring kigo in these parts—winters are hard and we don't get out much. Makes for big families! Here goes—it'll pop your top!

a mobile phone call
much to my surprise
the April night

scribbled on a beer mat
absent moon

The Author: I won't comment on the verses. The exchanges are the nub. Obviously these people are pleasant enough and enjoy each other's company, but what does Vinnie actually tell us about the hokku that isn't already evident at first reading? As it happens I've read that book by Donadei, but, if I hadn't, is Vinnie telling me that I wouldn't properly get the verse? Is recognition of the reference to *La Ragazza della Notte d'Aprile* essential? And what's that stuff about Fukuda? Given that he always had half an eye on renga as well as renku theory, it is highly probable that Fukuda-sensei did indeed say, or was hazardously translated as saying, something along those lines. But what's the relevance? Or is Vinnie just engaged on a bit of enthusiastic name checking in order to boost our estimation of his hokku?

The Author continues: Winnie certainly thinks so, and retaliates by citing Higginson. Mistakenly, of course. But the hokku candidate does at least get her vote. Provisionally. Minnie, less of an equivocator, is not prepared to wait until Winnie's sister returns from Guatemala with the loaned copy of the *Haiku Handbook* in order to check on the thingamibob. Instead she has felt compelled to write a responding verse. Minnie's enthusiasm is commendable. But even before posting the text she has told her partners that the verse is deliberately experimental, that the link back to the hokku is predicated on a given phrase, that this style of link should be compared to a specific Japanese technique, and that the seasonal reference may be rather oblique, but that it is nevertheless authentic because of the particular circumstances of her home state. Oh yes, and that they are certain to be stunned by the verse. Now that's a lot of priming! But how do said partners respond? Let's look at the putative opening pair again, then at the feedback:

a mobile phone call
much to my surprise
the April night

scribbled on a beer mat
absent moon

Vinnie: Yeah, no argument. It's everything you said and more. Hey but *absent moon*...

Minnie: I told you it'd be *much to your surprise*!

Winnie: Now I know for sure that we can't do that. I once ended up in a kasen with John Carley. He was pushing everyone around, like he does. But I remember him saying the moon had to be in a moon verse—it definitely had to be the main thing. You can't demean it. Or something. Because it's noble.

Vinnie: Yeah the guy's a pain. More to the point he's plain wrong. This isn't a kasen—we should experiment. Put a footnote in if needed. Come on Winnie, you're up next. What's in your sky?!

The Author: They bounce arguments back and forth about moon positions without actual moons until Winnie is placated. But, when she does settle down to write, the verse flashes back through the ether by return...

a mobile phone call
much to my surprise
the April night

scribbled on a beer mat
absent moon

a single swift
ghosts off the screen
at 13,000 ft

Vinnie: Woooah!

Minnie: Yeah, yeah. That's amazing. How does that work? I get it on some level but I just can't see how you work out the link.

Winnie: Well I was thinking of unusual absence—like the moon—and I remembered that swifts don't land for years after fleeing the nest. True. They even sleep when they're flying. Like the moon—lol. Which isn't in the sky either—like they're not in the nest. Anyway we need a nature verse. And it just came straight to mind.

Minnie: Truly. But it's pretty left field. I mean it's a great verse. But you know—even with a note—I'm not sure if people are going to be able to work it out.

Vinnie: Yeah, now you say that I'm not too sure either Min. I mean, it felt like a fit straight off. But when you think about it it's pretty… oblique. Even for you Winnie! Maybe we should, you know, vote on it. Or go another way here at #3?

The Author: Ah, but the problem with votes when there are only three participants is that it ends up as two against one. Which is perilously close to bullying. Our friends know this instinctively, and so begins an increasingly dilatory round of exchanges in which nothing is achieved beyond the realisation that the chaos which eats at the margins of our souls can only be kept at bay by ever more lavish pledges of mutual fidelity. As the protestations of sincerity grind ever more finely our poem slips quietly to its doom.

Which is a shame, because they had instinctively loved that third verse.

Really so careless

So we arrive at the point of this particular exercise in vituperation. Ladies and Gentlemen—are you concerned that the emperor may indeed be naked? Is renku nothing more than a conspiracy to self-deceive? Does the whole edifice crumble unless we lard our verses with explanation after explanation?

Hats off to anyone who has answered *Yes*. Why else would we want to surround our candidate verses with masses of additional information? If the extra content is essential to an understanding of the verse, doesn't that mean the verse is deficient? If the bumff is there simply to add gravitas to our candidate, doesn't that mean we fear the verse is weak? If we must lay claim to the authority of A. N. Expert, doesn't that mean we are unsure of our technique? If it is truly necessary to cite *tsuki no kage*, why not have done with it and write in Japanese throughout?

Similarly with prepping our colleagues for the quirks of the verse we are about to offer. The systematic management of expectations is best left to politicians. If you really think that *beer drinking* is a spring kigo the best thing to do is move state, take up macrame, and sacrifice your cat to the darkness. It won't make the slightest difference to the quality of your writing, but it will give the rest of us a laugh.

The same goes for lengthy expositions of the rationale behind our linkage. What can pre-loading the space between verses do other than limit the scope for resonance? Ladies and Gentlemen. Boys and Girls. What's the first lesson in a writing class? It's *show*. Show don't tell. If your linkage works it doesn't need describing or rationalising. If it needs describing or rationalising that's because it doesn't work. Write another verse. It's quicker.

The essential truth is so basic here that we are in danger of losing sight of it altogether. When we write renku our partners are not primarily respondents, they are first and foremost readers. A colleague cannot move on to the composition of an answering verse until they have first experienced the verse to which they wish to respond. It is better that said experience is theirs and theirs alone, without the encumbrance of specious justifications, special informations, cute insinuations, or emotional manipulations.

There's a very good reason for this. It is called *Basho*. Basho explicitly and purposefully moved the ground away from word links, object links, and analysis in his poetics to put intuition front and centre. Another word for this is *artistry*. If it feels good, it is good. If it doesn't feel good, that's because it is bad. Certainly—you can brow-beat the reader into believing that they haven't understood *a, b* or *c* because they have failed to go away and study the accompanying volume of footnotes with sufficient diligence. But you can only do it for so long. Eventually they will shrug and walk away. Hopefully to go and read something resembling poetry.

To be clear, I am railing here against something very specific. I am asking you to beware the temptation to engage in all sorts of extended analysis, description and rationalisation before the selection of a verse. And I'm not talking about discussion of the phrasing, or the cadence, or the wider phonics of the candidate verse, but about its meaning and the reasons for its linkage.

The white space of interpretation is where the real action of a sequence takes place. If we freight it with prepared opinions we diminish its power. If we wall it with precisions we impede imagination. That all belongs to the technical workshop. Not to the act of writing.

With his proposal of scent linkage Basho placed the magic of instinctual recognition at the heart of renku. Are we really so careless of the great man's legacy that we'll willingly explain it all away?

Exercises
snatching the pebble

Do I have to do them?

No. If you are already a renku genius there is absolutely no need to read or write anything further. Ever.

If however you feel there is still the teeniest bit of room for improvement in your technique these four exercises might prove useful. Two are traditional, therefore Japanese. Two are the work of the current author. All have been field tested.

The exercises are presented in a notional order of difficulty but can be tackled upside down and back to front. The reader might care to develop their own workout routine for those days when their renku buddies have gone to ground.

Copyright

The exercises require the participant to respond to the published work of others. In almost all cases the source materials will be under copyright. Therefore there are legalities to consider.

Copyright law varies between countries. Please check your particular jurisdiction. There are however certain commonalities. Where an exercise is conducted in a private space for personal reasons there is no cause for concern. If the workspace is open to all, in a physical or virtual sense, issues of public access might need to be considered. Closed groups are less likely to be problematic. Messages exchanged between individuals on social media platforms may be treated as publication if the exchanges are archived and those archives freely accessible. Group exercises, particularly in structured contexts which involve monetary gain for an individual or institution, are likely to fall foul of copyright restrictions.

Whilst limited exceptions apply in academic contexts, the general rule is that the work of others should never be offered for publication, in any form or medium, without the copyright holder's express permission. Please be aware that, in the case of translations, whilst the source text may be long out of copyright, rights to the text of the translation remain with the individual translator and, unless the translation itself is very old, are likely to be in force.

In this chapter therefore the translations of historic texts offered as resources are copyright to John or John and Edith Carley. Other named contemporaries have kindly ceded copyright for their verses to appear in this format for this publication only. The wider text of the present chapter, like that of the book itself, is copyright to John Carley.

Be in no doubt that to reproduce the work of others without their permission is theft.

Wakiokori—add a wakiku to a hokku

What

Wakiokori is a traditional exercise. The element *waki* means *support*. Readers will be familiar with the word *wakiku*: a supporting verse. In many instances, having adopted a hokku by an acknowledged master in order to honour a particular anniversary, place or undertaking, poets employing wakiokori will go on to write an entire sequence. Here *wakiokori* is intended in its narrower sense of *to put in place a wakiku*.

How

Choose a top quality hokku or haiku by someone good. You are next up. Try and compose a following verse. Now try and compose some alternatives. Keep at it until you have a broad range of choices. Three takes on the same idea don't count.

Resources

Below are translations from the Japanese of hokku by past masters. To get started try these as your head verses. When sourcing other materials to work with, please be alert to issues of copyright.

The chapter *Beginnings and Endings* might prove useful. As might *Cut or Uncut?*

waking not
from the dreamscape
— morning glories!   Suejo **hokku, Morning Glories. Translation: Carley**

November frost —
standing motionless
a line of cranes   Kakei **hokku, November Frost. Translation: Carley and Carley**

a darkening sea
the voices of the ducks
faintly white   Basho **hokku, A Darkening Sea. Translation: Carley**

the black kite peeps
peeps, the spirits too
perhaps make to depart   Issa **hokku, The Black Kite. Translation: Carley**

a trace of the dreams
of warriors past
ah, the summer grass   Basho **independent hokku, The Narrow Road. Translation: Carley**

Considerations

Before we can add a verse we have to enter into the verse to which we are linking. Hokku are always set in a season. As are most haiku. So what season is it? Always remembering that older poems in particular recognise a fifth season: new year.

How is the season indicated? Does the hokku or haiku you have chosen use a season word (*kigo*) with a specific palette of associations? Are there conventions around how one replies to such specific associations? Are there other forms of extra-textual allusion—sometimes referred to as *vertical axes*—present in the piece? Is any or all of the poem figurative? If so, what does it imply?

Does it make any difference if the verse you've picked was written as the head verse to a known sequence, as the verse element of a haiga or haibun, as a free-standing hokku, or as a relatively modern haiku? For instance, the hokku of many classic kasen contain coded greetings and allusions to the circumstances of composition. Is this is so in your case? Should you be trying to answer in kind?

More generally—what is the register of the chosen head verse? What is its tone? What is its intent? Do its structural or phonic properties require a particular form of response? And what style of linkage does it invite?

Less obvious is the question of what one intends to achieve with the added verse. Not all pairings function in the same way, or to the same end.

The tanrenga—*linked verse pair*—is often described as the shortest formal renga or renku sequence. The two verses of a tanrenga are more than complementary; they provide a poem that is complete in itself. Is this what we intend by adding our wakiku to the hokku—to close out the poem and generate a free-standing pair?

Hopefully you answered *no*. The poem should remain open enough to allow the possibility of a third verse. But a deliberately close proximity between hokku and wakiku are typical of Edo period haikai no renga and remain a feature of longer Shofu renku sequences. In this style of writing hokku and wakiku are essentially a single unit. The two verses share the same season, the wakiku limiting itself to the supply of further content specific to the scene established by the hokku. As the name suggests, the wakiku *supports*. The pair are rarely contradictory in tone. Never conflictual.

By contrast trends in modern renku are more radical. Especially in the context of very short sequences such as the junicho and shisan. Here the wakiku may be simply a linking verse, going so far as to challenge and move away from the hokku in a manner more typical of a conventional daisan. In these circumstances, far from generating a degree of closure with the hokku, the intention may be to maximise the pace of opening outwards.

How tight or how loose do you intend your wakiku to be? Why?

Mitsumono—three things

What

Meaning *three things* or perhaps *three states of being*, mitsumono is a traditional exercise.

In the history of renga the first three verses of any folio were afforded special significance. In the case of very long compositions of a thousand verses or more, there are many instances where only the first three verses of any given side were deemed worthy of preservation.

Whereas the term *mitsumono* may be correctly applied to the first three verses of any side of a writing sheet, for the purpose of this exercise it is taken to mean the first three verses of a kasen or similar. Therefore it indicates a hokku, wakiku and daisan written in a conventional Edo period manner.

How

One or more poets compose hokku, wakiku and daisan as if for a complete sequence.

Where only one or two poets participate, this exercise may be combined with wakiokori—the hokku being that of a past master or other poet of acknowledged merit.

Resources

Poets who wish to adopt a hokku by a past master will find some materials under the heading *wakiokori* above. When sourcing other materials to work with, please be alert to issues of copyright.

The chapters *Beginnings and Endings*, and *A Dynamic Pattern* address issues of intention. The chapters *Cut or Uncut?* and *Know Yourself* explore verse construction.

Considerations

When writing a full sequence the hokku always reflects the season in which composition is begun. However, for the purposes of the exercise, poets may compose a hokku in any season. What consequences does the choice of season have for the wakiku, and for daisan? Are there instances in the Edo style where the wakiku takes a different season to the hokku, or is non-season? How about for the third verse, daisan?

Might any of these verses be expected to take a principal fixed topic such as moon or blossom? If so, which season would be more likely to favour their appearance? And were they to appear, would one or other verse position be more conducive? Would moon or blossom be likely to appear in association with a non-season verse? And how about *love*—would that appear in the first three?

Many hokku of the Edo period code a greeting or augury. Should all hokku of this style do so? Does yours? If so, how does the wakiku respond? And what about daisan?

This exercise focuses on the more traditional approach to renku. What does the concept of *jo–ha–kyu* entail for these initial verses? What type of tonal and topical exclusions were typical of the Edo period? What was the purpose of these exclusions? What might a similar set of exclusions look like in your own cultural setting?

Hokku and daisan are referred to as *long verses*, wakiku as *short*. What do these terms signify? A hokku is often described as a *cut* verse. What does this mean? Can any or all of the first three verses be cut verses?

There is a Japanese convention that daisan ends with a verb taking the *te* conjugation. What is the point of this? Is it desirable to emulate this convention in English? If so, how might one do so?

In respect of the core generative dynamic of *link and shift* the daisan is sometimes described as the first *true* or *full* renku verse. Why?

Interjection—to add a bridging verse

What

Interjection is an exercise devised by the present author. It focuses on the fact that a renku verse must flow from the preceding verse, whilst giving rise to the following verse.

When writing renku it is important to look forwards as well as backwards.

How

Two long verses or two short verses are selected from different sources. The poet tries to interject a verse which bridges the two.

The new verse must feel as though it naturally follows on from the first of the selected pair. It must also give rise to the second of the selected pair in an equally unforced manner.

Where the selected pair are long verses, the interjected verse will be short. Where the selected pair are short verses, the interjected verse will be long.

EXERCISES

Resources

Below are some verses from a variety of sources. None are hokku or haiku. Therefore all are suitable as internal verses for a sequence and may be combined in any order.

Poets should select random pairs of long or short verses. Other internal verses (*hiraku*)—i.e. those which are not hokku or haiku—may be co-opted from any worthwhile poet or poets. When sourcing materials, please be alert to issues of copyright.

The chapters *Cut or Uncut?* and *Know Yourself* may be relevant to the way you construct your interjection.

penniless
the paper on the walls
gets daubed with verse   Buson **chouku**, Spying Maiden Grass. Translation: Carley

hard by the creek
at *Lone Retreat*
the worldly cast aside   Jugo **chouku**, November Frost. Translation: Carley

a famed bloom,
from her sleeve
a hint of aloeswood   Suejo **chouku**, Morning Glories. Translation: Carley

in every place
high season for the
third month's blossom   Ko'oku **chouku**, The Hawker's Goose. Translation: Carley

big straw sandals
small straw sandals,
holding them to my feet   Ippyo **chouku**, The Black Kite. Translation: Carley

beneath reed rooves
the charcoal mortars grind   Uritsu **tanku**, November Frost. Translation: Carley & Carley

my upstairs guests   Basho **tanku**, Plum Flowers, Fresh Greens. Translation: Carley &
having left, only autumn   Carley

away from Kyoto
love also ages   Chiyo-ni **tanku**, Morning Glories. Translation: Carley

lightly Chiyo-ni
touches her comb   Windsor **tanku**, Long Twilight

spread, red fall of leaves
like sacred prayer strips   Ippyo **tanku**, The Black Kite. Translation: Carley

the falling leaf
knows only now, and now   Darlington **ageku**, Between the Jagged Rocks

Considerations

The impression is easily gained that renku spends a lot of time looking over its shoulder. This exercise obliges the poet to look forwards as well as backwards.

The recommendation is that pairs of verses are drawn from divergent sources. How unrelated may they be? Does it matter if they are drawn from different linguistic and cultural settings? Does it matter if they are from different epochs?

The exercise states that where the adopted pair are long verses the interjection will be a short verse. And vice versa. But what do the terms *long* and *short* mean in practice? What is the effect if one of the nominal long verses is in fact much more contracted than the other? Or if one of the nominal short verses is rather verbose?

Do questions of metre arise, either within or between verses? And what about phonic qualities such as assonance or onomatopoeia—if they are present in either or both of the adopted verses, how might our interjection respond?

What do we do if our adopted verses are from different seasons? May more than one contain moon, or blossom, or love?

Which is more important for our interjection—looking backwards? Or looking forwards? When writing an actual sequence, why would you need to look forwards given that there are no verses already in place down the line?

Replacement—to substitute the middle verse of five

What

What indeed! What happens when someone falls out with the rest of the team and takes all their verses home?

One solution is to utterly disregard the miscreant's copyright and publish anyway. This is good because it gives the remaining participants a warm and spiteful glow. It is bad because it is illegal.

Replacement is an exercise devised by the present author. It involves the substitution of one verse for another in an established series. The exercise demonstrates the bivalent nature of a renku verse, which both flows from the preceding verse whilst giving rise to the following verse. It also highlights the fact that considerations of shift—of sufficient movement between a given verse and the verse before last—also operate in the opposite direction i.e. between that verse and the verse after next.

How

A five verse segment is taken from a renku sequence. The middle verse is removed. The poet seeks to write a replacement.

All aspects of the core requirements of link and shift must be met. The replacement verse must therefore flow from the preceding verse and shift sufficiently from the verse before last. It must also give rise to the following verse whilst not fouling or compromising the verse after next by anticipating some aspect of the form or content of that verse.

EXERCISES

Resources

Below are some five verse segments from a variety of sources. Poets are invited to use these extracts for the exercise or to select similar segments from any good quality renku sequence.

When sourcing and using other materials, please be alert to issues of copyright.

    a nearby porch,
    the next door neighbour
    heard to clear his throat   Doho

    the closer I draw in
    the more he grows po-faced   Empu

    abstract designs
    we learn to master them,
    Aizu lacquer   Ranran **replace**

    a patina of snow
    coats my bamboo clogs   Fumikuni

    once more in bloom
    but this year's party
    as yet to be settled   Yasui **all verses from Plum Flowers, Fresh Greens. Translation: Carley & Carley**

    Confucius he say
    haiku maeku shmyku

    the conversation drifts
    again
    from Kant to Camembert

    a quantum state
    defining both the   ***replace***

    avalanche!
    a particle of snow
    becomes a wave

    the slopes of Gstaad
    beneath the cosmic nose   **all verses** Carley **from the solo sequence The April Night**

RENKU THEORY AND PRACTICE

    predicting snow
    a used car salesman's
    great white smile   Lorin

    hurrying homeward
    chimneys crowd the sky   Ashley

    things get warm
    then warmer still
    under the kotatsu   John **replace (kotatsu: a heated throw or quilt)**

    the needle skips again,
    our last hiccup   Ashley

          predawn
        wakens
    to the sound of OM   Kala **all verses from Shades of Autumn: Ford, Capes, Carley, Capes, Ramesh**

    falling in fits and starts
    drizzle at the eaves   Yaba

    a carpenter
    with his oak saw
    tugging away at a knot   Ko'oku

    to see the moonrise
    over the bare mountain! Rigyu **replace**

    gourmet rice cakes
    still in good supply,
    the autumn breeze   Yaba

    firewood's cheap
    in a land of frozen dew   Yaba **all verses from The Hawker's Goose. Translation: Carley**

Considerations

The exercise embraces an arc of five verses. We know that our replacement verse (#3) must flow naturally from that immediately preceding (#2). It must also naturally give rise to the following verse (#4). Crucially the requirements of *shift* mean that it must also be comprehensively different from the verse before last (#1) whilst not fouling the final verse or our arc (#5) by preempting some aspect of its content or phrasing.

This exercise is difficult. There are a lot of things to think about.

Over an arc of five verses seasonal reference will be in play. Must the substitute verse necessarily adopt the same stance as the one it replaces?

What is the overall tenor of the passage of verse? How swiftly does it move? How intense is the verse we are replacing? What do these qualities imply for the substitute verse?

What are the person/place characteristics of the verse we are replacing? How much flexibility does our substitute verse have to adopt a different location and/or narrative perspective?

How is the verse written? What is the style of prosody? What is its style of diction? Do these qualities effect the way we construct our substitute verse?

Having established an overview, poets are encouraged to resist the temptation to simply substitute the original verse with a mirror image. The purpose of our questioning is to enable the creation of a completely new set of alternatives at #3—to explore different territory whilst still preserving a natural set of relationships with the surrounding verses.

To maximise the benefits of this exercise, participants should attempt to generate three replacement verses which are different from each other.

To paraphrase Master Kan: When you can snatch the verse from its setting, it will be time for you to leave. Grasshopper.

The Minimum Conditions
what does it take to be Shofu renku?

Shofu renku

Age 16. Essay. First define your terms. Is there anything more dispiriting? Yet to do otherwise is to court nihilism. Which, in the case of renku, has been snuffling around the back door for some time.

Though it had made the occasional guest appearance, the word *renku* was first popularised by Kyoshi as editor of Hototogisu in the early years of the last century. Like his mentor, Shiki, Kyoshi identified *renku* principally with the haikai no renga of the immediate Basho school, or that of later imitators. Like Shiki, he was agin.

During the 1920s, 30s and 40s, persons more sympathetic to linked verse began the revival of interest in the various genres. Again the term *renku* was most closely identified with the work of Basho and his followers.

However, in English at least, the term has recently undergone a substantial retro-fit. *Renku* may now be found scrawled across the manifest for any school, style or period of *haikai* linked verse. It may be bolted on to the medieval genre of *mushin renga*. And, worst of all, the truly benighted have begun to apply it to thematic linked verse—the absolute antithesis of Basho's mature style.

This is unfortunate. We wish abject confusion on our enemies, not our friends. So, to be clear, please note: these comments are directed towards Shofu renku only—*linked verse in the direct style and lineage of Basho*.

Not exactly auspicious

During the latter part of the last century a number of Japanese poets and critics addressed themselves to the fact that interest in Basho-style linked verse had begun to spread beyond the native language and culture. These novel circumstances raised the obvious question of what exactly constituted the core of the genre; what was it that made a piece recognisably Shofu renku?

At the heart of this conundrum lay the need to distinguish between the culturally specific facets of renku and those which were universal—a mode of analysis largely alien to the Japanese literary tradition which in the case of haiku had yielded little of value.

Renku fared no better. For the most part the genre was defined in terms of rules—all but a handful of the more gifted interlocutors being content to catalogue a plethora of effects rather than identify a nucleus of causes. In a classic reversal, the difficulty in communicating the resultant mass of injunctions was attributed to a lack of capacity on the part of the recipients. The conclusion being that said rules must necessarily be simplified. A process which deprived them of what little cogency they contained.

It is small wonder that many occidental poets view renku with suspicion. On the one hand we are told that there are a huge number of rules. And on the other that our sensibilities are such that we may never pretend to full knowledge. What, you may very well ask, has any of this got to do with *literature*? And wherefore such condescension?

Yet despite these inauspicious beginnings Shofu renku remains a fascinating literary genre which has been, and will be again, a vehicle for sublime artistry. Further, it may be written in any language, by people of any social background, without resort to a rule book, and in defiance of the suggestion that we adopt another's norms.

In describing the minimum conditions for a piece of poetry to qualify as Shofu renku, the following points seek to distinguish the genre clearly from earlier forms of medieval renga, from other schools of haikai no renga, and from the recent rash of enthusiastic English experiments—most of which bear imaginative names ending with *enga,* as in *False Etymologenga.*

The expression 'minimum condition' describes a requirement which must necessarily be met. Where a set of minimum conditions exists, as is the case here, all must be met for the requirement to be satisfied. Consequently the order in which the points are presented does not imply a hierarchy.

A Shofu shopping list

Artistic integrity: Shofu renku is neither a fiendish word game, a simple pastime, nor a purely performative act. It aspires to more. Three aesthetic principles have a particular bearing.

fuga no makoto—poetry as truth and art.

fueki ryuko—the unchanging within the ever changing. Truth endures in the fleeting. The churn of events contains the transcendental.

kogo kizoku—alert to the high, grounded in the low. Heaven and earth, refined and plebeian, form a single entelechy for the poet.

Dynamic structure: A Shofu renku sequence is not a string of random gobbets. Individual verses are carefully weighted to yield discrete passages. Prominent topics may serve as way-markers or fulcra to transition between segments of differing intensity. In the manner of a piece of music, longer poems may be organised into movements. Such forms of cohesion rely on tenor. Nowhere do they imply narrative development, thematic extension, or logical explication.

Ever moving: Shofu renku displays linear concatenation. A sequence reads sinuously onward. It is not conceived as a succession of recombinations in which each new pairing presents a cameo.

Expressive language: Shofu renku is not a purely imagist genre. It is more than the poetry of ideas. Word choice has significance, both within and between verses. Metrical proportions, controlled cadences, and the phonics of individual words and phrases, are used to enrich associations and inflect meaning.

Holistic: Judgements are made on the totality of the text rather than at the level of a word or phrase. Reductive analysis is resisted. Empathy prized over reason.

Mutuality: Though verses are ascribed to an individual they are the product of mutuality, often in the act of drafting, and always within the compass of the creative flame that lights the successful collective. So too in the relationship between poet and reader. A poem does not seek to astonish or scandalise. Rather it rearranges the psychic furniture in order to evoke new perspectives.

Sequence: Other than the first verse, Shofu renku verses cannot stand alone. The expressive power of renku lies in the transition between verses not on the content of verses. Unlike a collection or a series, if the verses of a sequence are reordered, all coherence is lost.

Variety and Change: A Shofu renku sequence reflects the fullness of natural and human creation. It is an iteration of the cosmic gestalt. Therefore it cannot embrace a pre-ordered or selective channelling designed to express a purpose. It is fundamentally, metaphysically, anti-thematic for the duration of the sequence. Even where a short run of verses share an aspect such as a season, that aspect is contextual only, never a conducting strand.

Conducting a Sequence
how to make enemies of your friends

Preamble

Perhaps you've flicked through the pages of this book at random and have arrived here by chance. Or you are one of those people who always start at the back. If not, and you've come all the way from the inside front cover, the fact you have stuck with it is really quite impressive—proof of the triumph of erm... thingie over what-not. Sorry, I can't do much better than that at the moment. If you think this book is heavy going as a reader, you should try writing it.

Anyway, this is the chapter that actually matters—full of handy hints for avoiding the blood feuds and suchlike that are a normal concomitant of writing renku. Shofu or otherwise.

What do I need to do or know before starting out?

Good question. Most people come to renku via haiku, which is not necessarily the advantage it may seem. The genres are more different than they at first appear. Even the form of the verses can be tricky (see *Cut or Uncut*). But a facility with some sort of short imagist verse is an advantage. Beyond that you need to:

- Decide on your purpose.

  Are you marking a ceremonial occasion? Trying for the highest level of artistry possible? Using the sequence in a teaching situation? Just looking for a bit of fun? Not all formats necessarily suit all circumstances.

- Choose your type of sequence.

  Skim through the types available. Factors in the choice will likely include the purpose you've already identified, and the time available. Run as a tight ship, and face to face, a kasen will take you a day—a junicho perhaps three hours. Remote composition—via social media platforms, email etc—depend to a degree on the number of time zones involved. One verse per 24 hours takes willing contributors and very decisive leadership. Otherwise, leave more time.

  The style you want to adopt may come into play too. With sufficient skill and experience, any type of sequence can be written in any manner. But some more readily lend themselves to the classic, others to the ultra-modern. The same holds true for the degree of difficulty—some are more forgiving than others. The appraisal section on each will inform your options.

- Decide your method of verse submission.

  How are people going to submit their verses? Japanese practice offers *degachi* and *hizaokuri*. The first means *winning out*. Everyone present puts in one or more candidates and the most appropriate verse is chosen. We'll come to by whom in a second.

  Hizaokuri means literally *passed from knee to knee*. Otherwise known as *by turns*. There is something of a convention attached that the person in the frame will submit more than a single candidate—three is a good number—and that said candidates should be widely divergent. Amongst other things this is really good discipline for the writer involved. Renku is always about plurality and potentiality. At a practical level it also helps oil the interpersonal wheels. Few things are more difficult than finding a polite way to say—*I'm sorry old chap, the sole candidate you have submitted is irredeemably awful. Please try again.*

A frequent solution is to mix competitive and allotted verse positions. The trick is to keep everyone sharp, whilst avoiding exclusion.

- Decide your method of verse selection.

So now you know how the verses are going to be submitted. But how is the choice to be made? Really this needs a heading of its own. There's a dedicated section just below.

- Check your grip on the basics.

In all cases you will need to have a glance at *How to Read the Schemas*, and pay attention to the description and appraisal that accompany the sequence you have chosen. Beyond that, an absolute minimum is a proper understanding of *Link & Shift:: An Overview*. It's only short.

Life would definitely be easier if you were also au fait with *Link: Making the Connection*, *More About Shift*, and *The Three Rs*. It is *not* necessary to have pored over the entirety of this book. Hopefully you will want to at some stage. But write some poetry first.

- Think about your verses.

Though the major part of the source literature, and most modern Japanese renku, uses tightly structured prosody, English Shofu renku can be written free-form—so willing. But there are implications for how the sequences perform. This is one of those areas where a good grounding in modern English haiku does not necessarily guarantee success (see *Know Your Enemy* and *Know Yourself*). At the very least you will need to be aware that phonic relationships stand alongside the semantic. Sound matters as well as meaning.

- Remember where the action takes place.

The real nitty gritty of a Shofu renku sequence takes place in the space between the verses. Which is the also the space between the reader's ears. It is all about suggestion and evocation.

If you have encountered the claim that each pair of verses forms a single scene—forget it. You will find instances of the technique in Basho's own work. And it can work to good effect in modern writing too. Occasionally. But as a guiding principle it belongs to medieval renga. If you have paid good money to be taught otherwise at university—consider litigation.

And that's it. Your are now ready to write renku. Apart from the small matter of the who, how and why of deciding on the actual selection of the verses. Oh yes, and then there's copyright... and verse attribution... and...

Methods of verse selection

It's all very well having the greatest set of verses since Tu Fu and Kikaku took on Pound and Ms Mountain—someone still has to score the round. Or do they? Verses may be selected by:

- Giving it your Best Shot.

The very best or very worst renku is a guaranteed outcome. Basho and Etsujin. Buson and Kito. Issa and Ippyo—all come to mind. If there are just two or three of you—and you can write to the standard of these gentlemen—simply taking turns to add a verse can work. You won't need multiple candidates either.

Things are less promising when the attraction of Buggin's Turn is that we're all far too nice to express an opinion. Or a certain party flies off the handle when faced with anything resembling a critique. Writing renku is a lesson in humility. It's like that ego-loss stuff that goes with scented candles. But for real.

key	verse position	submission basis	number of submissions	number of poets	adopted
degachi: competitive	hokku	degachi	9	4	original
hizaokuri: allotted	wakiku	degachi	15	4	redraft
original: as submitted by the author	daisan	hizaokuri	4	1	original
	vs 4	hizaokuri	4	1	redraft
redraft: altered after comments	vs 5 au mn	degachi	10	4	original
	vs 6	degachi	12	3	original

This chart shows submission and selection data for the first six verses of a nijuin led by an experienced writer. Me. You will notice that only at verse #3—daisan—was the original draft adopted from a lone poet. And that was chosen from four possibles. For the verse before—wakiku—four poets went head to head to produce a total of fifteen candidates. Yet the final choice still involved a redraft.

It is not impossible for poets relatively new to the genre to produce good work by simply taking turns. The fewer the poets involved, and the shorter the sequence, the more the chance of success. But a willingness to revise the text remains essential. And even so—for anything longer than a yotsumono—given that judgement has been eschewed, it takes a lot of luck.

- Arguing the toss.

Politely known as arriving at a consensus. With the right set of poets this can work. The interpersonal skills needed are high or else a dominant individual or faction will emerge, but it is better to operate in this environment than simply settle for turns. A little friction is inevitable, but it also beats working under a poem leader so dictatorial that participants lose ownership of the poem. Ooops!

There are two caveats. The first is that all involved need to have a general sense of what the genre entails, otherwise broad considerations get bound up with the specific and the whole thing becomes a nightmare. The second is that, even where everyone is on the same page, and reliably present in the same real or virtual workspace, too much discussion kills momentum and the poem becomes a chore.

We do well to remember that, for all it may sound civilised, compromise can come at a price. It was Alec Issigonis who pointed to the camel—a horse designed by a committee.

- A poem leader—a sabaki.

Dictatorial or otherwise, sabakis seem to have a bit of a bad name. It is true that, as renku has spread world wide, some of the self-appointed have sought to cloak their lack of knowledge with impenetrable mumbo-jumbo (see *On Backlink*). But the role has also been met with insensate hostility by the *year zero* brigade.

As for serious people... do we question the role of choreographer in a corps de ballet? An orchestral conductor? A theatrical director? A cinéaste? A record producer and sound engineer? Perhaps it is simply that occidental poetry has become so totally identified with interiority, with the existential angst of the lone scribbler, that it has become inconceivable for anyone other than The Solitary Sufferer to be seen to stick a finger in the mixing bowl of misery. And that goes for the audience too. They, at least, seem to have heeded the message and gone off to watch TV. Philistines.

The role of sabaki is fundamental to the evolution of the genre, and bears close examination. For the moment let's just observe that renku is a collective art form. It is closer to choral singing than soliloquising. As such, even when the singers have a great deal of experience, it often works best with an outline arrangement.

- Rotational leadership.

As the scary Ronseal Man would have it—*this does exactly what it says on the tin*. But, just like the product he was advertising, that's not as much as it seems.

The advantage of some form of rotational leadership is that it avoids the excessive level of chat that arriving at a consensus can demand. Things get settled. The poem moves on. Everyone takes their turn.

The disadvantage is that it seems to deliver the benefits of a well led poem, when in fact it does nothing of the sort. And no, that doesn't depend on the how and when of rotation, but on the fact of rotation itself.

Ah, and now we get to learn what the sabaki does... I just heard his jackboots in the hall.

The role of the sabaki

The word sabaki means *handler* or *guide*. This is a more modern and, in theory, more moderate turn of phrase than the earlier *sosho*—Master—indicating a less deferential attitude on the part of all concerned. It is pure chance that the German word Führer also translates as *guide*.

In practice there is not a great deal of difference between the competencies of the poem leader from Basho's day to the present. As to the way the role was exercised... A massive boom in the popularity of haikai no renga during the 18th century saw the rise of the professional renku master. In fact a glut. Rather like a town with too many piano teachers, this produced the sad spectacle of uncritical fawning on the part of those desperate not to alienate their clientele. Given that alcohol was also involved, there was a tendency for writing sessions to degenerate into sordid drinkathons tempered only by frequent resort to the all-you-can-eat buffet.

Not much top flight poetry there then. Just a nasty hangover. And a lot of maekuzuke or senryu. But that's a story for another day. Let's imagine that everyone is sober, and actually interested in Shofu renku. It is the role of the sabaki to:

- Generate *za*.

    Za literally means *place*. Anyone old enough to have smoked pot will understand this better as a *happening*, baby. Za is that creative state where an activity acquires a life of its own. Easier said than done. But at the very least a sabaki must communicate positive energy, smooth contact between the participants, and have contingencies in place for all eventualities. The more flexible the better.

- Choose the most appropriate verse.

    This goes beyond the idea of *best*. A renku sequence is not the same as a series of haiku. In the latter we are looking for poems that can be judged on their own terms, and placed together more or less loosely. A renku sequence is all about context. Verses are not in themselves stand-alone. Nor should they all be stand-out.

    The sabaki therefore needs to have sufficient understanding of the genre to avoid gross errors, such as stalling the poem by selecting a verse that goes backwards (see *The Three Rs*). But even more important is an instinctive sense for what seems to fit. If it feels right, it is right. And if that means sticking your fingers in your ears and blowing raspberries at tradition—do it.

    As variety and change in renku has so frequently been couched in terms *thou must not*, perhaps the least understood aspect of selection is the ability to identify the verse that most readily opens the way forwards. For this one needs a good sense, not of direction—Shofu renku is never thematic—but of potentiality. A working knowledge of quantum theory comes in handy. The verse as superposition. Easy!

- Outline what is next up.

    Upon opening the box, Schroedinger's cat was either dead or not dead. We all have our preferences. Were he a sabaki rather than a scientist he would have known that it might just as easily have turned out to be an armadillo, or a poorly bound copy of *The Book of Common Prayer*. But for all that, renku is not random. And at any one point, whilst the totality of the next verse is unknowable, certain aspects are more likely than others.

    The sabaki may therefore make observations about typical structural conventions such as a seasonal context or the appearance of a fixed topic. Certain subjects might also be unsuited to a particular passage or phase of a poem. The total annihilation of the human race, for instance, rarely sits well in the opening of kasen commissioned to mark Positive Thinking Week.

    Person/place considerations—ji-ta-ba—can be pretty fundamental (see *More About Shift*), as can the ideal dynamic tenor. The most important thing is that none of these oblige how a verse must be, they only indicate how elements of it *may* be. There is an art in knowing when to meet and when to defeat expectation.

- Tidy up the bits.

    If we get it right, the creative energy of the writing process—the community mind, the za, or whatever we want to call it—will carry us seamlessly through the poem. But there's still a little bit left to do.

Although verses mostly get settled as a poem progresses, the text is regarded as provisional until all queries, conundrums and alternatives have been discussed and resolved. It is vital that everybody ends up with the same hymn sheet.

The text will normally incorporate the poets' initials, or similar, as verse attributions—either in line or as an end note—plus a record of the when and where of composition. Full names appear for each contributor—sometimes the place of residence. Modesty aside, if anyone acted as leader, this is where they own up.

Then of course there's the slight matter of publishing. Avoiding multiple submissions. Keeping everyone in the loop. Clearly this can be undertaken by any of the contributors, but it is up to the sabaki to make sure everyone is in agreement. Common courtesy demands nothing less. So does copyright law.

Sabakis are facilitators. They do not ordain what must be done. But they have to perceive what *may* be done—and spread that understanding so that it empowers. Though different from a guiding ego that works towards a predetermined end, their style will effect the totality—the feel—of a poem. Even at the level of keeping the show on the road, rotational leadership cannot do this.

It is understandable that people are diffident about taking on the role of sabaki. After all, the wish to be a politician makes one unfit for office. But a truer analogy is to the conductor or choreographer. Will those arts be stronger or weaker if the roles are summarily abolished?

Oh, and another thing

Sabaki or no, there remain a few things that tend to come up in evidence for the prosecution. So let's take a very brief look at:

- Copyright.

    Copyright law varies from country to country. If you are working online, jurisdiction is generally held to belong to the country in which the servers hosting the platform are situated. But this is not universally recognised. Clearly you can check. The best tactic is to avoid any dispute in the first place.

    Though the point from which it is calculated—and the total length—differs from place to place, copyright lasts for a long time. Unless transferred by a duly constituted legal instrument, it belongs absolutely to the individual author. And not just to their verses either, but to everything they write—including critiques, commentaries and threatening letters. If wholly or partially transferred by a legal instrument, that whole or part belongs just as absolutely to the new copyright holder.

    Several things flow from this. One is that forfeiture statements of the *if you post your poem here we may use it as we wish* variety have no force in law. Ditto assumptions of collective ownership based on assertions of cultural precedent. More absurd yet is the oft heard claim that anything on the internet is fair game. The text of each verse belongs to its contributor. End of story.

    Beyond simple good manners, it is for this reason that the section above insists on the importance of all participants giving their full assent to the finalized draft of the poem. Quite rightly, magazine editors and competition organisers increasingly require sight of such a statement before accepting a piece for consideration.

    Be aware also that where a poem borrows a verse, a classic hokku for example from Buson or

Boncho, though the poet himself may be long since in the ground, the text of the translation belongs to the translator. Unless that is also very old, it is highly likely to be in copyright (see *Exercises*). There is a widespread misapprehension that in such cases it is sufficient to give attributions. This is tendentious at best—interpretations vary between jurisdictions. The smart thing is to get permission, *and* give attributions. The most polite too.

- Whose verse is it anyway?

This is the one the legal profession really would have a field-day with. In poetry workshops it is not unusual to encounter resistance to an edit or a redraft on the grounds that *it is no longer my own work*. Sometimes this extends to a reluctance to listen to any form of commentary.

Renku cannot be written under these circumstances. Well it can, using Buggin's Turn and Best Shot, but the chances of it being any good are infinitesimal. Yet even though our shrinking violets may be tiresomely precious—or perhaps just new to writing and understandably nervous—they actually have a good point. If we strip all the redundant and ugly words out of the average cat verse, will there be anything left?

This subject merits a chapter in its own right, but there's a chap outside with scythe who has been waiting for a while, so someone else will have to write it. Suffice to say that different people have differing views on what is and what is not acceptable. All of them have to be regarded as legitimate.

To a large extent copyright law simplifies the situation. If a person doesn't wish it to go forward, the verse cannot be used. Not against their name anyway. Where all agree, it may be attributed to the person who performed the surgery.

The official policy of *Renku Reckoner* is that the germ of a verse carries more weight than its execution. Almost any amount of rewording is therefore possible before it becomes inappropriate to attribute the verse to the original contributor.

But this is dangerous territory. Or it is if handled badly. Speaking of which—there is a recorded instance of an unnamed poet objecting to the meddling of one Basho Matsuo in just these circumstances. To which Basho is alleged to have retorted—*Even if all that is left is the word* of, *your name will be attached to this verse.*

Clearly, even St. Bash had his bad days.

- Overall gains.

If you write renku, hopefully you will want to write more for its own sake. But there are definite gains for your other writing too. Especially where, as with the majority of people, you come to the genre via haiku.

Renku can direct the writer's attention towards the relational aspects of phonics that have been so much neglected in haiku. There's also a feedback loop between inter-verse linkage and the scope for juxtaposition within a cut verse such as a haiku or a hokku. We can learn an awful lot about degrees of turn, and degrees of association. Doho called these *the going and the coming*, a mere three hundred years ago.

Writing with others—especially if they're good—also has a salutary effect. They are indeed *other*. It is impossible to anticipate the connections they will make to the things we had thought of as familiar. There are precious lessons to be learnt about assumptions and comfort zones.

Perhaps the best thing about renku is the almost certain knowledge that one's candidate verse is destined to fail. And not just once, but time after time.

Some people counsel that you can always keep these snippets of now and weave them into another when. Possibly. But the Shingon chaps wouldn't be happy.

After all, a candidate verse is just an iteration of the one true verse. And that's the one we've been trying to write all along.

where I tread
the barest footfalls linger
summer grass —

John Carley. Rossendale. Summer 2013

Publication Credits

The following, or earlier versions of them, previously appeared as follows:

Nijuin: Early Morning Heat	*Frogpond* 36:3, 2013
Imachi: Between the Jagged Rocks	*A Hundred Gourds* 1.2, 2012
New Junicho: Earthquake Season	*A Hundred Gourds* 1.2, 2012
Rokku: A Cup of Snow	*Frogpond* 36:2, 2013
Shisan: The Scent of Lemons	*Raw Nervz*, Sept 2004
Tankako: The Kite Contest	*A Hundred Gourds* 2.4, 2013
Triparshva: A Long Way Home	*Simply Haiku* 4:1, 2006
Yotsumono: Vivaldi	*Notes from the Gean*, Dec 2012
The Mechanics of the White Space	*Journal of Renga & Renku* 1, 2010
On Backlink	*Journal of Renga & Renku* 2, 2012
The Minimum Conditions	*Journal of Renga & Renku* 2, 2012
Explaining it all Away	*A Hundred Gourds* 2:3, 2013

The Intermission/Duration table in the chapter *Occurrence and Recurrence* is based on Table 4 of Herbert Jonsson's dissertation, *Haikai Poetics: Buson, Kitô and the Interpretation of Renku Poetry*, Stockholm University, 2006.

www.ingramcontent.com/pod-product-compliance
Lightning Source LLC
Chambersburg PA
CBHW080450170426
43196CB00016B/2752